JAPAN AS–*ANYTHING BUT*–NUMBER ONE

Japan as
–anything but–
Number One

Jon Woronoff

M. E. Sharpe, Inc.
Armonk, New York

First published in Japan by Yohan Publications 1990
Published in Great Britain by Macmillan Academic and Professional Ltd 1991

Published in the United States in 1991 by M. E. Sharpe, Inc.,
80 Business Park Drive, Armonk, New York 10504.

Printed in Hong Kong

Library of Congress Cataloging-in-Publication Data
Woronoff, Jon.
Japan as–anything but– number one / by Jon Woronoff.
p.   cm.
Includes bibliographical references (p.   ) and index.
ISBN 0–87332–872–8.—ISBN 0–87332–873–6 (pbk.)
1. Japan—Social conditions—1945–   2. Quality of life—Japan.
3. Japan—Economic conditions—1945–   4. Industry and state—Japan.
I. Title
HN723.5.W67   1991
306'.0952—dc20   91–2998
                                                                              CIP

Contents

4

Foreword

The modern myth of Japan is assuredly the biggest hoax of the present age. Here is a country one can freely visit, where one can meet and talk to the people, hear their hopes and fears, ascertain their likes and dislikes, examine their strengths and weaknesses, and describe the result as anywhere else . . . a mixture of good and bad.

Instead, we have been inundated by books, best typified by *Japan As No. 1*, that present an incredible and miraculous Japan. This is a place which has achieved far more than any other ever and promises to astonish us more in the future. It is a place with countless successes and rare failures (assuming any are conceded). It is a place where things work out for the best, harmony prevails, and incipient problems are solved in advance by farsighted leaders. In short, it is a fabulous place without parallel.

Yet, when you do visit Japan, and look around a bit, you keep on encountering flaws and failings. You stumble into all sorts of conflicts. You meet people who are anything but happy. And the media are full of complaints about nagging problems and warnings of imminent crises. What you see with your own eyes and hear with your own ears bears no resemblance to what you have read.

It would be nice to think that one day the truth will out, the myth will be dispelled, Japan will be dealt with like any other place. But that is not the case at present and the trends are very discouraging. When I wrote my first "crisis" book a decade ago, the favorable works outnumbered the critical two or three to one. By now it is easily four or five to one. There is an endless outpouring of views that mystify and mythologize.

Yet, in this same decade, things have patently gotten worse in Japan. The economy has obviously slowed down, income distribution has become skewed, while landowners have become rich ordinary families can no longer afford their own home. There are now poor people as well as many old people who are scared about what will become of them. Serious defects have appeared in the schools. Crime, drug addiction, AIDs, are also threats here. Pollution and environmental damage continue. Socially, gaps between age, gender and race remain wide and dissatisfaction with the ruling elite has intensified. Politics are sullied by corruption, sex scandals and, more generally, arrogance of leaders who ignore the concerns of the people.

Thus, the gap between myth and reality, fiction and fact, has only grown as ever more favorable books are written about a situation that is increasingly unfavorable. Yet, what happens when you point this out? You are told by the myth-makers that it does not exist. Or that it is exaggerated. Or that it does not matter. You are called a Cassandra and a Jeremiah for looking at the darker side of things. You are informed that you may well be a crank or worse—a Japan-basher—for making such a fuss.

Maybe so. But I would rather be labeled a critic and a pessimist rather than behave like a Pollyanna who can only see the good or a Pinocchio with an ever longer nose. Moreover, if I am a critic and a pessimist, I am one with a difference. I have been right more often than not in my criticism. I have been right more often than not in my forecasts. In fact, if anything, many situations have turned out worse than I predicted. My track record is infinitely better than those of the Japanapologists. And my books are still relevant while many of theirs were obsolete from the day they first appeared.

So, as a Cassandra and a Jeremiah, as a gadfly and a crank—but not as a Japan-basher—I will try again to show that there are two sides to Japan and that the side which the friends of Japan ignore can be rather dark while the only side they present is not quite as bright. This book, of course, is written primarily for foreigners. The Japanese already know the truth, although it doesn't hurt to remind them. But all too many foreigners have been taken in by stories which are so seductive that one is sorely tempted to believe them.

In so doing, I am not engaging in what is called "revisionism." It is not just a question of tinkering with the conventional wisdom to modify some views or shift the general thrust. I do not merely want to clear up details and add correctives. This modern myth, as I said, is manifestly a hoax. It is so wrong, on so many points, and so hopelessly distorted and bloated, that it has to be junked, scrapped, totally undone and abandoned so that we can fashion a more accurate understanding of Japan.

I do not think I achieve my goal this time. No more than I have succeeded in other books. But at least I will provide an alternative for those who seek the truth. And I sincerely hope that more will join me in this effort to put an end to the deceitful and harmful sham of Japanapology.

JON WORONOFF

1

Introduction
(Appearances Can Be Deceiving)

Welcome To Wonderland

Welcome to the most extraordinary place on Earth, where people are better and things nicer than anywhere else. To explore it, I will leave you in good hands. You will be guided by eminent ambassadors, academics, business consultants, publicists and authors. Admittedly, all of them are foreign. But they claim special insight into things Japanese.

Let us start with the late futurologist Herman Kahn, one of the most illustrious Americans to discover Japan since Commodore Perry. It was he who intimated that the 21st century would be the Japanese century, due to its exceptional economy which would assuredly be projected into other sectors. "I have come very close to a belief that the Japanese have, in effect, discovered or developed an ability to grow, economically, with a rapidity that is unlikely to be surpassed in the period at issue—and that might well result in the twentieth or early in the twenty-first century, in Japan's possessing the largest gross national product in the world. . . . it would not be surprising if the dynamism of Japanese growth were accompanied or followed by an equal dynamism in other areas—e.g. scientific, technological, cultural, and religious. Therefore if, as is not unlikely, the Japanese want to export worldwide influence, they may well succeed in doing so."[1]

This economic rise is usually traced to the emergence of dynamic companies, the *kaisha*. No name is more closely linked to this aspect than that of James Abegglen, who gave currency to the concept of "lifetime employment" and concluded that, more than anywhere, management and labor were one. The Japanese company "becomes in a real sense the property of the people who make it up . . . The *kaisha* is not simply an economic institution, but is a deeply social institution, working out its destiny in a competitive economic environment."[2] Rather than feel they are just cogs in a machine, according to former ambassador Edwin O. Reischauer, "managers and workers suffer no loss of identity but rather gain pride through their company. . . . Company songs are sung with enthusiasm and company pins are proudly displayed in buttonholes."[3]

This creates an exceptionally close relationship amongst employees, according to Bill Ouchi, author of the best-selling management primer, *Theory Z*. "Intimacy of this sort discourages selfish or dishonest action in the group, since abused relationships cannot be left behind. . . . Values and beliefs become mutually compatible over a wide range of work and non-work related issues. Each person's true level of effort and of performance stand out, and the close relationship brings about a high level of subtlety in understanding of each other's needs and plans."[4]

Progress, however, involved more than cooperation and hard work, it resulted from the pursuit of knowledge, according to Harvard professor Ezra Vogel. "If any single factor explains Japanese success, it is the group-directed quest for knowledge. In virtually every important organization and community where people share a common interest, from the national government to individual private firms, from cities to villages, devoted leaders worry about the future of their organizations and, to these leaders, nothing is more important than the information and knowledge that the organizations might one day need."[5]

This knowledge-based society is supported by an extraordinary educational system which, according to Kahn, combines American mass education with European quality.[6] Its significance can hardly be exaggerated since, as British sociologist Ronald Dore insists, it "stocks and sharpens their minds—and stocks a high proportion of them with scientific, technical, legal, and other industrially relevant matter. At the same time, simply as a set of selection filters, the educational system is highly efficient at putting top brains into top companies and ministries. . . ."[7]

Education is also important because it lays the foundation for a meritocracy. Japan, in the words of writer and educator Frank Gibney, "is a true meritocracy. One can move up, if one obeys the rules, and get quite far through sheer competence." Someone who excels in the exams can go to the best university, enter a top government bureaucracy or large corporation, and pull ahead. But Gibney adds that such achievement does not create an elitist who forgets his origins. ". . . he rarely turns his back on his antecedents. Family is family. Akita is still home. And, after all, everybody is Japanese."[8]

Others stress the degree of equality—indeed, classlessness—in Japanese society. Most Japanese claim to be middle-class and, according to Robert Christopher, journalist emeritus and Administrator of the Pulitzer Prize, they have a greater right to do so than others. Wealth is much more evenly spread, affluent Japanese mix with those less well off, there is no strong sense of class consciousness and, indeed, "there is no group in Japan really comparable to the Beautiful People of Western Europe and the United States."[9] Anyway, what is the point of talking of rich and poor? Business consultant Robert C. Wood tells us that the Japanese "have virtually eradicated poverty" through government aid to small business.[10]

The outcome is a rather impressive democracy, one much admired by Reischauer who, as ambassador, could observe it up close. He went on record as saying that "the Japanese political system . . . appears to measure up quite well as an effective system of democratic rule, not notably inferior to those of the West and perhaps stronger in some respects."[11] And Vogel argued "that Japan is now a more effective democracy than America."[12] This was, according to them and others, because of a supremely efficient elite bureaucracy.

One should not think that business is the only thing that interests the Japanese or that economic advance is the over-riding goal. Far from it, corrects David MacEachron, Pres-ident of The Japan Society. "The Japanese, more than their American counterparts, practice the goal of self-education. They are prodigious consumers of books and magazines. A considerable portion of the population are amateur musicians, and all sorts of visual arts from caligraphy to painting are practiced widely. Over a lifetime, there is without question more enjoyment to be derived from the pleasures of the mind than from pleasures of the flesh. The Japanese by no means neglect that latter, and, unlike many in this country who still suffer from a Puritan heritage, they have no guilt about en-joying them . . ." For such reasons, "the Japanese today are probably the largest body of contented people in the world."[13]

Yet, all the change and modernization has not destroyed the roots. "If what is new in Japan is astonishing, what is old contains even greater wonders and marvels," we are told by writer William Forbis. "At some quiet, still, central place in the Japanese psyche, the people of Japan hold, without concession, to esthetics, ideals, and societal bonds unchanged in twenty centuries. More than any other nation of the East, Japan has adopted, adapted, co-opted or even stolen the best

Welcome to Wonderland. Japan as all too many
admirers picture it.

Credit: Japan National Tourist Organization

of the West. But also more than any other nation of the East,
Japan has remained itself."[14]

Japan can thus serve as a lesson to us all. In the words of
former ambassador Mike Mansfield: "Japan alone among the
major industrial states has so far rejected the temptation of
costly nuclear armaments, substituting the positive promise
of economic gain in lieu of negative deterrence by military
threat. And the measure of future progress might well become

'net national welfare' rather than gross national product, with industries increasingly diverting to 'knowledge-intensive' electronics and computerized services in health, transportation, and banking, as well as in pollution control. If it all should come to pass, Japan may well be showing the rest of the world not only how to survive the twentieth century but how to prepare for the twenty-first."[15]

This makes for a rather nifty society. No wonder Ezra Vogel likens Japan to No. 1. "Those who have observed Japanese families and other groups in private have concluded that in zest for life, delight in carefree relaxation, and enthusiasm for recreation, the Japanese are no laggards. As they say of themselves, they like to work hard and to play hard. Many thoughtful Americans visiting Japan express amazement at the tidiness of urban facilities, the reliability of public transportation, the courtesy of commercial personnel, the affluence of department stores, the quality of restaurants, and the virtual absence of derelicts and alienated slums."[16] Yes, all this and the trains run on time!

That was not bad for a brief tour. And many more prodigies will be mentioned in the rest of the book. This makes the place as marvelous as Camelot, or Oz, or Wonderland. Like them, it also has the slight drawback that it does not exist, never has existed and never will exist. It is a special fiction that the Japanese call *tatemae*. *Tatemae* means appearances, things as they should be, idealization, pretense or illusion, depending on your mood and mind-set. Reality, things as they actually are, the humdrum workaday world, the truth are known as *honne*.

In Japan, both levels of perception exist. For everything, there is a *tatemae* and a *honne*. The *tatemae* is displayed on festive occasions, before important people who must be impressed or lesser beings who do not have access to the inside dope. It is usually the first version to appear in dealing with outsiders. Among these outsiders are foreigners or *gaijin* (literally, "outside people"). Only with insiders, those one is intimate with, who are themselves in the know, does one revert to *honne*. For Japanese dealing with Japanese, there is nothing dishonest or devious in proclaiming the *tatemae*. That is how things are done. Starting with the *honne* might, if anything, be rude and improper.

This does not mean that Japanese believe every *tatemae* they hear. To the contrary. Realizing that there are two levels, and the more attractive, presentable one comes first, they expect such pretenses and withhold judgment until they know what the *honne* is. Anyone who implicitly believed fine things like those referred to above would be regarded as simple-minded or deluded. Thus, it is quite possible to listen to the Japanese, or those who claim to speak on behalf of the Japanese, and get an absolutely fabulous and fantastic version of Japanese life that simply does not exist.

This sort of charade occurs elsewhere, although not as systematically or as spontaneously. In every society, there are things one does not tell outsiders because they are embarrassing, and there are other things one embellishes to gain their sympathy or impress them. You would not normally tell a stranger that your favorite aunt is dying of cancer or your son takes drugs. That is the *honne*. But a white lie like "my aunt is getting along quite well" or "my son is shaping up" sounds much better. That is a perfectly acceptable *tatemae*.

In fact, there are areas which are almost entirely given over to *tatemae* virtually everywhere. Solid citizens are patriotic about the homeland, bosses claim to be concerned about the welfare of their employees, salesmen only offer their clients the best deal, children all love mom and apple pie, soldiers brag that they are not afraid to die . . . even if they don't really mean it. When it comes to politicians and public figures, they seem to live perpetually in rhetoric and illusions. No one with any sense of reality would believe them, but few would point a finger and call them damned liars. That is part of the game.

However, there is a definite distinction between the attitude toward *tatemae* and *honne* among the Japanese and others. While, for the Japanese, it seems quite natural and normal, for many foreigners (Western more than Oriental), the former is stilted, false and futile, perhaps dishonest. The word hypocrisy might well express the feeling of some. After all, they were taught that there are only truth and falsehood, whatever is not true is false, and the truth is virtuous while lies are evil.

When Japanese apply *tatemae* to one another, there is not that much intention to deceive and they are so used to this practice that few are, in fact, deceived. They know it is not the truth, but it is not quite a lie. It is just another way of presenting things, a manner of speaking if you will. And since they do it to one another, neither party has much cause to complain.

When Japanese apply *tatemae* in dealing with foreigners, that is another matter. Foreigners expect to be told something closer to the truth and do not appreciate it as much. Indeed, since they are more accustomed to getting the truth, or something resembling it, more readily, they will perhaps be taken in. When they find out the real *honne*, they will be annoyed and complain of lies and hypocrisy. For such reasons, it would be preferable for Japanese not to use *tatemae* on foreigners. When they do, it can be ascribed to ignorance or lack of experience in communicating with foreigners the first time, and perhaps the second and third. But somewhere along the line it is not quite right.

When foreigners claim that an illusion, myth or bit of rhetoric is the truth, the absolute truth, and a truth they have personally discovered and are revealing to the world, it is hard to regard that as benignly. They know perfectly well the difference between truth and fiction, *honne* and *tatemae*, and claiming one is the other is downright dishonest. They are, indeed, liars and hypocrites. But first you have to find out . . . .

Distinguishing *Honne* From *Tatemae*

Since there is such a thing as *honne* and *tatemae*, and the former can be assimilated to reality and the latter to illusion, why would anyone bother producing the latter? What point can there be to creating, refining and spreading fables and myths? More significantly, why is it that those who provide a rosy, glowing, false vision of Japan have been gaining on those who go out of their way to uncover what is wrong as well? And this to the point that they are shaping the general consensus and conventional wisdom?

I have been reflecting on this for many years. And, try as I may, I can only find two possible reasons, each with many intriguing variations, namely ignorance and dishonesty.

For one, an amazing number of Japan "experts" have not lived there very long before writing their flattering works. For some, a year at best. Others went on a six-month tour of the country. But an increasing contingent spent only a few weeks researching or visiting (occasionally on organized, packaged tours) before taking word processor to hand. Most journalists start writing authoritatively from the day they arrive. And, by the time they actually know what they are writing about, they are posted to another country only to be replaced by novices. But they are not as bad as the visiting firemen, hot-shots from the visual media, who flock to Tokyo for an election or summit and provide instantaneous coverage. Worse even are the editors and producers back home who give preference to what appeals to their taste or sells best, namely Japan as an "economic miracle."

Yet, even living there for an extended period is not necessarily adequate. It depends very much on where one lived and how. It is very easy for a foreigner to lead a rather peculiar life in Japan. He can inhabit a *gaijin* ghetto complete with foreign-style apartments, schools, shopping centers, etc. He will then mix mainly with other foreigners. But even living amongst the Japanese is not enough since it is possible to move about in a "bubble" of sorts since everyone treats the *gaijin* with great respect. That is pleasant. But it creates a distance from the normal currents of life.

This is a particular threat (if that is the word) to foreigners who enjoy higher status and are treated with yet greater deference. They are given the deluxe version of the standard *tatemae* and since they are surrounded by so many subordinates and flunkies they may never make contact with reality. This applies especially to those who can influence world opinion, like big-name academics, journalists for prestigious publications, managers of high-powered companies and, of course, your ambassadors, visiting ministers and other dignitaries.

Among the rank-and-file, including substantial numbers who have been in Japan for years and years, there is occasionally too much naivete. These people came to Japan because they were attracted by the *tatemae*. They believed that out there on a far-distant island dwelled a magical race which fashioned a marvelous civilization like none other. It was truly based on knowledge, meritocracy, respect and mutual obligation, harmony and so on. Most were idealists. Others romantics, tapping into martial arts, traditional crafts or zen. Whatever the explanation, all too many never perceived the *honne* . . . or really cared to.

It would be nice if one could ascribe the predominance of the idealized and glorified version to mere ignorance and naivete. But that is actually the lesser part. The biggest names in the literature are those of people who have lived in Japan for extended periods, know a fair amount about it, often speak the language and have perhaps married a Japanese, and yet churn out material they know does not stand up to factual examination. This is the category of opportunism and dishonesty.

There are good reasons for presenting Japan in a favorable

light, good not intended here in the moral sense. Many long-time "friends" of Japan feel that they must explain the country and, somehow or other, explaining ends up being a mixture of praise for what has been accomplished and excuses for any failures. Rather than remain specialists (*chinichika*), they become advocates (*shinnichika*), making Japan's case to the world. Rather than remain Japanologists, they become Japanapologists, a term I coined some years back and has caught on. There are far too many Japanapologists to name them all but the venerable master of this school is clearly Edwin O. Reischauer. His essential message was conveyed by a faithful disciple, Nathaniel Thayer. "Never, never, never be anything but wildly optimistic about Japan, about its capabilities, about what's going to happen next."[17]

Others don't really care about Japan, they care about themselves and their standing back home. Thus, prophets and gurus of all sorts come to observe and, my word, suddenly discover that Japan is a success because it has adopted some theory they propounded that is either ignored or ridiculed at home. Japan has proven them right! Others are delighted to use Japan as a stick to whack their fellow countrymen over the head with, because Japan is doing right what the folks back home are supposedly doing wrong (despite repeated admonitions from the critic).

However, the best reason (again not in the moral sense) is that supporting Japan pays. It pays very well. In a great variety of ways. And much of this untaxed (and unreported). It is possible to give lectures on virtually anything or nothing and pick up handsome fees. You can be interviewed by a newspaper, magazine or television show and get rewards for that. If your book is translated, the Japanese royalties could exceed those for the original edition. And this is peanuts compared to what can be earned if you make yourself useful by providing valuable advice, helpful consulting services, or congenial public relations. If you can influence your own people and government, the sky's the limit.

Of course, in keeping with time-honored custom, not every transaction is monetary, just an exchange of favors. It is possible to be invited to a seminar, where you give a short talk, and receive a free trip, hotel and meals plus an honorarium. Or your university may obtain scholarships which you distribute among your favorite students while grabbing a study grant for yourself. There may even be an endowment, in exchange for a suitable display of zeal, which greatly expands the power base of Japan studies and gets you the position of department head. Think tanks may be asked to prepare reports and naturally receive dues. As for consultants, an introduction to clients with money to throw around is a welcome counterpart.

Of course, the Japanapologists have justifications and rationalizations for what they do. Everybody already knows what is wrong, they say, it is necessary to show what is right. It is thus appropriate to concentrate on the finer aspects and perhaps draw lessons so that others may learn from Japan. The foreign public is distressingly unaware of the merits so it is indispensable to explain in greater detail. Moreover, there are already others who write critical stories on Japan. These are the Japan-bashers. So the best excuse is the need to counter these scurrilous tracts.

However, when you look for the Japan-bashers, they are harder to find. They are greatly outnumbered by those who write positively on Japan. Admittedly, there were nasty books before, during and after the war. But that has gone out of fashion except in two narrow sectors, trade and defense. It is exceedingly rare to encounter foreigners who criticize Japan's educational system, or management style, or labor relations, or family, or society, or anything else. It makes one feel that the Japan-bashers are not only fewer than claimed but largely a pretext for others to espouse more positive views.

Oddly enough, when you want to find serious criticism of Japan, you don't have to go abroad. Look to Japan. There you will encounter innumerable critics from all walks of life and all shades of the political spectrum. They range from radical students to prime ministers, from irate citizens to establishment types. They can be seen on television, heard in the Diet, or read in countless books and articles. They find fault not only with Japan's trade or defense policy but virtually every aspect of its national life. Indeed, the foreign friends of Japan would be most distressed by what they say (if they bothered listening).

So, anyone who is intent on understanding Japan, knowing what makes it tick, and getting by in a very confusing society will have to separate the *honne* from the *tatemae*, reality from illusion. That is not easy. Claiming it could be accomplished by following some simple rules would be grossly misleading. It actually takes years to peel off enough of the surface to perceive what lies underneath and more years to comprehend that level. But certainly a start should be made, and the sooner the better.

The first thing to remember is that there is always a *honne* and a *tatemae* for everything. Each is a complete, self-contained version that leaves nothing out. So it would be wrong to assume that just by finding some bits of reality or uncovering some lies you have solved the problem. You must work systematically until you have discovered both levels, illusion and reality. Then you can navigate freely from one to the other, comprehending each, but basing your own action on the more solid *honne* rather than the *tatemae* that is often there to ensnare you.

The only saving grace is that, in principle, the *tatemae* is designed to be more attractive. Thus, you can judge when things are just too good, when the behavior is just too unique,

when the Japanese appear to be supermen as opposed t(
mere mortals who exist elsewhere. This does not mea:.
you should always look on the dark side, only be interested
in flaws and defects and conclude that they are the sole reality.
But they should definitely be integrated in your view and they
should probably be weighted more heavily than the positive
aspects because they are the sort of things that are frequently
denied or hidden from sight.

In this process, it helps to be wary of probable sources of
tatemae. They include official spokesmen of the Japanese
nation, such as politicians, bureaucrats, business leaders, as-
sociated think tanks, coopted academics and so on. There is
no need to enumerate further, everyone knows who they are.
Yet, in Japan, there is a tendency to give more credence to
them than elsewhere when one should do just the opposite
. . . for their task is to purvey the party line.

When approaching material written by foreign ''experts,''
be exceptionally cautious in selecting the right ones. You
have to look for those who at least have the minimum
credentials in terms of how long they have been in Japan
before writing and what sort of relationship they have to
the country. That is, are they just superficial observers or
did they do something that could give them genuine insight?
If not, don't waste your time. The second, more essential
question is, do they have such a firm commitment to the
regime that they cannot be trusted to provide honest opinions? This will knock some more supposed authorities off
your list.

For what it's worth, you are more likely to obtain useful
and truthful views from those who are more actively involved
in Japanese realities such as businessmen or journalists (but
not their editors). Diplomats vary, with the underlings usually
better informed than the higher echelon. Business consultants,
at least those who earn their keep from Japanese clients, are
knowledgeable but not very trustworthy. Paid lobbyists are

Yes, dear readers, Jon Woronoff really
did live in Japan.

worse. The biggest disappointment, however, are the academics. They often remain distant from everyday life, absorbed with theories and paradigms, too busy endorsing or
refuting one another to bother with matters that interest the
general public.

Above all, be wary of those who claim that the Japanese
just don't know how lucky they are to be living in such a
wonderful country and then proceed to highlight those wonders for them. Something like "most Japanese understate
their successes because they are innately modest." If the
Japanese do not know, how should anyone else? And, if
the Japanese are not satisfied, why should anyone else tell
them things are great? After all, this is their country, they
know it best, and certainly their views should be taken into

account. Especially if these views run contrary to those of foreign "experts."

By the way, it is not that hard to ascertain what the Japanese think. There are English editions of the major dailies. Weekly and monthly news magazines are even more explicit and revealing. There is no shortage of books by Japanese on Japan. And you can actually speak to Japanese, get to know them, and find out what they think. Of course, you have to establish a proper relationship. And alcoholic beverages will certainly loosen their tongues. But it can be done. And when they hold forth, don't expect them to sound like a page out of *Japan As No. 1*.

Naturally, the process of dispelling illusions and destroying myths is a long and tiresome one. It is nice to have some help and perhaps get a head start by considering the conclusions drawn by someone who has already spent years seeking the elusive *honne* without admittedly having reached the end of his quest. That is the primary purpose of this book. The following pages examine twelve prominent institutions which are presented "warts and all," as they say. The warts do not disfigure or uglify them, they simply betray hidden realities.

While virtually everything is downgraded compared to the overblown presentations of the Japanapologists, the intention is not to discredit but understand. Good, bad and indifferent institutions are included and some are surely worthy of emulation even after removing the cosmetic support. Others, which may have been praised as wonders by more enthusiastic admirers, should be avoided. The result is a Japan that is not No. 1—but also not at the bottom of the list. It is probably close to the middle.

These various institutions are arranged as in a report card starting with those that are good, then those that are just satisfactory (but not quite good), those that are unsatisfactory (but not outright bad), and those that really are pretty bad.

NOTES

1. Herman Kahn, *The Emerging Japanese Superstate*, pp. 2–3.
2. James Abegglen and George Stalk, *Kaisha*, pp. 207–8.
3. Edwin O. Reischauer, *The Japanese Today*, p. 133.
4. William Ouchi, *Theory Z*, p. 54.
5. Ezra F. Vogel, *Japan As Number One*, p. 27.
6. Kahn, *op. cit.*, p. 119.
7. Ronald Dore, *Flexible Rigidities*, p. 65.
8. Frank Gibney, *Japan: The Fragile Superpower*, p. 79.
9. Robert C. Christopher, *The Japanese Mind*, pp. 141–2.
10. Robert C. Wood, "Strength of Small Business in Japan Aids Lower Class," *Christian Science Monitor*, January 7, 1981, p. 11.
11. Reischauer, *op. cit.*, p. 327.
12. Vogel, *op. cit.*, p. 97.
13. *Speaking of Japan*, November 1984, p. 13–4.
14. William H. Forbis, *Japan Today*, p. 4.
15. Ibid., p. ix.
16. Vogel, *op. cit.*, 20–1.
17. *Daily Yomiuri*, October 27, 1985.

2

Japanese-Style Management (Fact or Fiction?)

How It Really Works

There is virtually no country whose management system has aroused more interest than Japan. It is depicted as a modern miracle, a system that satisfies both the needs of the company and the workers, a success unique in the annals of industrialization. There are so many boosters of Japanese-style management that it is impossible to mention them all. And they have become enamored of so many aspects of the system that it is impossible to deal with all of them. But certainly some of the most prominent should be looked at more closely.

There is probably no characteristic that has become more widely known, and firmly rooted in popular misconceptions, than "lifetime employment." This was discovered by James C. Abegglen, then an obscure student who proclaimed it in *The Japanese Factory* back in 1958. Over the years, he has held to that view and steadily built on it. He still insists that the Japanese system is based on "three pillars" of career employment, seniority-based pay and promotion and enterprise unions.[1] Let us see.

First of all, employees are recruited directly from school on the whole rather than being drawn from a general labor market which, in practice, hardly exists. This means that, among other things, most have no previous work experience and are fresh to the company, "virgin" is perhaps a more accurate expression. Once within the company, they are rotated from job to job. These transfers occur every few years and most employees thereby obtain a very broad exposure. They get to know the company well and meet large numbers of co-workers. Over time, they develop a strong company ethic.

During the earlier phase, company employees tend to rise almost automatically and at the same pace from year to year. Wages increase as a function of seniority. At specific points, they will be given promotions and the titles and perks that go with them. This is the famous "escalator" where the dull advance about as quickly as the bright with no chance of getting onto any "fast track." Only at higher levels are they sorted out when some become top managers and directors and others. . . . Well, let's leave that until later.

Of course, while this standardized career pattern does exist, there has been a regrettable tendency to overlook the fact that there are actually four escalators and not just one, as I pointed out in *Japan's Wasted Workers.*[2] Male college graduates step onto an escalator that eventually takes them to managerial positions and, if they are lucky, the very top. Male high school graduates start much further down and rarely reach more than foreman or lower-level management. And most females are dumped on two escalators that never get anywhere, one for college, the other for high school graduates. They do the same humdrum jobs for a brief period until they marry or have children and "retire." Finally, as the Japanese know all too well, top jobs are not distributed on the basis of experience or skill but favoritism and connections.

Since workers stay with the same company, are assigned their jobs and given promotions by the company, they feel much more company men (we can safely forget the women in this context) than specialized workers. They are, in short,

Mitsubishi-men or Hitachi-men as opposed to electricians, bookkeepers or software specialists. This means that enterprise unions make more sense than trade unions or industrial unions. And, if this were not adequately convincing, management would see to it that unions were restricted to enterprise level anyway.

Since they will stay with the company throughout a career, the company is willing to train them for whatever work is required. As jobs are rotated every few years, this training occurs not only once but many times over the years. With their fate tied more to the company than their own skills (which few possess), workers are willing to sacrifice more of their time and energy. They will mobilize for productivity drives and join quality control circles.

But it is a big step from saying things happen this way to claiming that they occur spontaneously and voluntarily. There is no better example for dispelling this myth than the QC Circle, so highly touted among foreign management gurus. Here is the inspirational definition one of them gave.

"The quality circle itself is a completely voluntary body. Nobody is paid to join, nobody is forced to join, and nobody is penalized for not taking part. The motivation is solely the desire to do a constructive job of work and to find satisfaction in seeking the results of effort. The circle, once formed, sets its own terms of reference; selects for itself the problems it wishes to tackle; and, in due course, presents its recommendations for their solution. In other words, it functions organically—according to its own perceived needs—rather than compulsively in response to externally determined criteria."[3]

How delightful! If only it were true. Alas, this description is wrong in all particulars. Any worker in a factory that has QC circles has to join, no excuse is acceptable for abstaining, and refusal could result in an aborted career. Most circles were initially created by management and not workers and each is run by a leader, often a foreman, which means that ordinary workers had better participate actively. As if this were not enough, there are guidelines on what sort of projects should be undertaken and if they are frivolous or inadequate progress is made, it will displease the higher authorities who supervise the process. Moreover, QC groups compete against one another within the company and from company to company so their members have to keep up.

The suggestion box system is similar. It is not just a question of coming up with good ideas now and then. Workers are expected to turn in suggestions regularly. Indeed, many factories have quotas for the number required and those who do not meet the quota are talked to by the foreman and may come to regret it. No wonder companies claim to receive not only hundreds but thousands and tens of thousands every year.

How do I know? Simple. I have visited many factories which sported banners proclaiming the official goal, such as twenty suggestions each this year (and perhaps thirty next). I saw charts with cute little flowers drawn by working girls who were allowed to color a petal each time they made a suggestion. Once I even saw little girl figures, stark naked at first, but gradually clothed with a dress or blouse each time the owner submitted a suggestion. It is not only the figures which would have shivered if not enough suggestions were produced. If you don't believe me, just look at the corresponding photo.

This makes the romanticized views of chief guru Bill Ouchi look downright silly. But they are quoted again to show just how far this school can go, although having already reached Theory Z it can hopefully proceed no further.

"When economic and social life are integrated into a single whole, then relationships between individuals become intimate. . . . Intimacy of this sort discourages selfish or dishonest action in the group, since abused relationships cannot be left behind. People who live in a company dormitory, play on a company baseball team, work together in five different com-

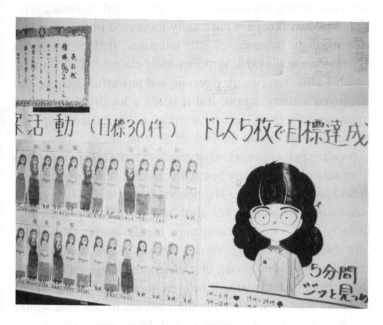

Just make five suggestions and your doll won't
have to shiver in the cold any more.

Credit: Jon Woronoff

mittees, and know the situation will continue for the rest of
their lives will develop a unique relationship. Values and
beliefs become mutually compatible over a wide range of
work and non-work related issues. Each person's true level
of effort and of performance stands out, and the close relationship brings about a high level of subtlety in understanding
of each other's needs and plans. This mixture of supports and
restraints promotes mutual trust, since compatible goals and
complete openness remove the fears of or desires for decep-
tion.''[4]

What fluff! Still, what can be expected from an ''expert''
who—like so many others—never lived in Japan, worked in
Japan or even seriously studied real Japanese companies be-

fore proclaiming his message to America's gullible managers. Yet, while workers are not totally immersed in the company in a wholistic manner, as Bill intimates, it does not mean that they are not loyal as is more widely claimed. This loyalty, which I also concede, is vigorous and powerful, shaping the employee's every action. But it is not a loyalty that springs spontaneously from the soul so much as one that is imposed by circumstances and the lack of alternatives.

As already mentioned, most employees are taken in directly from school and, if they botch this chance, they are unlikely to find another as good. The general labor market is severely constricted, so looking for a job at a later date is not easy. In fact, most "good" companies hardly recruit mid-career personnel. Once having earned several years' seniority, an employee would be giving up considerable wage increments, fringe benefits and status if he were to leave. And he would probably start closer to the bottom anywhere else that would hire him. So there is nothing gained. Moreover, without special skills or transferable experience, why should any other company bother hiring him? Of such considerations is loyalty made.

If you do not like my cynical criticism, why not turn to a Japanese expert like Kunio Okada, Professor emeritus of the University of Tokyo and one of Japan's leading sociologists? His book on Japanese management first had to debunk the views of overenthusiastic foreign admirers before explaining the problems and possible solutions. His concerns included excessive employee dependence and suppression of individual creativity, discrimination and impediments to a free labor market, harmful effects of the escalator system of promotion and "work that gives no joy and seemingly has no meaning."[5] Similar views were espoused by many other Japanese experts and even the Japan Productivity Center. What a pity their opinions carry no weight with the Japanapologists.

Not Quite Lifetime Employment

Dare we assault the most cherished premise of the system, lifetime employment? Why not? After all, although it is presented as a "typical" practice, it is anything but. It actually only covers a small share of all workers, a point that is carefully sidestepped by management gurus like Abegglen, Ouchi, Pascal and others. Just how small is hard to say because no one ever signs a "lifetime contract." Everything is tacit. Workers are assumed to stay on, but they may leave. Companies are assumed to keep them, but they may not. So it is impossible to quote figures.

Still, there is obviously no point in speaking of lifetime employment in agriculture, especially since most farmers are self-employed. So are most shopkeepers. The same applies to countless artisans. Civil servants usually have tenure throughout a career, but that is true of most countries and not only Japan. In the services or construction, the labor force is much less structured and the system is less entrenched. It is really only in manufacturing, high finance and large-scale distribution that one can speak of lifetime employment having much significance.

And even within those sectors it is not so widespread. In order to bring in batches of fresh graduates annually and work them up through the company over thirty years or so, it is necessary to have a huge staff. It makes no sense for firms with only hundreds or even thousands of employees. This means that the supposedly typical system only applies fully to large companies which happen to account for 1% of the total number, albeit with some 30% of the workers. Then perhaps to some of the medium-sized enterprises. But it is missing from the vast majority of smaller firms with about half the labor force.[6]

If we could stop here, then one might speak of a dual

structure where large companies have something akin to "lifetime employment" while smaller ones do not. Alas, even in big companies not everyone participates. As indicated, most women retire after a few years. When they return after having raised their children, they often only hold part-time jobs. So do some men. Others just have contracts that are periodically extended. And the worst off do piecework. These temporary employees, perhaps a third of the work force in big companies, do not enjoy the same relationship as regulars and their careers may be terminated at short notice.

By the way, "lifetime" is just a manner of speaking. Large companies enforce compulsory retirement at the age of 55, or sometimes 60, while most Japanese continue working another five, ten or fifteen years. As Rodney Clark explains, on the basis of what he saw with his own eyes while studying a real Japanese company, "they take the best and most productive years of their employees' lives, and then leave them to look after themselves in their period of decline."[7] This contingent could account for as much as a quarter of the work force by the 21st century.

Finally, although the principle is that regulars are not laid off when times are rough, management has found many devious and compelling ways of having them withdraw. One is quite simply to hint that if they do resign voluntarily, they will receive a substantial bonus whereas if they do not, they will not, but they will go nonetheless. Or, at the ripe old age of fifty, they are stripped of their title and asked to serve under younger men, or given an empty office with nothing to do, or transferred to some god-forsaken place in the sticks with a cut in wages and not enough money to bring their family. And so on.

By process of deduction, it would seem that the share of workers covered by the "typical" Japanese system is not very substantial. Only employees in half of the economic sectors at best, and then only those in fairly large companies, not including women, or temporary staff, or older men, or some unlucky devils would have anything resembling lifetime employment. You only end up with about 15% or 20%. That makes Japanese-style management as glorified in *Theory Z*, *The Art of Japanese Management*, *Kaisha* and other learned tomes decidedly atypical.

What sort of employment system exists in the smaller companies which cannot afford lifetime employment? Good old hire and fire. It's not their fault, they don't have any choice. They are expected to expand more rapidly in good times and cut back more drastically in bad. They may also have to make way for excess or inefficient employees dumped on them by bigger companies. Not only that, their workers know that they have no job security and may develop the habit of switching whenever they can get better pay or conditions or merely tire of the old job. Just like the West, only worse in some ways because the normal labor market is truncated and regulation looser.

While I hardly expect to launch a counter-trend, I think a more accurate and fairly neutral term would be the "core" system. It consists of two basic dimensions which reinforce one another.

The "core" in one sense is the select group of employees recruited directly into the company upon graduation and who are expected to stay with the company no matter what. After all, every organization needs certain key personnel. The "peripheral" staff consists of part-time workers, contract workers and any other temporary personnel as well quite often as employees picked up along the way after having initiated their career elsewhere and who are not quite assimilated.

Of course, within the "core" there are different levels. Only men are really expected to stay on. And only men are really given jobs of consequence. Women frequently do petty tasks that are beneath men or brighten up the office. They become the "flowers of the office." College graduates, whether men or women, stand above high school graduates, men and especially women. But these distinctions are not hard to follow because, on the whole, college grads end up working in the head office while high school grads are relegated to the factories. Finally, and not to forget, older workers rank higher than younger, although age is not enough for a woman to pull rank on a man.[8]

Within the broader company "family," there is also a "core." That is the big company, with the prestigious name and control over other branches. The "periphery" consists of subsidiaries and subcontractors. Naturally, the larger the subsidiary and the closer to the parent company, the greater its status. And it may also have its own subsidiaries. Meanwhile, there can be more than a dozen layers of subcontractors, each one passing work it does not want down to the next.

The advantage to this concept is that the "core" system actually shows how Japanese companies function internally and with one another. The core workers will devote themselves to the company because they have a disproportionate share of the power and benefits. They become an "aristocracy," an expression used regularly by the Japanese public. The core company will always prevail because it can manipulate the others to its benefit. That makes the system very powerful. It also makes it amazingly resilient because there is so much vested interest. Moreover, the system can last forever because it is possible to shrink or expand the core depending on business circumstances without abandoning the principles.

Unlike "lifetime employment," which only emerged in the past few decades, the core system goes right back to feudal times when shoguns and clans surrounded themselves with vassals. And it embodies the Confucian tradition which is based on distinctions of sex, age and education. This might be remembered by the theoreticians who presume that a worker is a worker and a company a company anywhere. It is not that simple. The Japanese system really is different enough so that phony experts should consider the differences before drawing conclusions. As for those who go to the other extreme, exalting a Confucian ethic in Japan, like Ron Dore, it is necessary to consider what Confucianism means.[9] And one should not praise the positive aspects without considering the negative.

Harmony Or Else

Of course, if a company hires workers for life (which it doesn't, but let the proposition stand for argument's sake) then, or so reason the "experts," the company must belong to those who run it and not some all-powerful boss or absentee shareholders. This is the view that Japanese capitalists—yes, they do exist—like to foist on the public and it has been adopted by noted Japanapologists like Jim Abegglen. After muddying the waters over "lifetime employment," he has moved on to bigger and better things. Although by now a reputed business consultant who should know otherwise, he glibly explains that harmony not only can but must prevail because workers and company (*kaisha*) are one.

"The *kaisha* becomes in a real sense the property of the people who make it up. It will not be sold, in whole or in part, without the specific approval of all of its directors, acting on behalf of all of its employees. Earnings of the company go first as a return to investors with the entire balance going to ensure the company's future and thus ensure the future of its employees. The *kaisha* is not simply an economic institution, but is a deeply social institution, working out its destiny in a competitive economic environment."[10]

Here, too, it is necessary to introduce certain correctives. After all, as just noted, the *kaisha* could not possibly exist for all of its employees since it only worries about regulars as opposed to part-timers, contract workers, temporary work-ers, and so on. Even if the parent company is eager to keep the subsidiaries and subcontractors alive, this is in its own interest and not theirs. In a pinch, it would not hesitate to sacrifice them. More essentially, even if workers become managers and directors, the objectives at the base and at the top are simply not the same. One wants bigger wages, the other bigger profits. One wants more leisure, the other de-mands overtime. And so on.

Another fundamental issue is whether the "typical" Jap-anese company really is the bureaucratic type so widely prop-agated. That is, the company where top management derives purely from inside promotion of hardworking salarymen who joined it so many years before on leaving school. This is what is claimed and I have rarely heard anyone propound the contrary. Yet, I have noticed an awful lot of companies whose bosses are not terribly different from bosses anywhere else as concerns their prerogatives. Many, in fact, are founders of the companies of which they own a considerable chunk. It may even occur that, not only are they the president or chairman, but their children, relatives and in-laws are com-pany officers and future presidents and chairmen.

There is no shortage of examples. Matsushita, the premier electronics firm, was founded by Konosuke Matsushita who ran it with an iron hand. Sony is run with a velvet glove, but no less decisively, by founder Akio Morita. Toyota is the fief of the Toyoda family. And everyone should know that Soichiro Honda created the motorcycle company of that name. The president of Casio Computer is a chap named Kashio and Reijiro Hattori recently succeeded his father at the head of K. Hattori, the maker of Seiko watches. YKK is the creation of Yoshida-san. Kenichiro Ishibashi or "Bridge-Stone" in English and his family own a lot of that company. Masatoshi Ito founded and runs Ito Yokado and Isao Nakauchi, Daiei, two of the top retailers. Meanwhile, the Tsutsumis hold sway over the Seibu empire. Most construction (Ohbay-ashi, Maeda, Magara) and pharmaceutical (Taisho, Mochida) companies are controlled by their founders and Kikkoman and Suntory are family firms. Not bad for a start. And this is just a small portion of the major companies that could be mentioned. Virtually all the smaller enterprises follow this pattern.

This means that bureaucratic companies are not so typical. Most of them stem from prewar *zaibatsu* that were taken from their owners and split up by the American occupation forces. But even many of them are run strongly from the top. Toshiwo Doko turned Nippon Steel into the world's biggest producer without asking his subordinates what to do at every turn. Yoshio Ohno, who heads Shiseido, was described as overtly aggressive, as opposed to other Japanese bosses who do not let it show. Ryoichi Kawai, the chairman of Komatsu, was feisty enough to dismiss the president when he was seventy years old and should have been relaxing. Nissan is more bureaucratic than Toyota, but bosses are still bosses. And the head of Mitsukoshi department store was denounced by the employees as a tyrant some years back.

Nonetheless, even entrepreneurial companies were grad-ually institutionalized and internal decision-making came to depend less on the dynamic founders. While some of the grand old men refused to let go and gave orders into their dotage, others had the wisdom to delegate authority. Natu-rally, the more bureaucratic companies where ownership is more diffuse, tended to spread control more widely. This internal system, which is rather different and exotic, gave rise to another myth much admired by the Japanapologists—bottom-up management.

The system has been so intensively documented that there is no need to present it in detail. As per usual, the stress is on positive elements that motivate workers, that make them strive for their company's success because, like the three musketeers, it is one for all and all for one. We have *ringi-sho* or memos written by lower level personnel and channeled upward for approval. And the endless meetings or *kaigi*. And most popular, *nemawashi* (or root-binding), where someone promoting an idea consults individually with those concerned, winning them over one by one. It is all very exotic. All very Japanese.

Unfortunately, the notion of bottom-up management is also very overdone. Yes, *ringi-sho* do emanate from further down, but they will never be enforced until vast numbers of superiors approve them or at least acquiesce. Meetings draw in all and sundry. But the decision will not be reached until the higher-ups agree and anyone lower down who speaks out of turn is in for trouble. Moreover, when questions are discussed, it is the management which has the crucial information. As for *nemawashi*, why can't a boss ask his subordinate to submit an idea just to make it look as if the idea came from the base. Does this happen? You bet it does!

But why quibble over whether bottom-up management operates in a pure or diluted form, whether it springs from below or is manipulated from above? The essential drawback is that it is not very efficient. It simply takes too long to hold all those discussions and get all those approvals. And it takes up too much time. According to Dentsu, executives spend 40% of their time in meetings which is far too much.[11] They should be doing other things instead. That is why bottom-up management is limited to relatively secondary questions. Really crucial ones, especially those involving personnel and profits, derive from smaller circles. More interesting yet is that those companies where there is less—not more—bottom-up management have been among the most dynamic. The management gurus might consider that before they urge foreigners to copy Japan.

This brings us to the third element of company dynamics, much admired by the Japanapologists. It is the enterprise union which cooperates happily and voluntarily with management. Sounds good, huh. Still, by now most rational observers must realize that the unions have very limited influence. In fact, it is easier to state what they cannot do than what they can do, an approach taken by a Japanese authority Hirosuke Kawanishi:

"The enterprise unions in key industries do not play an effective role in tackling members' problems such as wages, working conditions, and shortening of working hours. Nor do they implement internal democracy. Rather they function as an auxiliary to management in the personnel sector. The positive assessment of such unions contained in the established theory is contradicted by a wealth of evidence gained in systematic, empirical investigations."[12]

Of course, none of this will keep Japanese managers from waxing poetic, in well-worn and oft-repeated phrases, about how the company is the father and the workers are the children, how the company cares for and nurtures the workers, how it strives to give them what they need. And there may be a recitation of Hideyoshi's noble words: "the people are the walls, the people are the moat, the people are the castle." Or an announcement that having climbed Mount Fuji the company now intends to scale Mount Everest. Then perhaps a rousing round of the company song and a stirring pledge to carry on to guarantee the future of the company and its loyal personnel. After all, this is just *tatemae* and it is routinely presented and just as routinely swallowed.

No less routine is the applause of foreign admirers who don't seem to realize that this is only *tatemae* and not to be taken seriously. Yet, they write as if it were *honne* and Japanese workers could truly be reckoned among the most fortunate in the world. Just get a load of this quotation from that venerable elder statesman Edwin O. Reischauer.

"A job in Japan is not merely a contractual agreement for pay but means identification with a larger entity—in other

Exercise! It's good for you. Then
get back to work!

Credit: Matsushita Electric

words, a satisfying sense of being part of something big and
significant. Employment for both management and labor is
likely to last until the normal age of retirement. For both,
this brings a sense of security and also pride in and loyalty
to the firm. There is little of the feeling, so common in the
West, of being an insignificant and replaceable cog in a great
machine. Both managers and workers suffer no loss of identity but rather gain pride through their company, particularly
if it is large and famous. Company songs are sung with

enthusiasm, and company pins are proudly displayed in buttonholes.''[13]

But why ask managers if the workers are well looked after and happy? And why ask foreign sycophants? Ask the workers! I have done that hundreds of times. And I have repeatedly been treated to an avalanche of griefs. Others have tried the same thing and come up with the same results. And if you want to check it out, just go to one of the bars where salarymen or factory workers meet in the evening for a drink and to unwind. You will hear the younger ones griping about the job, the company, the pay, the hours, the conditions, and especially the boss. Older ones will grump that younger workers don't strive hard enough. I have yet to hear of anyone boasting that he was the luckiest guy on earth because he worked for such-and-such a company.[14]

If this is too anecdotal, you can always check the surveys and polls. There are dozens of them and I have never found one that flatters the Japanese system. For example, a survey of younger workers by the Labor Ministry showed that one out of three wanted to change jobs and two out of three were only working to make a living. This was confirmed by a poll by Sumitomo Bank, with two-thirds of the respondents stating that the primary motivation for work was to earn a living. Only 11% were interested in ''making a contribution to the company.'' Well, if they were working for money, did they feel that their present level of income was adequate? Two-thirds answered ''no,'' only 7% said ''yes.''

If the situation in Japan was not very upbeat, it was even more dismal when compared to other countries in various international studies. In one survey of workers' attitudes in ten countries, the Japanese only ranked fifth for loyalty, sixth for willingness to make an extra effort for the company and eighth for degree of satisfaction with working life. In another, covering younger workers, 52% of the Americans and 66% of the British were satisfied with their job, but only 16% of the Japanese. The Japanese were also considerably less satisfied with their chances of promotion, income and working hours.[15]

Not exactly what you would expect if you read the bestsellers on Japanese management. But, if you ever worked for a Japanese company, or at least spoke to people who do, it is perfectly comprehensible. And, if the management gurus were to realize the flaws in the system, they could no longer write their books.

Less Lovable Than Effective

Anyone who is familiar with how the Japanese corporate system functions in practice—not in theory—realizes that the foreign management gurus have it all wrong. They present a view which not only deviates from reality but turns it inside out. To explain this we have to consider who and what make the greatest contribution to production.

According to the literature, it is the big company which is supremely efficient and generates masses of fine products. It is true that the productivity is high in big companies. But you must then ask: why? Well, that is because they produce at very large scale standardized articles that can be manufactured in huge quantities with the latest machinery. This is done in immense factories which could be constructed because these companies have access to abundant, cheap capital.

There is another reason as well. It is that smaller companies, their subsidiaries, subcontractors and suppliers, provide the various parts and components which cannot be mass produced. These articles require a lot of time-consuming, elaborate and costly manual labor. It is therefore not surprising that most small companies are rather cramped and backward affairs, especially at the lower levels, because they cannot afford better installations or equipment. If their low productivity were averaged in with the high productivity of those they serve, Japanese industry would not look so efficient. But nobody does that.

So, to be fair, the real backbone of Japanese industry is the small-and-medium sized enterprises, a fact conceded verbally in the big companies and bureaucracy, but which does not lead them to give smaller firms a fair share of the pie. To the contrary, big companies keep their prices down (and profits up) by squeezing small companies for the cheapest possible terms and just-in-time delivery. Then they pay up late. And, if any article can be mechanized, they bring it in house and leave the supplier to shift for itself.

Contrary to the conventional wisdom, it is not the noble salaryman who is the driving element in the work force. He is a white-collar worker employed in the office and Japanese offices are notoriously inefficient. They do not follow strict and streamlined decision-making procedures. Rather, everything is nebulous and vague due to the endless meetings, *nemawashi* and *ringi-sho* so dear to the heart of management gurus. These are all methods which are far too cumbrous and provide solutions which are more often too little and too late. As for productivity campaigns, quality control circles and suggestion boxes, that is beneath them.[16]

Things can be even worse. Anyone who visits a Japanese office unannounced, as I have deliberately done hundreds of times, will find much of the personnel well, frankly, goofing off. They may be sitting around chatting, having tea, reading travel brochures, searching for papers in a pile, even snoozing. In the coffee houses and restaurants of the business districts you can see countless salarymen doing apparently nothing while in the subway many more are commuting to and fro. In fact, the best time to find the average salaryman at his desk is 5 o'clock, i.e. closing time. He returns to beaver away in the hope of earning overtime and outstaying his boss, since he does want to get a promotion. If he stays late enough, he may actually do an honest day's work.

None of this fooling around with the blue-collar workers. They appear on the factory floor not on time but early to get their tools ready. They start work at the bell. When time comes for a coffee or lunch break, they voluntarily shorten it. If necessary, they stay on to finish the job. All this while, they are glued to the machinery, they follow a set routine that has been worked out in minute detail. Then, after the day's work is done, they attend pep talks or quality control circles which they know damn well will only come up with innovations that push them harder still. This makes the blue-collar worker the unsung hero of Japanese industry.

But there are those whose lot is even harsher and contribution perhaps greater. That is virtually everyone in the peripheral sector.[17] A regular factory worker does the nicer, neater, more mechanized jobs while temporary or seasonal staff is called in for the really nasty chores. Work which is merely dull and monotonous is relegated to females, many of them part-timers since the fresh young things serve as "flowers" of the office or factory. Outside, other women are working at home, striving and straining to churn out as many pieces as they can each hour.

It is thus the "core" system operates. The function of the core is not only to hold things together but to push the periphery to work as diligently as possible. It is the function of the white-collar workers to keep the blue-collar workers busy enough to make up for their own sloth. Regular employees bear down on temporary employees and other outsiders. The parent company pressures the subsidiaries and subcontractors which, since there are multiple layers, do the same to those underneath them.

Most management gurus do not realize this and it makes their advice not only useless but dangerous for those foolish enough to trust them. They assume that it is the big companies which are breathlessly efficient in their own right. Stripped of their suppliers and distributors, they would be worse than many foreign companies (which cannot manipulate the system as well anyway). And it is not the white-collar workers who should be emulated; that would be disastrous. *Ringi-sho*, *nemawashi*, bottom-up antics and the rest should be shunned. Only the nuts-and-bolts of factory productivity is outstanding, although again Western companies could not possibly manipulate their workers as effectively.

That is why I have developed my own theory of Japanese management which I call Theory A to distance it as much as possible from Theory Z. Theory A companies do not hesitate to surround themselves with lesser companies which they force to perform. Theory A companies hire a small core of regulars to make outsiders work all the harder. Theory A managers speak fondly of kindliness and generosity, but they realize that compulsion can be so much more effective. Theory A managers also know that every time they meet Theory Z managers they can knock the hell out of 'em.

So then why list Japanese management as superior? Because, in a sense, it is. It is the most ruthlessly efficient management system existing today. It produces more goods, of better quality, at cheaper prices than any other productive machine. It arranges repeatedly to outperform and then crush weaker foreign competitors. That it also makes many of its own companies and workers suffer is unfortunate and something I personally regret more than any of the gurus. That is why I find it far from perfect. But I must still concede its merits.

NOTES

1. See James Abegglen, *Kaisha* and *The Japanese Factory*.
2. Jon Woronoff, *Japan's Wasted Workers*, pp. 16–23.
3. David Hutchins in *Management Today*, January 1981, London.

50

4. William Ouchi, *Theory Z*, p. 54.
5. Kunio Okada, *Japanese Management: A Forward Looking Analysis*, Tokyo, Asian Productivity Organization, 1987.
6. If you cannot take my word for it, see what Ezra Vogel had to say before his conversion, in *Modern Japanese Organization and Decision-Making*, p. xviii.
7. Rodney Clark, *The Japanese Company*, p. 174.
8. For more on the treatment of women, see Woronoff, *op. cit.*, pp. 111–47.
9. See Ron Dore, *Taking Japan Seriously*.
10. Abegglen, *Kaisha*, pp. 207–8.
11. *World Executive's Digest*, May 1986, p. 58.
12. Hirosuke Kawanishi, "The reality of enterprise unionism," in Gavan McCormack (ed.), *Democracy in Contemporary Japan*, p. 156.
13. Reischauer, *The Japanese Today*, p. 133.
14. Anyone who wants to know what the life of a factory worker is like, from the worker's viewpoint and not the manager's, should read Satoshi Kamata, *Japan In The Passing Lane*. But skip Dore's inexcusable foreword.
15. *Manichi*, August 9, 1986, *Japan Economic Journal*, April 12, 1986 & December 21, 1985, and *Yomiuri*, August 16, 1989.
16. For the foibles of white-collar workers, see Woronoff, *op. cit.*, 24–65.
17. The best description of these workers and how they are used by the system is in Norma Chalmer's *Industrial Relations in Japan: The Peripheral Sector*.

3
Japanese Companies
(The All-Mighty Kaisha)

Company Families

Hail, the All-Mighty *Kaisha*. This is the corporation which the gurus tell us is the finest of its species, bound to rise to the top in a jungle where only the fittest survive. As to why Japanese *kaisha* are so strong and effective, we are given many reasons. There is the stress on quality. Nobody cares quite as much about quality, and nobody goes to the same effort to see that each unit is superior, if need be by destroying inferior units, but preferably by preventing defects and bringing them down to zero. There is also efficiency and productivity. Every effort is made to use the best machinery and see that it interacts as smoothly as possible with the work force. Finally, technology. Companies go out of their way to incorporate the best in their products and their production.

Before readers get nervous, let me state that I do not disagree with any of the above. I have visited hundreds of factories, I have seen workers plugging away on the shop floor, I have observed quality control activities and I have naturally bought their products. Not only that, I have also written numerous articles on these phenomenal producers, all of them positive and I would stand by the conclusions still.[1] What concerns me is that, as per usual, this is not the whole picture.

It is not even half of the picture. It is merely the more agreeable portion that Japanese and the Japanapologists like to show.

Another part of the picture actually reveals that Japanese companies are more effective and powerful than commonly thought. Not omnipotent, but as close as you can get to it in this world. To do so, it is necessary to consider just what a corporation is.

Unlike Western counterparts, a *kaisha* is not simply a legally incorporated entity with its capital, personnel, know-how, etc. It is much more. Each big company—and those are the only ones the fans of Japanese management really care about—has three additional dimensions which define it in the Japanese context.

One is vertical, namely the host of suppliers, be they actual subsidiaries or supposedly "independent" firms. This may well consist of several layers, with primary, secondary, tertiary suppliers and so on, acting as subcontractors to the parent company. Secondly, there is the network of distributors, some wholly-owned, others reputedly "independent." Thirdly, there is the horizontal grouping known as a *keiretsu* (the modern equivalent of the ill-fated *zaibatsu*). This consists of truly autonomous companies but which have close relations through crossholdings, exchange of personnel, joint ventures and other linkages.[2]

Japanese *kaisha* are already among the largest companies in the world, to judge by the listings of *Forbes* or *Fortune*. Indeed, many of them are among the top ten in their sector worldwide. But that ranking does not do them justice. Considering the close integration between the core company, its subsidiaries, suppliers and assorted subcontractors, its distributors and the allies within the horizontal grouping, each one is easily two or three times as big as it looks. This makes the *kaisha* much more formidable than at first appears and helps explain why it can overpower big foreign companies with relative ease.

To see this in more concrete terms, let us consider one fairly typical *kaisha*, Mitsubishi Motors. It is chosen specifically because it is one of the less prominent automakers and also because its structure follows the standard pattern. This should be a relief from the management gurus who purposely select one of the top companies or an exceptional pioneer, a Toyota, Matsushita or Sony, and then have the nerve to pass it off as the "typical" company.

Mitsubishi Motors is not particularly large per se. But it does have several hundred suppliers, each of which may have dozens of subsuppliers. It also has a considerable distribution network, with dealers who sell nothing but Mitsubishi cars. Naturally, it is a member of the Mitsubishi Group which includes companies in industry (steel, aluminum, chemicals, shipbuilding, electronics, etc.), commerce (trading, transport, wholesaling), finance (banking, insurance) and so on. With some of these, namely the steelmaker, the electronics suppliers and the bank, it has very close relations, with others less so.

It should be noted that it is not only Mitsubishi Motors that functions this way. So do Toyota, Nissan, Honda, etc. And it is not only automakers that have supplier and distributor networks, so do producers of electronics, ships, watches, chemicals, toys, cosmetics, etc. As for the Mitsubishi Group, it is not the only *keiretsu*, there are a dozen other large ones and many more smaller groupings. This pattern, in fact, is quite typical of Japan's corporate hierarchy.

Why do these additional dimensions make the *kaisha* not only bigger than it appears, but also more powerful? That is because each "core" company can use these links to its own advantage. Particularly since, as intimated, the suppliers and subsidiaries are not really "independent" no matter what the formal structure implies. Nor are the distributors. Many of the suppliers are wholly or partly owned, which means the parent company can dictate the conditions. The others depend so heavily for orders that they "voluntarily" accept its will. Distributors are kept in line because they owe substantial debts and anyway, since they only sell the goods of one producer, they would be ruined if the supply ceased.

This means that, for example, the "core" company can keep its prices lower by forcing suppliers to reduce their prices, a measure which has been taken time and again. Subcontractors can be forced to adjust their activities to the parent company's every need. Distributors can be made to sell at the producer's fixed price and usually pressured into meeting a sales quota. Practices like this are unethical and some are even illegal. But the laws are not effectively enforced by the authorities and the underlings are in no position to resist.

Within the *keiretsu*, relations are more equal but there are good reasons for cooperation. The manufacturer, for example, wants to obtain basic materials like steel, aluminum or glass at cheaper rates. It wants access to finance through the group bank, again at cheaper rates. And it hopes to sell its products to other members, giving it a guaranteed market (even if it must reciprocate with somewhat cheaper prices). In return, the steelmaker is pleased to have a guaranteed market for part of its output. And the bank, insurer, trader, etc. are eager to do business with a prominent manufacturer.

This is not said merely to expand the reader's knowledge of Japan's corporate dynamics. It is crucial in understanding both why and how Japanese companies succeed. And that is not primarily due to quality or productivity. After all, they only explain why Japanese companies might do better than foreign ones in some particulars, if not others. It certainly does not help us grasp why some Japanese companies beat other Japanese companies, since they all strive for quality, productivity, etc.

The true keys to success happen to be quite different, if

less often mentioned and less admirable. They are access to finance and control over distribution. And that is what these linkages provide.

Japanese goods are not sold on quality per se but on quality for a given price. With equal quality, the cheaper product prevails; even if better in quality, if it is too expensive it would not sell. Thus, like everyone else, Japanese companies must strive to hold down costs. This is done through managerial pressure, productivity drives and so on. But it comes far more from introducing more efficient machinery, automation and robotization. And it is capped by scale: the larger the scale, the greater the economies. The amount of machinery and scale a company can invest in, however, is a direct function of its finances.

In the earlier years particularly, but also today, much of the cash was not generated internally but came from the banks. Thus, a company with access to a big bank could obtain more and the closer the relationship, the better the terms. Belonging to a strong *keiretsu*, with a rich bank, was therefore essential in enhancing efficiency. It was even more crucial if the company went into long-term projects whose payoff might be quite remote. And it was never more vital than when it had to engage in price wars with rivals to drive them out of the sector or expand its own market share.

Access to a vast distribution network was equally important since, in Japan, there is a dearth of independent distributors that will sell the goods of any maker who comes along and meets standard conditions. Quite to the contrary, it is a nation of exclusive outlets which handle the goods of one producer only. This is also illegal, but allowed, so that a firm without access to retailers simply could not sell no matter how good or cheap its products. And suppliers without access to end users would be in like straits. It goes without saying that the companies you read about in the foreign press or treatises on

56

Japanese management are systematically those with good connections.

The Seven Cs

Why have Japanese companies succeeded? Or more exactly, and the nuance is extremely significant, why have those Japanese companies which succeeded, succeeded?

There are many explanations depending on the guru you fancy. For some it is love of quality, harmonious company relations, concern for the consumer, and other management traits referred to earlier. For Dore, it is the Confucian ethic. For Ouchi, it is Theory Z, which I never quite understood because it is written in business school jargon. For Abegglen, it is the ability to compete, which is true. But where that comes from is another question. For Pascale and Athos, it includes such intriguing Zen virtues as indirection and vagueness. It is also neatly summed up in the "seven Ss"—superordinate goals, strategy, structure, systems, skills, style and staff.[3]

As indicated, we think it lies somewhere else, in a direction most management experts never even look. It is intimately tied up with finance and distribution, in Japan at least. Having explained how companies achieve this, let us see how it is used. In so doing, we can cite several case histories which are already well known but very poorly interpreted.

The most famous contest is between Matsushita (National, Panasonic) and Sony.[4] In this epic struggle, the former has repeatedly won. The question is: why? Both produce much the same products, of about the same quality, sold for roughly the same price. They worship the consumer and honor their workers. So none of this explains the results. They can best be traced to the fact that Matsushita has a vastly larger distribution network, for one. With a bigger production base and company family, it also has considerably more cash whenever it is necessary to cut prices and with more varied articles it is easier to cross-subsidize whatever the loss leader may be.

To survive, Sony has had to be—in the words of Jim Abegglen—different if not better.[5] It has had to come up with one innovative new product after another. It has done so with the transistor radio, the Walkman, the first video tape recorders, 8mm camcorders, compact disks and so on. Matsushita has launched fewer new products. It has simply waited for Sony and others to come up with them. One of these others is Victor Company of Japan, a Matsushita subsidiary which produced an alternative VTR system. But it has not hesitated to pluck ideas where it finds them, like the bread cooker more recently. With its imposing size, access to finance and distribution network, it then manages to push back the originators and claim the lion's share for itself.

What is the secret of Matsushita's success? According to Abegglen, "Matsushita generally allows its competitors to experiment with new product concepts. When potential is demonstrated, Matsushita enters the market with state-of-the-art products backed by large investments and sales targets geared to make the company the volume leader in two or three years."[6] It eventually becomes the dominant producer (of somebody else's invention) while the likes of Sony has to find something else. Pascale and Athos exquisitely refer to this strategy as "followership."[7]

Japanese commentators, who are not quite as refined, refer to such companies as "copy cats." Matsushita is not the only one. In fact, in virtually every sector there are one or two and, in most cases, they are the biggest and strongest.

Toyota is the largest automaker; Honda is much smaller. Honda is extremely innovative, constantly coming up with new concepts and designs that make its cars popular for a while, until they are integrated in everybody else's cars, especially Toyota's. After all, it provides more models, in more price categories than anyone else. It has the biggest cash hoard and also the broadest distribution network. When it comes to motorcycles, the shoe is on the other foot. There, Honda is top dog. It was only challenged once, by Yamaha a few years ago. Honda threw back the attack by introducing more models and cutting prices deeper, something it could afford because in that sector it had more dealers and could cross-subsidize motorcycle losses with automobile profits.[8] In cosmetics, Shiseido is known for adopting the proven products of its competitors.

Beyond manufacturing, where such examples are clearest, the big boys with the deepest pockets and the best market access also manage to keep ahead. Dentsu has always been the top advertising agency, not the most creative, because of its control of the media and customers. Dai-Ichi Kangyo has broader access to cash with more branch offices and a rather impressive *keiretsu*. The Mitsui and Mitsubishi trading companies cannot be beat for mass imports and exports because they service so many group manufacturers. Nomura sends out more securities salesmen and sells more shares. And so on ad infinitum.

The winners almost always possess the two indispensable prerequisites: finance and distribution. Nowhere in any of these illustrations could the success of one, or the failure of the other, be attributed to quality, concern for the customer, superior management, greater productivity, Theory Z or the Seven Ss. Indeed, they seem almost irrelevant, most obviously in the case of Sony's VTR. The format was superior to that adopted by Matsushita according to most technicians. And it was the favorite in America and Europe where consumers buy what they like and retailers carry everybody's brand. It was only in Japan, where the market is manipulated and controlled, that it lost out decisively.

Which brings us to the question of superior. Abegglen refers to Matsushita as the company which embodies "better" over against Sony's "different." What can possibly be the meaning of better in this context? Certainly, it does not fit the Western notion of what better is. For most Westerners, Sony or Honda would be regarded as better. The very idea of pursuit of excellence is tied up with such innovation and creativity. But it is not in Japan. So let this be a warning to all foreign (and native Japanese) companies which are so naive as to believe the conventional wisdom.

They should never forget that in Japan what counts is access to finance and control of distribution. That implies bigness in all its manifestations as opposed to skill, or ability, or quality, or caring, or being different or anything else.

Thus, to help those who truly wish to fathom the Japanese management system, I have come up with my own formula. This is known as the Seven Cs, of which I am inordinately proud. They are as follows. Cash—to finance a company strongly. Collateral—to hold on to the distributors by advancing them loans they cannot pay back. Control—self-evident. Collusion—with competitors to rig prices (when there is no serious rivalry). Connivance—with the government, in order to get away with the above. Copying—this is not original with me, it is borrowed from the concept of "followership." Concern—you know, telling the public that everything you do is for the good of the consumer, you just want to provide fine products, you don't care about the money; or telling the workers that you just want them to have a good job, you don't care about profits.

If you follow the Seven Cs, in Japan at least, you cannot lose. If you do so elsewhere, you may go broke or end up in jail.

When Better Is Worse

It is strange how reporting on companies is skewed in Western literature. For America and Europe, you read about successes and failures, with perhaps a slight stress on the latter and what mistakes to avoid. For Japan, to the contrary, you are told endlessly about the marvelous success stories but hardly ever about failures. There are good reasons for that, "good" obviously not meant in the ethical sense. Most foreign management gurus and business journalists focus on the big companies, where failures are relatively few. They pay scant attention to smaller firms, where the going is much rougher. But, more to the point, they are writing for a public which apparently only wants the good news.

In addition, Japanese corporations and business organizations keep the foreign "experts" well supplied with information about every expansion, new product, advanced technology and export breakthrough. You have to hunt for the blunders and fiascos, which is more work. Worse, just to prove how wonderful Japanese companies are, many writers fail to distinguish between the ordinary and the exceptional. They write about top companies as if others are just as good. They write of innovative management techniques as if they are widespread. They write about sophisticated technologies as if everyone has them. Most awfully, they write about "model" factories as if they were typical.

So, off they go in droves to visit the Zama automobile plant of Nissan, probably the facility that has been written about most. Or they traipse through Yamazaki's latest operation, which is so thoroughly automated you rarely see a human being. And they spend some time at Fanuc's splendid robot factory where, they proudly tell their readers, "robots are making robots." Alas, I have also been to those and other factories and they bear no resemblance to the rest of the factories of the very same companies, let alone the factories of lesser companies, or most especially the factories or makeshift workshops of their subcontractors.

Equally inexcusable, the writers fail to point out that the only reason that Nissan, Yamazaki or Fanuc can have such highly automated plants is that suppliers and subcontractors are providing the bits and pieces that cannot be automated and perhaps also assembling them. Thus, the claims of factories where robots make robots are utter nonsense. Robots only make certain parts, humans make the rest. Robots are poor at assembly, so much of that is left to people. But let us not blame the Japanese for fooling the foreigners, the foreigners wanted to be fooled so they could peddle a hot story or sell clients on Japanese-style management.

Still, amidst all the successes, there are failures. And they are not limited to relative failures, such as Honda, Sony or Yamaha, which could not quite make it to the top. There is no shortage of out-and-out failures, undisguised failures, failures due to sheer stupidity and gross inefficiency. So, since foreign journalists and management gurus tend to gloss over them, we must pause a moment to consider the situation.

First off, and this is completely logical, there must be more failures than successes in Japan because there is such concentration in most sectors. By now, just two, three or four companies have managed to dominate the market which implies that many others have either disappeared or moved elsewhere. Just as an example, there were once a hundred motorcycle makers; now there are only four. There were once dozens of sewing machine makers; now only two really large ones exist. And so on. This means that the rise of big, powerful *kaisha* was accompanied by the demise of vast numbers of weaker brethren. It also means that, no matter what the Japan boosters may say, the triumphant *kaisha* are just a tiny minority of all companies.

In some cases, failure can be traced to stupid moves and poorly conceived actions such as occur everywhere. For example, the sewing machine maker Riccar went bankrupt because it diversified too much and forgot about its main line. Mitsui Ocean Development, which did nothing but oil rig and marine projects, collapsed because the sector declined.

62

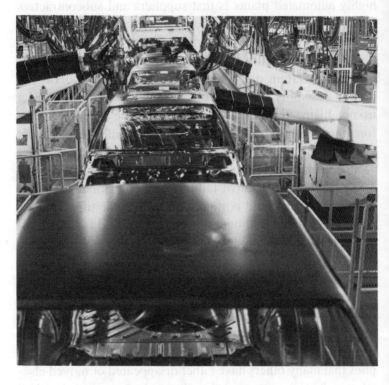

Nobody here but us robots. If you want to see
human workers, try the subcontractors.

Credit: Honda

More significantly, Kojin (textiles) went under because it
speculated in land and Heiwa Sogo (banking) got into trouble
because it issued irregular loans. All the shipping lines were
hurt by the recession but Sanko compounded this by ordering
more tankers at the wrong time. There used to be ten general
trading companies, but that was cut to nine when Ataka invested in an Alaskan oil venture that turned bad.

This just goes to show that Japanese businessmen can make
mistakes such as are encountered everywhere. The following

examples are far more serious because they are more typical of Japan and systemic.

Most smaller manufacturers could be regarded as relative failures even if they survive. Their machinery is less productive and older than in big companies, their personnel is less trained and skilled, with a lower educational level and weaker morale. Admittedly, they sometimes get cast off machinery from the parent company and advice when necessary. They may even upgrade over the years. But what's the point? Whenever suppliers or subcontractors manage to produce smarter or cheaper they are forced to lower their prices so they never get ahead.

Outside of manufacturing, there are huge sectors which are not particularly efficient and may not even boast quality products. This applies to distribution, aside from very large outfits, where the amount of business handled per person is much smaller than abroad and it is necessary to service masses of retailers. Stores, especially the small, but also larger ones, are grotesquely inefficient because of cultural hangups that require excessive staff to deal with the honorable clientele. Most service establishments are tiny, poorly organized and grossly backward by Western standards. Construction is not much better, with a preference for small projects and manual labor to large-scale, prefabricated developments. And farming is ridiculously wasteful.

This is not too surprising. More worrisome for Japan is the apparent failure of the latest class of entrepreneurs, the venture capitalists of only a few years back. Surely, you remember them! It was impossible to pick up a business magazine without reading about Sord, "the computer industry's rising star," or Toshio Kono, Dainichi's "whiz kid who aims to build a better robot." Or a bit more established, Kyocera, the ceramics maker. Alas, Sord was bought up by Toshiba, and Dainichi went bust, while Kyocera was recently described as follows: "ceramic idol chipped." What a pity new companies have such trouble making it. But that is hardly surprising where big is beautiful.

Then there is a whole subcategory of firms which, while they still exist and sometimes even prosper, only do so abroad. In Japan, they have almost disappeared. One is Uniden, which produces telephones and the like in Southeast Asia for sale in the United States. Others still produce in Japan, although they do not sell much there, including Akai Electric, Crown and Shintom.

But even the supposed "stars," so lavishly praised in the Western media, occasionally get into trouble. That was noted for Sony with its video tape recorders and Yamaha with its motorcycles. More broadly, many of the attempts at diversification, especially when too many companies diversified in the same direction at the same time, have been rather disappointing. That occurred for numerous entrants in biotechnology, new materials and robotics. Even those who succeeded in highly successful sectors, like computers and semiconductors, often invested so heavily that the returns were meager. More generally, the big companies are afflicted by failings that are well known in Japan, if hardly mentioned abroad, such as an excessively bureaucratic Mitsubishi, Nissan regarded as stodgy and Toyota as "feudal," an NTT that is no less bloated and inefficient than AT&T was, and Matsushita whose organizational structure is hopelessly complex and clumsy.

Finally, there are the *gaijin*. Foreign companies exist in Japan, slews of them, but they could scarcely be regarded as successes on the whole. That is not always evident given a massive publicity campaign by Japan, Inc. to highlight every real or alleged success which is echoed by complacent foreigners like Robert Christopher in *Second To None*, arguably the worst bit of investigative reporting ever. Alas, foreign companies have only done well in very narrow sectors or ones they dominate through proprietary technologies, like

Coca Cola, McDonalds, Gucci or IBM. Anyone selling more competitive goods has failed to penetrate much. Even today, foreign companies only hold a few percent of the market for electronics, automobiles, textiles, liquor, banking, insurance, pharmaceuticals or any broad sector.

Is this because the smaller manufacturers, the firms in more backward sectors, the budding entrepreneurs and the foreigners "do not try hard enough," as is claimed of the latter? Perhaps so. More likely not. Anyway, no matter how hard they try, they cannot possibly get into the market without access to the proper distribution channels. If their goods are not displayed in the stores no one will ever know how fine they are. And, if most manufacturers mainly buy from within the company family, they cannot sell parts or products no matter how reliable and cheap a supplier they might be.

What really proves the point is the supposed success stories of foreigners. Some of them, like IBM and Johnson & Johnson made it on their own, but only because they had the financial backing to hang on and develop alternative channels. Most others only succeeded because they accepted to be an appendage of an existing entity, quite often a rival. This they did by entering joint ventures, with the partner handling distribution. Or, like Schick, they were lucky enough to find the right independent distributor. Of course this was better than nothing, but less than going it alone as they regularly did in other foreign markets.

Why have the Japanese *kaisha* done so well abroad? Is it because they try harder? Maybe. But it was more often because they did not have to try as hard. They were operating in markets where quality and price really did count and established relationships were easily broken once the Japanese could offer even a modest discount. This they could readily do by cross-subsidizing initial losses abroad. As for finding suitable distribution channels or getting their goods on the store shelves, that was rarely a problem. No wonder they managed to expand market share at a prodigious rate.

Does this make the *kaisha* superior to mere foreign corporations? Not really. The competition is not fair and the playing field is not level, to borrow cliches that are more accurate than commonly assumed. The Japanese only have to compete on one front, namely abroad, since they have effectively tied up the home market. The foreigners, operating in more open, transparent systems, do not have such advantages when facing Japanese rivals on their own shores. Nor can they respond adequately when Japanese firms engage in tactics like dumping or predatory pricing, which can easily be done because the home market is protected. If the initial positions were more balanced, it is questionable whether the *kaisha* would be so invincible.

Moreover, even if they eventually win in the sense of penetrating markets and expanding market share, it must be remembered that there is more to business than that. In some other aspects, the *kaisha* are quite mediocre. After all, companies exist not only to produce but to profit from their production. Very few companies make such intense efforts to sell and have so little to show for it on the bottom line. Japanese profits are much worse than those of comparable American, European or Asian firms. And that is one good reason, aside from the moral aspect, why they are not quite perfect.

In fact, Japanese profit margins are so small that this has become worrisome for many. But it is hard to expect anything else. *Kaisha* want market share more than anything else, and that forcibly reduces profits. They want scale, which is expensive; they want new factories, which is expensive; they want the latest machinery and technologies, which is expensive. They are willing to sell for extended periods at cost or even a modest loss to establish themselves. All that is bad for profits. The only reason that profits are not worse is that Japanese consumers, unlike most foreigners, accept or at least tolerate high prices. They pay more for nearly everything they buy either because it is produced inefficiently by backward (and protected) companies at home or marked up by efficient producers that want to subsidize exports.

Under these conditions, it is hard to understand what is meant by "success." It is even harder to understand why the gurus present Japanese companies as models for foreign companies when the *kaisha* do such a lousy job at what the foreigners regard as essential, making profits. As for foreign consumers, they should just pray that their own companies do not become equally successful by ripping them off to finance competitive battles with the Japanese.

NOTES

1. See Jon Woronoff, *Inside Japan, Inc.* and *The Japan Syndrome* and articles in *Asian Business, Modern Asia, Oriental Economist,* etc.
2. See *Industrial Groupings in Japan*, Tokyo, Dodwell Marketing, periodic.
3. A.G. Athos and R. Pascale, *The Art of Japanese Management*, p. 202.
4. See Athos & Pascale, *op. cit.*, and various books, articles, etc. on Sony.
5. James Abegglen, *Kaisha*, p. 8.
6. *Ibid.*, p. 9.
7. Athos & Pascale, *op. cit.*, p. 30.
8. Admittedly, Abegglen has a different view of this. For his version, see *Kaisha*, pp. 46–52.

4
Industrial Policy
(Promoting and Meddling)

Targeting Techniques

If you ask foreign rivals what Japan's most awesome weapon is, you will be told "targeting." The government and private companies get together, decide on certain projects behind which they throw their full weight, bring new products out in massive quantities and at ridiculously low prices, and then crush the competition. One view of this was expressed by Sir Terence Beckett, Director-General of the Confederation of British Industry. The Japanese, according to him, "adopt a laser beam approach, concentrating on particular targets and virtually obliterating those industries one by one."[1] To Marvin J. Wolf, it was a "conspiracy" and a "plot to dominate industry worldwide."[2]

While this may be a bit of an exaggeration, it is hardly more so than the claims made by Japan's backers who boasted that targeting, or more broadly industrial policy, was one of its finest achievements. Like Chalmers Johnson, who mistakenly attributed Japan's economic miracle to MITI's promotion of industrial policy.[3] Or Norman Macrae of *The Economist*, who talked of bureaucratic superplanning and praised Japan's economy as the "most intelligently *dirigiste* system in the world today." We do not entirely disagree or we would not have listed it in the superior category. As per usual, we merely have some quibbles about the results. But more about that later. First, it is necessary to clear up some of the misunderstanding purposely injected in the debate by the so-called "experts."

For starters, this is not some miraculous new weapon. Japan has been engaged in targeting for well over a century. In fact, even before its opening local lords were impressed by foreign cannons which they promptly had copied and produced in as large quantities as possible. As of Meiji days, the government systematically chose industries which were useful to strengthen the nation's defense or, less often, wealth. They included mining, steel, shipbuilding and shipping, silk and textiles, etc. This continued for decades until the lead was taken by the targeters of the Munitions Ministry, who directed the whole economy toward military production for World War II.

The nefarious MITI (Ministry of International Trade and Industry) became the direct heir to this tradition. Indeed, its top officials and some ministers had gotten their training in the wartime economy and to them nothing could be more natural than for the state (i.e. the bureaucrats) to meddle in the economy. They pursued various programs and projects which allowed them to play a significant role. But the attempt to make industrial policy the law of the land was decisively rejected by the Diet, at the behest of the private sector which had had quite enough of being dictated to.

Despite the impression one may get from Johnson's book, MITI is not the only practitioner of industrial policy. It is undertaken by virtually every ministry and agency within its own sphere. Thus, the Ministry of Transport promoted shipbuilding and shipping; the Ministry of Construction looked after cement and housing; the Ministry of Health encouraged a local pharmaceuticals industry; the Ministry of Finance reinforced banking, securities and insurance; the Ministry of

Defense assiduously built up the armaments industry; and the Ministry of Agriculture targeted not only tractors and fertilizer but cows and oranges. And that is only part of it. This makes MITI just one of many, although certainly more noticeable and highly publicized.

There is no doubt that during the initial postwar phase, the government (i.e. bureaucrats) took the lead. After all, factories had been bombed, the workforce dispersed, and companies were poor and technologically backward. They needed a central authority to concentrate efforts and provide support. But that was long ago. Now the private sector is quite able to get along on its own and more determined than ever not to come under bureaucratic control. But industrial policy has not ceased. It is simply that the managers tell the bureaucrats what they want done, a point obviously missed by the bureaucratophiles.

The idea that targeting is somehow a thing of the past was deliberately inculcated by, of all people, MITI officials. Japan was coming under too much criticism for manipulating the economy, which is a no-no for liberal economists. Worse, the industries it targeted were allegedly crushing their foreign counterparts because of improper government support and unfair trading practices. So, just when outsiders began to figure things out, MITI backtracked verbally. And some of the Japanapologists chimed in, especially those theoreticians who had always insisted that all economies are alike and the Japanese economy cannot be any different no matter how it may seem.

One of them is Gary Saxonhouse, who fed this very dubious information to the International Trade Commission: "Examination of the familiar instruments of industrial policy indicates Japan gives less formal aid and comfort to its high technology sectors than do the governments of most other advanced industrial economies. Targeting is largely reserved for agriculture."[4] Even more astounding was the about-face of the *Economist* writer who stopped praising Japan for its superplanning and intelligent *dirigism* and now complimented it on becoming the country with the "lowest level of government interference." What about his former claims? That was "always balderdash."[5] A pity he didn't tell us before.

No more targeting? Nonsense! Just look at the official documents coming out of MITI and other ministries. More important, look at their budgets. All that has happened is that sectors which were sufficiently strong to get by were dropped and new ones picked up. Japan went from coal and steel to shipbuilding and heavy machinery, then to electronics and computers, and on to machine tools and semiconductors, followed by robots and biotechnology. Recently, it added superconductors and aerospace. And there is no end in sight.

And a final demystification. Japan is not the only place that engages in industrial policy. It is also practiced, to a much smaller extent, in more liberal economies when they hit upon a project where only government backing can achieve a breakthrough, say, developing spacecraft or thermonuclear weapons, but also high-speed computers or an AIDS cure. Something similar can be found more widely in developing countries which adopted import substitution, picking those imports they wanted to have produced locally and giving them appropriate support. As for the centrally-planned economies, they are doing it all the time.

What is different about Japan is that it does a far better job. For one, it only targets a few products at a time and then moves on to others. This means that it does not disperse efforts as widely as developing or Communist countries while still making more of an effort than Americans or Europeans. In so doing, its industrial policy became more refined and the targeting machinery more efficient. It also developed some techniques others do not use, as we shall see. But it is incorrect to claim, as Chalmers Johnson does, that Japan is "plan rational," selecting only sectors where it can succeed and where it is worthwhile succeeding.[6]

The initial step is obviously to pick the right sectors. That is done, according to the foreign fans of industrial policy, by the bureaucrats. But the bureaucrats don't know much about industry or technology. They know even less about business and trade. So they depend heavily on the views of the private sector which means that they ultimately pick those areas companies wanted to get into anyway. No wonder it is so easy to enroll them in government-sponsored projects.

Even if private companies were hesitant, the clincher is that the government provides all sorts of incentives. Once this was outright subsidies, since discarded due to foreign objections. It was followed by loans that companies never bothered paying back, then loans they did pay back but at low interest rates. They also joined in cooperative research projects which were partly financed by the government, but entirely devoted to commercial goals, in which enough company research workers were involved for them to produce something useful.

The next step is actually more crucial. The government wanted the new products to contribute to the economy, and businessmen wanted to make money, so there were various arrangements to guarantee a market. The ministries, for example, bought Japanese computers only. So did the local administrations. So did the telecommunications monopoly NTT. So did large corporations instructed to buy Japanese by the bureaucrats. And this was done whether the quality or price of domestic computers were competitive or not in early years. It was also done for Japanese steel, and ships, and chips, and chemicals, and anything else that arrived.

Just to be certain that these new products which had been targeted were a commercial success, the government erected tariffs and other trade barriers not only once they were in production but before to create an artificial demand and keep foreign rivals from getting in first. Since these barriers could easily be 10% or 20% and even 30% or 40%, this meant that Japanese goods could be sold at absurdly high prices and thereby reimbursed the companies for their efforts while making them beholden to the bureaucracy.

Finally, and this is where Japan really differed from the developing and planned economies, it immediately began exporting. The only way to attain substantial economies of scale was to sell on the world market. If the initial articles were not that good, or production costs were still too high, that was easily overcome by government subsidization or financial incentives. Moreover, since products could be sold 10%, 20%, 30% or 40% more expensively at home, they could be sold that much cheaper abroad. By taking one item at a time, and then selling massively and aggressively on one market at a time, it was possible to pick off the competitors one at a time.

There you have it, the laser approach. Nasty? Yes. Unfair? Hard to say. Effective? You bet.

Industrial Overkill

In theory, there is no doubt about it, targeting and industrial policy are absolutely extraordinary weapons. That is what Chalmers Johnson presumes in *MITI And The Japanese Miracle*. But it is foolhardy to judge any institution only in theory, one must consider the practice. And this Johnson does not do. There is not a single case history in his learned treatise. Indeed, he does not even bother explaining what industrial policy is, how sectors are picked, how they are promoted and what the results were. That does not seem to interest him although he admires the system enough to advocate its adoption in the United States.

So we have to turn to Ezra Vogel and others, some of whom were swept away by the grandeur of it all. Just think.

Crushed and devastated after the war, Japan rose up out of the ashes to forge the world's premier industrial establishment! It created one industry after the other, not just ordinary ones but high-tech!! And production boomed!!! All of which is true. But they overlook the cost of these operations. And they forget that there are two types of industrial policy—one to promote emerging sectors, the other to ease the demise of declining ones.

Let us start with the at least apparently brilliant successes. One which follows the pure theory of the government intervening to save the nation is the linkage of coal and steel right after the war. It was impossible to produce steel without coal or to mine coal without steel machinery, and thus the economy was stymied. Seizing the initiative, the bureaucrats adopted laws promoting both industries, financing them and getting production back on track.

This was followed up by MITI in its first major program of boosting the steel industry yet further. This implied not repairing old mills but tearing them down and building new "greenfield" steelworks with the largest scale and latest technologies. Naturally, that sort of thing was expensive, but the state provided lavish tax incentives and subsidies and the Japan Development Bank granted cheap loans. To have all this steel consumed, the market was protected by tariffs and exports were encouraged. By the 1970s, Japan boasted the world's finest steelmills and produced almost 130 million tons a year.

Meanwhile, the Ministry of Transport was working to revive shipbuilding. Here, too, rather than repair old yards brand-new ones were built, including the world's largest which could handle huge supertankers. To help finance the effort, companies also obtained tax relief, subsidies and JDB loans. For exports, the Export-Import Bank provided low interest rates. But just to be sure ships were sold, MOT forced the shipping companies it was also promoting and subsidizing to buy Japanese. By the 1970s, Japan's shipbuilding industry was No. 1, producing almost 18 million tons a year.

MITI came back for an even more glorious round of programs to promote the electronics and computer industries from the late 1950s to the present day. Even before products were made, it set up tariff walls to keep out superior foreign imports and only IBM managed to produce locally. Meanwhile, it saw to it that Japanese goods were bought by the government and companies. The real thrust, however, was to overcome technological limits through an endless and very costly series of research projects, from components, to computers, to semiconductors, to software. It is presently engaged in the highly touted Fifth Generation Computer project.

Less visibly, but no less effectively, the Ministry of Health nurtured a pharmaceutical industry. This it did partly by making it a very lucrative sector. Not hard. It simply saw to it that the national health insurance scheme paid exorbitant prices for locally-produced drugs which were still cheaper than imported ones because of the high tariffs. Blocked by tariffs, quotas and innumerable non-tariff barriers, foreign manufacturers could only enter the lucrative Japanese market through joint ventures. The result was that local producers "borrowed" their technologies, upgraded and became tough competitors. Now that biotechnology is all the rage, MITI has chipped in with research projects.

Well, that is one side of the story. The only side you hear much about. Let's try the other. This consists of some outright failures and also questionable successes.

One of Vogel's favorites is coal mining, which was condemned to disappear eventually, but where MITI brought about an orderly retreat.[7] How noble. But why it bothered is beyond me. Coal mining was never sensible in Japan. Coal seams are remote, small and low yielding. Manpower is costly. The price of domestic coal was thus much higher than imported coal, let alone cheap oil. Instead of wisely winding

Happiness is exporting more
than you can possibly import.

Credit: Foreign Press Center/Kyodo

down the industry in a decade or so, MITI stubbornly held
on for four until it finally collapsed in the mid-1980s.

Another is aluminum, a pet project of MITI which probably
hoped it could repeat its achievements with steel. True, it
was possible to build modern smelters and expand output to
a million tons a year, making Japan the number three producer. And bauxite could be imported cheaply. But this industry consumes enormous quantities of electricity, which is
exceedingly expensive in Japan. So it was never going to be
competitive, any more than for zinc, copper or nickel which
the bureaucrats also dabbled in. By the 1980s, all these sectors
were dying.[8]

Other MITI programs were even more questionable like the grandiose Sunshine Project, initiated in 1974 with high hopes of making quick breakthroughs for alternative sources of energy. One form was geothermal, given the many fields located in Japan. Some small power stations were built but they were disappointing, generating little power and even the fields gave out. Solar energy was even less promising since Japan is not a very sunny country. Despite generators on countless rooftops, not much came of it. Nor was there greater success with wind power, biomass or ocean tides. All that was produced for sure were jobs for superannuated bureaucrats until some joked of this as being a "moonlight" project.

More striking, and embarrassing, are some of the failures in major high tech fields. No project has ever been launched with more extravagant expectations than the "fifth generation" computer. Here, with thinking computers and artificial intelligence, Japan could surely pull ahead. Indeed, its coming accomplishments were celebrated in advance by books like *The Fifth Generation*.[9] But progress was slow and now, the director informs us, we will have to wait not only ten years but well into the 21st century.[10] The targeters also made a mess of plans to develop aircraft, creating nothing new and doing so at an absurd cost. Yet, that did not keep them from introducing ever more ambitious projects like hypersonic planes, huge rockets and inevitably putting Japanese into space.

Still more futile were the attempts of the Ministry of Agriculture to diversify farming. It was obvious that there was too much rice production but, rather than merely cut back or get farmers out of the sector, the bureaucrats came up with one hairbrained scheme after another. Instead of rice, they urged wheat production. But the land and climate, let alone the size of farms, were even less propitious for that. Then they tried cattle, in herds of a dozen at best, which proved unprofitable. Next came citrus fruits, for which the weather was not always ideal. And all the time the government kept out imported produce while subsidizing its farmers more than any others in the world.

Alas, we cannot stop here. We have to go back to some of the "success stories" which have come upon hard times and, once having been built up, are now being cut back. When we left off, Japan had the world's biggest shipbuilding industry and the world's biggest shipyards. By the late 1970s, however, it had rather few orders and supertankers were out of fashion, making its giant yards white elephants. So the government stepped in, forming cartels, rationalizing production, reducing capacity to a quarter the former level, and subsidizing all the way. By the late 1980s, it faced similar problems with petrochemicals and perhaps steel. And others would come by and by.

Why did this happen? It is incorrect, and intellectually dishonest, to pin the blame on the 1973 oil crisis. Japanese companies were still building new, larger facilities after that and the supposedly far-sighted industrial associations and bureaucracies were making wildly optimistic forecasts of the coming upturn. The real problem is that this system, which subsidizes increased production and artificially raises the returns of domestic sales, sends the wrong signals. It lets businessmen believe that they can succeed by following government directives and not what the market tells them. So they regularly end up with excess capacity that ultimately has to be shed.

This means that the system is incredibly wasteful. It pumps in tremendous amounts of money to subsidize, support, and protect projects which themselves are exceptionally expensive because every company wants nothing but the biggest and the best. And later some of this has to be scrapped. The worst example is probably shipbuilding, another one of Vogel's favorites, which never made a penny. It was heavily subsidized while it was built up. There was a period when ships were selling well, but due to excessive competition margins remained slim. Then came a long downturn when losses were accumulated year after year.

Who paid for all this? The government? Of course not. It has no money of its own, it only has tax revenue it gets from the public. The companies? Not really. They got everything subsidized and could sell products dear on a protected home market. So it was the taxpayers and consumers who paid. In short, this system can be a heavy burden on ordinary citizens. And there is not much they can do about it.

Just how successful targeting and industrial policy were depended on how intelligently each individual project was designed and run. Some were, indeed, worthwhile. Others should never have been undertaken. The clearest rule is the less the state intervened, the better the results. If the bureaucrats want to pat themselves on the back for their great accomplishments, and academics like Johnson and Vogel want to applaud them, let them do so. But don't be taken in. While the Japanese did a better job than most, it was hardly flawless.

NOTES

1. *Japan Times*, June 12, 1981.
2. See Marvin J. Wolf, *The Japanese Conspiracy*.
3. See Chalmers Johnson, *MITI And The Japanese Miracle*.
4. Gary R. Saxonhouse, *Tampering with Comparative Advantage in Japan?*, ITC Investigation 332–162, 1983.
5. *Daily Yomiuri*, April 30, 1986.
6. Johnson, *op. cit.*, pp. 17–26.
7. For this and other case histories, see Ezra Vogel, *Comeback*.
8. For a very sober assessment, see Richard J. Samuels, "The Industrial Destructuring of the Japanese Aluminum Industry," *Pacific Affairs*, Fall 1983, pp. 495–509.
9. See Edward A. Feigenbaum and Pamela McCorduck, *The Fifth Generation*.
10. *Financial Times*, September 8, 1988.

5
Economic Progress
(Onward If Not Upward)

No More Growth Hero

Japan, the land of the rising sun, seems also to be the land of the rising economy, the land of eternally dynamic growth, the land of ever onward and upward. It is hard to open a book or newspaper without getting extravagant appraisals of Japan's growth potential. One of the most famous was issued by futurologist Herman Kahn back in 1970. "It seems to me at least as likely as not that by 1975 the Japanese—and most of the outside world—will be expecting Japan to enjoy another twenty-five years of much the same growth rates. Or even if by 1975 the Japanese—or others—no longer expect Japan to match the greater than 10% per annum growth rates of the 1950-75 time period, they almost certainly will expect close to 10% and substantially more than the 'usual' 5% or so. . . ."[1]

As we know, Kahn's prediction was grossly mistaken. Growth slackened dramatically, partly, but only partly due to the oil crisis. Yet, although growth was down, optimism and wishful thinking were as buoyant as ever. In 1974, when it should have known better, the Japan Economic Research Center (better known by its acronym JERC), forecast as much as 9% annual growth for the coming decade.

And it was not entirely alone. Other independent forecasts were in the 6% to 7% range. The Economic Planning Agency, the official government source, came out with targets that high or higher. Even today we get spurts of bullish enthusiasm. Consider this analysis in the normally sober *Financial Times*.

"The Japanese economy might well be considered one of the wonders of the world. It responds rapidly to radically changed circumstances without producing inflation or undue pain to those affected by the changes. . . . the yen has doubled in value against the dollar, initially causing enormous anxieties in many sectors of Japanese industry. But today the Japanese economy, far from being hurt by the strong currency, is growing at rates not seen since the early 1970s and is virtually free of inflation. Most economists in Tokyo are forecasting real growth of slightly better than 5%. . . ."[2]

This shows just how risky it is to go against the conventional wisdom. While everyone else was predicting solid growth in the 1970s, I wrote *Japan: The Coming Economic Crisis*. Was I praised for my foresight? No, I was criticized and ridiculed. Journalist colleagues would ask me when the economy was going to collapse, as if I were 'Chicken Little' waiting for the sky to fall. What happened later was even more distressing. The economy did slow. Did I get any credit for having foreseen that? No. Obviously it had to slow down, Japan was a mature economy, it was unreasonable to expect endless growth, etc., etc. This from the very same folks who had been expecting it. And now they become inordinately proud when Japan attains the 'usual' 5%.

Nonetheless, I will again go out on a limb by rating Japan's economy a mere satisfactory and not a brilliant superior. This will not endear me to the experts, quasi-experts, would-be experts, have-been experts and others who live in the lofty realms of rosy scenario. Still, let me explain my reasons.

First of all, while Japan's growth did not fall as low as that of other advanced countries, it did fall more sharply. The deceleration was acute, from 10% or more before the oil crisis to only about 4% or 5% thereafter. That was a loss of more than 5 percentage points or considerably more than was suffered by any OECD country. Over the past decade or so, Japan's growth has only been slightly better than the OECD average. But it was not even as good as some more vigorous European countries. And it was downright mediocre compared to 10% and up in the East Asian "tigers," Hong Kong, Singapore, Taiwan and Korea.

So there is no cause to get ecstatic about 5% growth as the *Financial Times* did. That is not an exceptional rate and the fact that admirers can wax poetic about such ordinary growth shows that they have lost their bearings and praise Japan no matter what. It is great when it attains 10%. When it only achieves 5%, that is also great. Whatever it does is great, for them. But for me it only rates a satisfactory.

The same applies to other aspects of the Japanese economy. It was mentioned that there was not "undue pain." I assume this means no massive layoffs and unemployment. But unemployment did creep up to 2.8%, low by international standards, but twice Japan's earlier levels. It was also "virtually free of inflation." Perhaps there was little sign of inflation during the early 1980s, when oil prices were declining, but it was only compensating for the runaway, oil-fueled inflation of the late 1970s. So the decrease in inflation was actually a correction from excessively high levels.

If we stop here, then the Japan claque may have some right to applaud. But we cannot. Now we must make our first foray into the thicket of Japanese statistics. In so doing, we must remember the fallacy of comparing apples to oranges, one made all too often by the media and supposed "experts." For Japanese statistics do not always (read: almost never) count the same things as the rest of us.

One grotesque example is the unemployment rate. I included a whole chapter on this in *Japan's Wasted Workers*.[3] And a knowledgeable specialist, Koji Taira, provided a more technical explanation.[4] The upshot, however, is the same. There are many workers we would count as jobless which the Japanese do not. They overlook those who have been laid off, those who will be employed within a month, those who turn down a job offered by the labor exchange, those looking for work during the month but not the week of the survey, and some others. Moreover, "unemployed" means not having done even one hour's work during that week, which is a bit restrictive.

If you include all the jobless counted elsewhere, and exclude some categories the Japanese add to the employed, you would get a much higher unemployment figure. According to Taira and others, it would be at least double. If you were to add the masses of women and other discouraged workers who have given up seeking a job, or are simply too demure or uptight to admit that they were looking, you could easily get a figure three times as high. Whether you opt for doubling to about 5% or tripling to about 7.5%, Japan no longer appears so extraordinary. Quite to the contrary, its unemployment level would be about average for the OECD countries and high for the East Asian NICs.

The situation for inflation is similar, although harder to analyze exactly because every country has a somewhat different "basket" of goods whose prices are followed to determine inflation. Still, in Japan, it is clear that this basket is heavily weighted toward ordinary household expenses, including local foodstuffs, and oil. On the other hand, it does not include much in the way of indicators of housing prices, whether land, construction, rental or housing loans. Nor does it adequately reflect the supplementary costs of education.[5]

This makes the consumer price index almost useless in

Trends in Land and Consumer Price Indexes
(index, 1980 = 100)

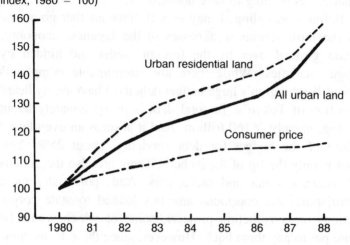

No, we don't have any inflation,
just rapidly rising land prices.

Source: *Economic Statistics Annual*,
Bank of Japan, 1988.
Credit: *Facts and Figures of Japan 1989*, p. 80.

measuring cost of living changes for most Japanese. There is no expenditure which exceeds that of buying a home or paying off the mortgage. It can easily run 30% of the household budget for many families. Those with children in high school or university spend about 10% on that. Yet, as everybody knows, land prices have been climbing at an incredible pace and housing prices have also risen substantially. The same applies to educational costs. This makes an official inflation rate of 1% or so completely meaningless.

Now, if inflation is really higher than claimed, certainly 1% or 2% more than admitted, other figures must also be skewed. The most significant is "real" growth. This is determined by correcting "nominal" growth, which is actually measured, by a deflator which is tied to inflation. If this deflator should be higher, then Japanese "real" growth should be lower. And real "real" growth of 3% or 4% rather than 5% is nothing to rave about.

Before concluding, I may as well have another go at one of the most serious weaknesses of the Japanese economy, again glossed over by the foreign media and hidden by bogus statistics. While there are interminable complaints about Washington's huge budget deficits, I have rarely heard mention of Tokyo's. Its total debt is proportionately about as big, namely ¥160 trillion. And it absorbs an even larger share of the budget for debt servicing, about 25%. Yet, that is only the tip of the iceberg. There are also the deficits of villages, cities and prefectures. And, potentially more worrisome, the enormous amounts loaned to state corporations or construction projects, some of which would be sore put to pay them back. However, since these loans come from the Fiscal Investment and Loan Program they are off-budget.[6]

So, the economy is not that impressive. It is certainly not as sound or dynamic as claimed. But, and this must be conceded, it has had a bounce recently even if not one that would justify the overblown language of the *Financial Times*. What actually happened was not that the Maekawa report, urging a revamping of the economy toward domestic-led growth, was suddenly implemented. Rather, after having painstakingly restrained budget growth and partly restored the financial situation under Nakasone, his successor was able to throw lots of money at various sectors. Not surprisingly, Takeshita gave public works the lion's share.

A bounce or even steadier growth around 5% (or maybe 3%) does not make Japan a growth hero. That is still down significantly from the high-growth period, it is well below the levels achieved by other Asian countries and even lags some Western ones on occasion. It is good, not great. Thus, I rank the economy as satisfactory, not superior.

Good Sectors, Bad Sectors

It is disconcerting that the Japanapologists, even while claiming that Japan has the greatest economy in the world, manage to find alibis for any failings or adopt the official excuses issued by Japan, Inc. So, before seeing what the most serious problems are, let's get the more common excuses out of the way. In so doing, we do not claim that they lack all validity but rather that they have been exaggerated or serve as red herrings to keep observers from looking in the right direction.

One of the favorite explanations, of course, is the oil crisis. Japanese speakers, who like to start their pep talks from a historical turning point, constantly begin with reference to the dramatic events of 1973, when Japan, the world's most oil-dependent country, found itself threatened with destruction as the flow was cut off. Yet, by making absolutely extraordinary efforts, it was ultimately able to "overcome" the oil crisis and go from strength to strength.

There are only a few flaws in this scenario, scarcely worthy of mention, but enough to turn it upside down. True, Japan was more dependent on imported oil than most but still basically in the same position as European countries like Germany or France which also lived through the crisis. The first thing it did was to make friends with the Arabs. After that, it was just a question of money, of which it had plenty, and industrial rationalization, at which it is formidable but not quite the only country to pull it off. Thus, Japan managed to muddle through just like the rest of us.

But it did not really "overcome" in any demonstrable way since growth dropped sharply and 1973 marked the end of the high growth period. What is more intriguing is what has happened since. During recent years, oil prices have stabilized or fallen while being eroded by inflation, so that they are only about where they were in real terms back in 1973. Yet, Japanese growth has not snapped back. This leads me to

88

believe that, oil crisis or no oil crisis, the economy would have slackened.

It seems that Japan always needs a crisis to mobilize, and speakers got tired of referring to the same old crisis, so mercifully they were blessed with *endaka*. This is the "high yen," a yen that doubled in value against the U.S. dollar as of 1985, and appeared poised to crush the economy again. Yet, by pulling in their belts, rationalizing production, saving here and there, the Japanese could resume the march forward. Splendid. Admirable. But Germany did the same thing. And so did even less celebrated countries like Great Britain, France and Italy.

So, getting through *endaka* with a buoyant economy, the phenomenon highlighted by the *Financial Times*, is not so exceptional. Especially not when it represents a bounce after some slower-than-average years. Moreover, and this point should not be forgotten, the period of yen appreciation followed a period of yen depreciation, bringing it back to where it was and a bit beyond. After all, the yen is traditionally kept undervalued and every once in a while it must respond to reality and strengthen. This was not the first time. And it will not be the last.

Another popular excuse is protectionism. To hear the Japanese tell it, foreign countries are ganging up on them because Japanese products are too good and too cheap and they simply can't take the heat. There may be an element of truth in that. But it cannot be assumed that others will stand idly by as their industries and companies are crushed one by one. Anyway, Japan had no end of warnings in the form of nasty conflicts over televisions, and automobiles, and steel, and ships, and semiconductors, and computers, and a mass of other products with countries as varied as the United States, France, Indonesia, Korea, Taiwan and the People's Republic of China.

Moreover, it is a bit hypocritical to complain that trading

partners closed their markets to Japan when it had been so tardy in opening its own. It was among the last advanced economies to eliminate its tariffs, quotas and, just recently, some of its non-tariff barriers. Even now, national producers still defend their turf through the Three Super-Cs, connivance, collusion and control of distribution. Worse, after having finally opened the market a fair amount, worried producers in backward sectors are urging the government to protect them from the newly industrializing countries and a whole new series of barriers is going up.

Now we reach something more serious and pervasive, that is the maturation of the economy. This has taken various forms. One is that, after having spent decades developing products that had been invented by others, Japan began running out and had to create some of its own. Another is that, after having spent decades buying, borrowing or stealing foreign technologies, it had to conceive some of its own. The third is that, after having spent decades conquering new foreign markets, there were not many more left.

There is no doubt that such maturation has put a crimp in its economic expansion. Each additional step was harder to take and the path ahead was no longer clearly blazed by those who preceded it and with whom it had now caught up. But this sort of thing is natural. And maturation comes to every economy, so it is silly to complain about it. Moreover, although admittedly younger and more vigorous, it is amazing how other Pacific economies managed to maintain relatively high growth even after Japan slipped.

The last explanation, however, is by far the best. Yet, it is overlooked by the Japan claque. It is that the economy is grotesquely unbalanced and distorted. All we ever hear about are the magnificent, highly productive, strongly capitalized, superbly organized, big company-dominated high tech industries oriented toward exports. Or perhaps the giant banks, the indomitable trading companies (*sogo shosha*) and some

advanced service enterprises. But that is not the whole economy. It is not even half. It is probably not even a quarter.
And the rest is much less impressive.

As was mentioned, the industrial sectors just referred to
are only a portion of manufacturing as a whole. Aside from
that, there is a series of rather backward sectors, many of
them patently artisinal, which produce ordinary articles for
everyday use like tatami mats, porcelain, kimonos, furniture,
and so on. Other sectors like cement, paper, light metals and
petrochemicals are not particularly efficient. Finally come the
declining sectors, which were once very competitive but have
gradually lost their edge and weakened, textiles and garments,
footwear, fabricated metals, fertilizer, shipbuilding, etc.

There is also construction, which ranges from fairly advanced to absurdly primitive. Most housing is produced on
a small scale, one office building or detached house at a time,
which makes it hard to engage in mass production techniques
or prefabrication. Indeed, if you walk about a housing site,
you will find the carpenters, roofers, plumbers, etc. exercising
their trades in almost medieval style. For public works projects, whether highways, bridges and ports or schools and
administrative buildings, the methods are not overly productive and the organizational techniques far worse, with numerous layers of subcontractors and each lower level a
throwback to yet earlier times.

Distribution, as everyone must realize by now, is exceedingly inefficient. Despite a supposed "revolution" and the
emergence of more department stores, superstores, chain
stores and the like, there are still far too many retail units
and the bulk of them are "papa-mama" stores. Japan still
has 1,630,000 or so retail outlets which is much more for the
size of its population than other industrialized countries.
Thus, each unit serves 69 persons in Japan as opposed to 136
persons in the United States, 166 in West Germany and 240
in Great Britain.

The services sector is divided between large and small units, with huge banks and tiny consumer finance firms, imposing hotel chains and modest bars and restaurants, sophisticated airlines and simple trucking companies. It is also divided between advanced sectors, like advertising, leasing and software and backward ones, often related to personal and household services. There are far more of the smaller firms and backward sectors and they are as inefficient as can be imagined. In fact, in certain ways, efficiency is not even the goal as opposed to "service" in the Japanese sense of endless time and care lavished on making the customer feel good.

The worst of the lot, however, is agriculture. It is hopelessly inefficient although quite large compared to other advanced countries. There are too many farmers for the amount of land and not enough consolidation to create viable units. No quantity of equipment or agrochemicals can make up for that. Yet, it grows too much of certain crops, like rice and wheat, which must then be stored at great expense. And it does not produce enough of things that are in greater demand, like meat, fruits and vegetables.

So, if you look at the whole Japanese economy, you get a very different picture. The modern, efficient portion is relatively small; the rudimentary and inefficient, much larger. No wonder the economy is not progressing as rapidly when it is so heavily burdened down. And this is the fault, not of the Arabs, or the Americans, or the European Community but Japan. For over a century it has had a dual economy and, despite claims to the contrary, that situation has not changed. This means that any economist who points only at the more admirable side and overlooks the rest—as frequently happens—is either incredibly misinformed or incredibly dishonest. On a more objective, balanced view the Japanese economy is just fair-to-middling.

Peasant farmers—the only endangered species
Japan is actively protecting

Credit: Foreign Press Center/Kyodo

Productive, Not Fruitful

Developing and expanding the economy is one thing. Actually
deriving benefit from it is another. So far the Japanese have
been rather good at the former and quite poor at the latter.
They have fashioned an economy in which the most extraordinary products are made in profusion but only bring in rather
paltry returns. That is why I have repeatedly stressed the
seemingly odd concept of an economy that is productive, not
fruitful.

The essential reason is easy enough to grasp. Japanese

business does not aim, like Western business and many others, to achieve the greatest possible profit. Profit-maximization is not now and never has been the principal goal. Originally, back in Meiji days, it was to create a sufficiently strong economy to defend Japan from the West, with businessmen being patriots of a sort. Now, saddled with an extensive core staff, vast and expensive production facilities, and generally high overheads, the important thing is to sell more and expand to justify this expenditure.

But the root cause is the urge for market share. Just about every Japanese company wants to expand so that it can gain a bigger piece of the market. With larger sales, it justifies scale, lowers costs and can ultimately reap greater profits. Before that "ultimately" happens, however, it must engage in fierce competitive battles because no other company is willing to lose market share. For, if it did, and if it were pushed back enough, it would disappear. Thus the idea that companies are fighting for "survival" so often expressed by Japanese executives is true.

Market share is a very harsh taskmaster. While, in a profit-oriented economy, every company can enhance profit by reducing costs, increasing sales, charging more or whatever, there is no way that everyone can enhance market share. There are only 100%. For one company to gain another percent, some other company must lose. That, more than anything else, explains why Japanese companies are so competitive, an aspect overlooked by Abegglen and others but well-known to the businessmen who engage in, but dread, what they call *kato kyoso* or "excessive competition."[7]

It is this rivalry, at home and abroad, which keeps their profits much lower than in most Western countries or places like Hong Kong and Taiwan. According to various statistics, they are lucky to get a return of 1% or 2% on sales while others obtain 5% or more. In fact, Japanese businessmen are regularly stunned by how their foreign competitors can actually lose market share yet boost profits. This for the larger companies. According to the tax authorities, half of Japan's small and medium-sized firms have been declaring losses for years. While you cannot trust their tax returns, they are not really thriving.

How then do Japanese companies earn such profits as they do? Primarily by only engaging in these competitive struggles intermittently. There are periods of intense rivalry in early days, when numerous companies rush into a new sector. But the inevitable shakeout comes and only about a dozen or so real contenders remain. Over the years, there will be more bouts of *kato kyoso* when a lower-ranking firm tries to boost its position or the top ones decide to get rid of smaller entities until only a few are left. Otherwise, it is live and let live and they recoup the costs and even make tidy profits for a while.

Indeed, they may even do better if they are adept at the three Super-Cs of connivance, collusion and control of distribution. This is done in various ways. Manufacturers which sell through dependent outlets will fix the sales price in their own stores and see that there is no discounting. Meanwhile, explicitly or tacitly, they will agree with other makers to hold to similar prices. Even in those stores which offer a variety of makes it is hard to find bargains. The only time prices are marked down is when *kato kyoso* rears its ugly head.

The Three Super-Cs are even crasser in the construction industry where contractors get together to decide who will get which project and, since there really is only one bidder, he can charge pretty much what he wants. In distribution, it involves especially so-called luxury goods whose sales are restricted to artificially boost prices. In farming, it is mainly the connivance which works, since the farmers inveigle the government into paying higher crop prices than are justified. But connivance exists throughout since it is the government which allows the manufacturers and contractors to break antitrust laws or lets banks pay low interest rates and insurance companies charge high premiums.

Obviously, this sort of thing is much more difficult (but not impossible) in foreign markets where there is also an indigenous industry and governments may supervise antitrust rules more strictly.[8] That is why exporting, rather than being an abundant and lucrative source of earnings, has so far brought rather mediocre returns. The Japanese undercut fiercely to get into the market initially. Subsequently, they could charge the going rate and make a nice profit and they probably would if they were only competing with local companies that want to maximize profits. Alas, they are pitted against the same nasty rivals from back home and the competitive wars quickly spill over onto distant shores.[9]

It seems that the only way Japanese exporters can make fat profits is when they maintain a worldwide monopoly or oligopoly (motorcycles, VCRs and chips, for example) or when a foreign government intervenes to protect its own market and forces Japan to accept restraint. This usually results in quotas which limit the quantity sold and, relieved of the urge to enhance market share, prices and margins can be raised. The best illustrations were the controls on semiconductor prices and auto exports to the United States.

The outcome is admittedly "managed" trade. And it is becoming the norm. More and more foreign governments have imposed formal or tacit quotas on Japanese products and each time this halts the drive for market share and encourages greater attention to profits. By now, dozens of sectors are covered. Indeed, MITI already regulates so many products that, in August 1988, an advisory group suggested this might be institutionalized and MITI could control exports even before formal complaints were lodged. This was rejected angrily and indignantly by the business community, but the process still continues on a case-by-case basis.

This failure to keep prices at a profitable level unless

obliged to by foreign governments or MITI or achieved by squeezing domestic consumers only constitutes one side of the equation. The other is cost.

While there has been much praise of Japanese efforts to rationalize production, use more machinery, reduce inventory and so on, there has been little criticism of certain phenomena we mentioned earlier. In Japan, rather than merely expand or upgrade facilities, the companies are for ever tearing down or scrapping old ones and building brand-new greenfield factories. This process is considerably more expensive. And it becomes ridiculously so when keen competition forces manufacturers to change designs and models at short intervals, requiring even more investments.

As was also mentioned above, it would not matter so much if the companies merely wanted to upgrade or modernize. Instead, they insist on boosting scale each time as well. This has two negative effects. For one, the factory is obviously more costly than otherwise even if unit costs can be reduced. The other, more serious, is that they now have to sell more units than ever before. To do so, they may have to cut unit prices beneath the lower unit costs in order to win market share from competitors which have probably also increased scale at the same time. In this unnecessary bout of *kato kyoso*, some of the rivals will withdraw or go under which means that the extraordinary sums spent on huge, new, costly installations will be wasted.

There is only one way to boost profits without all this hassle and risk, that is to reduce labor costs. And Japanese companies—for all their love of the happy company family—have become masters at this. They are constantly decreasing the amount of manpower going into their various products by replacing workers with machines and robots. In so doing, they spare no effort. And they enroll the workers in their own demise by having them suggest ways of raising productivity. Thus, each time I visit Japanese factories, I see fewer human beings on the assembly line and some facilities are already entirely automated.

In addition to eliminating jobs, it is possible to save on labor costs by having the work done by workers who cost less. Thus, for example, older employees are retired and replaced by younger workers who, under the seniority system, are paid less. Or, if one does not wish to fire loyal workers, they can be sent off to a remote branch, special subsidiary or subcontractor where they earn less. Meanwhile, whenever money can be saved, jobs requiring more manpower are passed down to suppliers which pay their own employees considerably less.

Finally, to keep the general level of wages at an "acceptable" level, managers fight tenaciously to hold annual increments within bounds. One year, they complain that wage hikes cannot be larger because of the oil shock, another because of the high yen, and yet another because it might contribute to inflation. There is always a good excuse. Sometimes they link wage hikes to productivity, other times to inflation, whatever gives the lowest result. Since the company unions are fairly subservient, and the national centers rather weak, management has kept wages from rising too rapidly. So labor does not get much out of any gains aside from rare periods when business is booming and it is hard to find enough staff.

When you take these various elements, namely the weaker, sloppier sectors covered in the previous section and what has just been described here, such as costly investments, excessive scale, ruthless competition, cheap exports and often expensive domestic prices, unimpressive profits and even more miserly wage hikes, it is easy to understand that the Japanese economy is not very fruitful. It generates incredible quantities of goods. But those who produce them, whether the companies or workers, have less to show for their efforts than most foreigners. This is one more strike against Japanese-style economics, although it will only make sense to those who believe that an economy is meant to serve the people and not the other way around.

NOTES

1. Herman Kahn, *The Emerging Japanese Superstate*, p. 2.
2. *Financial Times*, September 28, 1988.
3. See Jon Woronoff, *Japan's Wasted Workers*, pp. 229–61.
4. Koji Taira, "Japan's Low Unemployment: Economic Miracle or Statistical Artifact?," *Monthly Labor Review*, July 1983, pp. 3–10.
5. See Woronoff, *Inside Japan, Inc.*, pp. 232–51.
6. See Woronoff, *Politics, The Japanese Way*, pp. 240–6.
7. See Woronoff, *The Japan Syndrome*, pp. 53–7.
8. Admittedly, this does not entirely prevent collusion as when Japanese television producers agreed on prices and markets for the United States, the source of one of the conspiracies described in Marvin Wolf's *The Japanese Conspiracy*.
9. See Vladimir Pucik, "Management Practices and Business Strategy in Manufacturing Firms," in *Strategic Management in the United States and Japan*, Cambridge, Ballinger, 1986, pp. 115–28.

6
Education
(What is Learning?)

World Champion Test-Takers

No aspect of Japanese society has been singled out for more lavish praise (and less criticism) than the educational system. One of the best known expressions thereof was penned by Edwin O. Reischauer in his habitual "never be anything but wildly optimistic" style.

"Formal education and examinations have taken the place of class and birth in determining which organizations and career patterns one qualifies for—in other words, one's function and status in Japan's modern meritocracy. High literacy rates and excellent educational standards are also major reasons for Japan's success in meeting the challenge of a technologically more advanced West in the nineteenth century and for its subsequent achievement of a position of economic leadership. Nothing, in fact, is more central in Japanese society or more basic to Japan's success than is its educational system."[1]

But it was Ezra Vogel, joined by Cummings, Duke, Lynn, White et. al., who not only applauded the educational system for its contribution to Japan's success but proposed it as a model for others.[2] It is therefore necessary to consider the evidence *Japan As No. 1* adduced for this. Seemingly, the most impressive and irrefutable are readily measured: the number of schools, students and graduates, which is very high. Another, almost as imposing and solid, derives from results on cross-national comparative tests in which, according to Vogel, "no country outperformed Japan overall."[3] You can't argue with numbers, can you? Well, maybe you can.

Certainly, on the face of it, the situation for school enrollment is admirable. Just about every child receives primary education, although this is also compulsory in all advanced countries and many developing ones. But 95% of the Japanese go on to secondary school and 90% graduate, which is a very high percentage compared to the United States, with 77%, and European countries, with much lower figures. By now, some 40% of the high school graduates proceed to college, lower only than the American level of over 50%, but much higher than the levels in Europe, which are considerably below 30%.

However, counting the number of students in each category has drawbacks which the Japan claque tends to overlook. For one, we are again mixing apples and oranges. Half of Japan's colleges, with a fifth of the students, are only "junior" or two-year colleges which hardly entitles them to comparison with bona fide universities. This is particularly so since they are mainly frequented by female students and males who could not make it elsewhere. In Japan, they are widely regarded as finishing schools for young ladies or diploma mills.

Far more significant is that in Europe, as opposed to Japan (and the United States), secondary and tertiary education do not imply the same thing. European students have two more years of schooling before entering a *lycee* or *Gymnasium* and they enter and graduate from university two years later. On the whole, it is felt that a good *lycee* or *Gymnasium* education corresponds to getting halfway through a Japanese (or American) college and a European university diploma can best be compared to a master's degree. Thus, the smaller number of high school and university students is very misleading. Europe is at least on the same level as Japan numberwise.

Far more serious than this, and here we are comparing apples not to oranges but watermelons, is that the apparently plain and unambiguous term "graduation" has a remarkably different significance in Japan. In the West, it is quite normal to regularly narrow the stream of students, indeed, to erect barriers for the specific purpose of eliminating the less capable, if need be by flunking them. This is not done in Japan. There, virtually everybody who gets into a high school or college will graduate if he or she does not pass away or voluntarily withdraw.

This can be explained by a markedly different social environment which observers would be unwise to ignore. In Japan, having a "good" education is far more important than elsewhere since education is not only the main, it is almost the sole criterion for advancement in society. No student can afford to fail. And no parent would accept this. They would put the blame for failure on the teachers and administrators. Rather than bearing the opprobrium for apparently not being able to fulfill their duties, rather than flunk students, the schools let them carry on.

Ez Vogel, bless his soul, sees this as an accomplishment. The schools ". . . ensure that virtually every pupil achieves minimal standards. No student is failed, and all students of the same age proceed together up through grade nine."[4] Actually, as Japanese educator Nishio Kanji explains, this does not work to the advantage of the students. Rather than being put on a slower track where they can proceed at something closer to their own pace or have time to catch up, weaker students are hurried along and have to keep up not with average students but the best in the class.[5] The result is that everybody graduates. But graduation has scarcely any meaning other than having sat in school for the requisite number of years. The same applies at the university level, with everyone who wants one eventually getting a diploma.

This makes comparing numbers of students or graduates silly and claiming that everybody meets minimum standards completely ridiculous. That is a statement hardly any Japanese educators would support. Indeed, how could they when personal observations and authoritative surveys show just the opposite. The situation was best summed up by Father Gustav Voss, a noted foreign educator in Japan, who complained about what he called the "*shichi-go-san* system" whereby only 70% of primary school children can follow the lessons, only 50% of junior high school students can do so, and a mere 30% of senior high school students can perform at the expected levels.[6]

He may have been unduly generous. Motofumi Makieda, then president of the Japan Teachers' Union, regarded "dropouts" as one of the most worrisome educational problems. By this he meant not dropouts in the Western sense, namely those who actually leave school, but dropouts (*ochikobore*) in the Japanese sense of students who remain in the classroom and cannot keep up. This contingent was estimated by the Japan National Association of Educational Research Institutes at half the students on the basis of a poll of high school teachers.[7] And a survey by the Prime Minister's Office found that only 26% of the primary and secondary students understood their lessons.[8] But the most revealing insight comes from a Japanese high school teacher who describes the situation in a manner completely different from the foreign "experts," but in terms that are perfectly familiar to Japanese students, teachers, parents and the media.

"There are many students going to high school who have totally lost the will to study even back in middle school. I think there are many high schools where it would be counted as above average if there are five students per class who promptly take notes and prepare properly for study. The rest of the class is either dozing off or absorbed in loud chatter. Or else they spend the time fooling around or taking walks, paying no attention to their studies. I wonder why students who hate to study have to be forced to attend high schools. . . ."[9]

So, having lots of schools, and lots of students, and lots of graduates is not proof of a superior educational system. Is passing tests more reliable evidence? It depends very much on whether good test scores are a result of having learned a lot or just knowing how to pass tests. These were the two alternative explanations for the amazing ability of Japanese students not only to score high on cross-national tests but to continue raising their scores proposed by Richard Lynn, a professor of psychology, who recently jumped on the "learn from Japan" bandwagon. He hastily concluded that the key factor was the exceptionally demanding educational standards.[10] I beg to differ.

As we saw, anyone who enters a Japanese high school is likely to graduate, so receiving a high school diploma is no great shakes. If you want to succeed, you must proceed on to the next level, college. To get into college (as opposed to getting out of high school), you have to pass incredibly stiff exams. And, unlike other countries where previous educational achievements, recommendations by teachers or civic leaders, or extracurricular activities may help, in Japan the only "narrow gate" is the college entrance exam. On the other hand, once in you can coast along.

Thus, the focus of secondary education becomes preparation for exams that are given once a year and which vary from college to college. These exams consist almost exclusively of multiple choice questions and the more correct answers in the shorter time, the greater the chances of success. Most students therefore do everything they can to amass the specific information required and to bone up on the techniques of passing tests. To some extent, this can be done in school since the examination material covers the basic subjects they are studying. But it can be done much more effectively, purposefully and successfully at specialized cram schools or *juku*.

Gradually, as they approach the exams, high school students devote more and more time to cramming. The *juku* courses supplement school classes and may run one or two hours a day at first, three or four later on. Many students also spend Saturday and Sunday at the *juku* to do mock exams for the specific college they hope to attend. The number of students engaged in this and the time devoted to it has kept rising during the whole postwar period. Now, no students would be so bold, or fcolish, as to try out for a college without suitable preparations. And, if they fail the first time, many will spend another year, or two, or three as *ronin* further ingurgitating facts and refining their test-taking techniques at special preparatory schools.

This means that, without a doubt, Japanese students are the world's champion exam takers. So, it is not surprising that they should perform well on cross-national comparisons. But they are not as good as Vogel and the rest claim. Just consider the results of the latest tests of the International Association for the Evaluation of Educational Achievement, administered in 1984 to students in 22 different countries. The subjects included were physics, chemistry, biology and general science. At the primary school level, Japan tied for first place with Korea. At the more crucial high school level, however, it only came in sixth. Its students had tough competition not only from Korea but also Hong Kong, Finland, Sweden, Hungary, Canada, Holland and Great Britain.[11]

Such minor mishaps are overlooked by the Japanapologists. They like to compare Japan's results to those of the United States, which were much poorer. Why they do so is hard to grasp if they are really interested in comparing educational achievement. But they are not. They only want to show Japan in a good light, if necessary by reference to an educational system whose weaknesses everyone acknowledges. And it would never occur to them to launch a campaign to "learn from Korea" or "learn from Finland."

Lower Higher Education

Naturally, Vogel and the others did not limit their justification for praising Japan's educational system merely to head counts or tests. It was also the approach to education which was worthy of emulation. The schools produced students who were knowledgeable and showed great artistic ability, mastering no less than three musical instruments, according to William Cummings. They also learned self-discipline and were "expected to be courteous and considerate to their teachers and to other students." The Japanese were internally motivated to succeed, mindful of their responsibilities to their parents and the school and genuinely enjoyed learning (putting in extra time when necessary). In summing up, said Vogel, "the nation acquires a large reservoir of well-trained people with a substantial core of common culture, people who are curious, teachable, disciplined, and sensitive to humanistic and civic concerns."[12]

To look into these features, of course, it is indispensable to consider just what is the meaning of a good education. In most Western countries, and I admit that there is a degree of rhetoric involved, education seems to connote not only acquiring facts and skills but also understanding essential phenomena, reasoning and figuring out solutions on the basis of what has been learned. That is also the *tatemae* in Japan, but the *honne* is thoroughly different. In school, the emphasis is not on reasoning but absorbing the officially prescribed material, often by rote memory. There is little time devoted to individual efforts or figuring things out. Tests are usually of the multiple choice variety and writing essays or holding discussions is hardly done. Nor is there much stress on practical applications or realistic exercises.

Anyone who has taught Japanese students, or worked with them later on, knows that they have instant access to vast quantities of often disjointed information. But they are notably lacking in useful skills. They are nowhere near as good in application of their knowledge as the average foreigner. Worse, many do not even possess common sense. These conclusions are not purely anecdotal. There is ample evidence thereof in the same cross-national tests referred to above. They repeatedly showed that the Japanese did well on abstract points but poorly on applied ones, even such an elementary question as what creates rust.

The huge gap between theoretical and practical knowledge is painfully demonstrated by their performance for foreign languages, an example nearly everyone must have personal experience of. Japanese students can barely speak or even comprehend English and their reading ability is not that much better. Yet, they know an incredible amount of English grammar, English syntax, English spelling, even American colloquialisms, indeed, anything that can be learned from books and dutifully memorized. They simply cannot apply that knowledge in the most purposeful manner.

There is another crucial question which must be raised, namely, what should be learned to become an intelligent and useful person? To judge by the comments of some Japanapologists (and Japanese), the only worthwhile subjects are mathematics and science. That happens to be where the biggest efforts are made and the greatest glee expressed over any achievements. But there is more to life than that.

There is certainly much less emphasis on the social sciences in general. This includes history, political science, geography, sociology or ethics. Arts, philosophy, literature and the like are also downgraded. Yet, they are important for very real reasons and not just social uplift. Without them, it is impossible to understand one's place or role in society or to deal intelligently with the broader world beyond the Japanese isles.

One of the worst failures is clearly history. And this is not entirely accidental. Japanese students are thoroughly drilled in the names, dates, events, etc. of the bygone eras and empires. They can tell you anything about ancient history. But modern and contemporary history are almost a blank. They know little of the colonial period, the militarism and dictatorship during the war, or even the development of postwar Japan. In short, they are deplorably ignorant of the most delicate (and shameful) periods, the ones every foreigner would expect them to be fully aware of.

If there is any subject the Japanese should be good at, it is English. They have studied it longer than anything else. And, coming from an insular society speaking a language not widely known abroad, they need it desperately. Yet, this effort has been a failure, as even Reischauer concedes. "It seems significant that, despite the extraordinary amount of time devoted to the study of English in Japanese schools, the results are meager. People are produced who, through painful reading, can acquire knowledge about the outside world and, if required, can develop their abilities into rudimentary speaking skills adequate for necessary economic negotiations in English. But the Japanese educational system turns out few Japanese who can participate actively in the intellectual life of the world."[13]

Obviously, there is more to education than just book learning. It is vital for youngsters to know how to get along with others, not only those in their class or school but people they have never met before. They must acquire certain social graces and an understanding of and perhaps compassion for those who are different. They should develop some ethical and moral values and, since this is the best time for it, even a bit of idealism. These aspects receive scant attention during the earlier years and any pretense of concern for the broader or deeper personality is discarded in the runup to the college entrance exams when anything that does not contribute directly to passing them is cast aside.

This period, which the students refer to as "examination hell," is so given over to memorizing and mock tests that there is no time to lead a normal life. They cut back on sports, art and music (so much for playing three instruments) and engage, in the rare moments of relaxation, in less demanding activities like watching television or reading comics. The intensive competition also separates them from classmates, all of whom are potential rivals for the same schools. Indeed, they have few other human contacts. Yet, although everything is focused on "learning," it certainly does not generate any love of learning.

At this point, another cross-national study is most instructive. It compared the interests and activities of Japanese and American high school students. According to the Japan Youth Research Institute, the Japanese were most interested in comic books, listed by 68%, whereas Americans preferred sports magazines and only 15% bothered with comic books. The Japanese limited their circle of friends to classmates while Americans joined clubs and had friends outside of school. The Americans were interested in politics and social affairs, which hardly concerned the Japanese. More surprisingly, 46% of the U.S. students felt that it is important to improve grades at school even if that meant sacrificing play or social activity, compared with a mere 8% for the Japanese.

According to Tamotsu Sengoku, who interpreted the results, "it appears that U.S. high school students gradually wake up to an interest in politics and society, and begin to take a broader view of their society." As for the Japanese, "as they get older and more preoccupied with entrance examinations, studying begins to lose its original appeal. When they read comic books, perhaps they are looking for a way to escape the heavy pressures of examinations."[14]

These conclusions would appear to contradict Vogel's promise of "people who are curious, teachable, disciplined, and sensitive to humanistic and civic concerns." But it does tally rather well with the conclusions of a genuine authority who spent considerable time visiting and observing Japanese and American high schools. Here, in the words of Thomas P. Rohlen, is a useful and useable comparison.

"Exam-oriented Japanese students become virtual information junkies, drinking in as many facts as possible. They learn to listen well and to think quickly, but not to express their ideas. Neither speaking nor writing is encouraged. Speculation, controversy, and interpretive relativism do not enter the classroom. Thought is weighted in favor of memory and objective problem solving with little official curricular interest in creativity of a humanistic or artistic kind. The pedagogy may seem Confucian, but the real explanation is the matter of passing entrance exams.

"The avowed goals of American teachers are radically different. Although we, too, have lectures and facts to memorize in high school, they are just part of the story. Classroom instruction in the United States ideally includes discussions, digressions, and personal opinions. In our better schools it means essays and research projects and debates. Considerably less well-informed than his Japanese counterpart, the American student is much better prepared to express a personal opinion and think of a question as having more than one answer."[15]

The oddest thing about the debate on Japanese education, however, is that Vogel, Duke, even Rohlen, focus on the primary and secondary schools as if that were where the most valid comparisons could be made. Admittedly, in passing, they all conceded that higher education leaves much to be desired. But they did not draw the conclusion that one should concentrate on the culmination of the educational process,

I passed the exam! I passed the exam!
I got into Todai!!

Credit: Foreign Press Center/Koydo

the students and schools at the top as opposed to somewhere in the middle. This would ordinarily mean that the focus should shift to the universities and graduate studies.

The Japanapologists do not like to discuss this level for very good reasons. Japan's tertiary system is pretty mediocre. From everything I have read or seen personally, it is a bit of a farce. College students spend most of their time relaxing and recovering from the grind of high school and examination hell. They wake up late, skip many lectures, do hardly any homework, spend hours having coffee or playing mah jongg with fellow students, watch television or read comics to kill time, and then turn in late. The more active ones may join a club or engage in sports. But it is only the odd eggheads who strive to learn.

There is no need to take my word for it when there are untold thousands of observers who report much the same phenomena. In fact, you can ask any student; they don't hide it. Or try Michio Nagai, former president of the University of Tokyo and Minister of Education, who condemned the system in a book that foreign academics seem to have overlooked.[16] Even Reischauer, in his ripe old age, had a change of heart when he criticized "the squandering of four years at the college level on poor teaching and very little study."[17] Yet better are the pragmatic comments of an American professor in Japan, Stan Gold, who witnessed the routine first hand.

"One clear tendency among about 90% of the Japanese students I've taught is their strong determination not to study. . . . For these students the four years of college life represent a prolonged respite—a kind of moratorium period during which they spend their time trying to make as many social friends as possible, thus working to develop skills they have ignored while arduously preparing over a period of years for college entrance exams. Many devote themselves to club activities, almost totally neglecting their academic studies."[18]

If there is little reference by admirers of Japan's educational system to the universities, there is even less to graduate studies. Maybe it is because there are so few graduate schools and so few students working for a master's or doctorate. The explanation is simple. There is no market in Japan for students who have wasted their time on advanced studies not required by companies and bureaucracies that employ personnel. And thus graduate studies become a one-way ticket to unemployment or an academic career.

This makes Japan the only country whose educational system becomes progressively weaker as one rises. Its primary schools, according to cross-national tests, were tops. Its secondary schools shared the honors with other countries. Its universities turn out graduates, who, in many cases, do not even leave with as much information as they had when they entered. Indeed, I think it would be exceedingly embarrassing if Japanese college students were subjected to cross-national tests. And it would become much harder to flog this anomaly as No. 1.

Education Or Induction?

If Japanese education has so many drawbacks and defects, how come it has contributed to the country's economic rise? And why do I rate it satisfactory rather than unsatisfactory or worse?

That is because the system has several aspects which were glossed over or played down by the Japanapologists. They manage to compensate for some of the weaknesses and, for certain users at least, actually appear as a "saving grace." It should, however, be remembered that what the Japanese regard as positive may not coincide with the views of foreigners.

While foreign admirers put forward better teachers, better schools, better courses or better students to explain Japan's supposed success, much of the answer resides elsewhere. It is simply longer hours. Japanese students go to school five-and-a-half days a week, this includes Saturday morning. They attend school 240 days a year, compared to only 180 days in the United States. It was thus estimated that, by the time they graduate from high school, Japanese students have put in four more years than their American counterparts. Perhaps it is only two or three compared to Europeans.

But even this underestimates the actual input. Japanese students, like those elsewhere, break for summer vacation. Unlike the rest, they are not free to relax and have fun. They are given massive homework and special projects to prepare during the summer and, smack in the middle of vacation, they have to return to school to show their teachers that they are making progress. During the school year, there is the normal homework, which can amount to two or three hours a day. On top of that, any special courses in cram or prep schools, which can add another hour or two a day plus, for the most determined, Saturday and Sunday during the final phase. Nowhere in the world do you find kids who spend half that much time. So they cannot help but "learn" a lot.

Foreigners will complain that this sort of routine is almost inhuman, that it prevents the development of other talents or social skills, that children need to develop a well-rounded personality and a sense of being, or quite simply and banally that "all work and no play makes Jack a dull boy." That is doubtlessly true. And most Japanese would concede it. But this is yet another saving grace for the future employers who receive people who are used to doing what they are told, who show considerable diligence, and who don't mind putting in long hours and even going without vacation if need be.

Obviously, Japanese students are not doing this, as Vogel suggests, out of love of learning or to become "educated" in any abstract sense but to qualify for the next higher level which is induction into a company or bureaucracy. Since the "good" employers only accept students who have graduated from "good" schools, they have no choice but to go through the routine. Employers, while they do not like the quality or quantity of knowledge the new employees bring with them, and have to supplement it later, nonetheless approve of the system.

After all, they are not looking for candidates who are particularly bright or dynamic or have specialized knowhow or skills. They seek employees who can be moved around the company or bureaucracy as circumstances require. Too much knowledge would be wasted or might even get in the way.

114

That this view predominates can be seen from the preference for graduates of general studies as opposed to specialists. It is the former who are put on the escalator leading to top posts while the latter are relegated to some technical job they are less likely to stray from.

Admittedly, this means that the company or bureaucracy has to make up for any gaps or lapses in the school education. Having the employees for an extensive period, they seem to mind less and, somehow or other, they all think that their own methods are so special and different that only they are worth learning. Thus, young workers or bureaucrats are put through the equivalent of apprenticeship, assigned to older employees and instructed to follow what they do. If there is a need for more formal training, that can be provided by in-house courses for the most part.[19] If that is inadequate, companies would not hesitate to send employees to an institute or university to study, probably abroad because that is where the best advanced studies are available.

To judge by both word and deed, the ideal Japanese employee is not one with particular intelligence, spirit or imagination, not one who knows a lot, not one who can move ahead on his own, characteristics that other educational systems encourage. Rather, he is someone who feels best within the group, who does not try to stand out, who follows orders from above without asking too many questions, and who shows loyalty. That is what the Japanese educational system produces, another saving grace. This was clearly stated by Benjamin Duke, a long-time professor at International Christian University in Tokyo.

"One of the predominant traits of the Japanese—be it at work, school, or play—is loyalty to the group. It transcends all layers of the society. It is the stuff of 'being Japanese.' . . . The course for developing group loyalty begins in school with the very first day of grade one. . . . The first grade *kumi* (class) represents the beginning of the formal process of group training, Japanese style, that is, developing ties that bind the individual to his group in order to achieve the ultimate goal, group harmony. It is, in every sense, the initial stage in school in the long task of preparing the future Japanese worker for the harmonious adjustment of employer-employee relationships characteristic of labor relations within Japanese industry.''[20]

While the schools are not as specifically geared to turning out good citizens, they certainly contribute to creating the sort of citizenry the Japanese establishment fancies. These are people who do their work, obey the laws, accept whatever sacrifice is necessary for the greater good, don't mix in politics except to vote, and especially do not question the right of the ruling party to dominate politics or the value of its policies. Once again, this may not be what other societies regard as good citizens, but it is manifestly in the interests of the Liberal Democratic Party and the government bureaucracies.

The final result has been what Western sycophants refer to as a "meritocracy." On the basis of education, the more capable elements go to "good" schools and enter "good" companies or bureaucracies and rise to the top of the social ladder while the rest find their natural position further down. Since this is done by an impersonal and objective examination, and everyone has the same "fair" chance, there is no cause to complain about one's lot in life.

What naive creatures the foreign academics are. They really don't seem to know their *tatemae* from their *honne*. But one can easily understand why they like the system. It is based, in theory at least, on educational attainment. And who has accomplished more than they? They are also *sensei*. In the Japanese hierarchy they would be at the top, or so they imagine. Much nicer than being placed toward the bottom at home, under people who do rather than teach, like businessmen, professionals, politicians. Who knows? The pinnacle in the

United States might be reserved for professors from Harvard. Ez Vogel and cohorts would be No. 1 then!

Alas, most of these ideas are mistaken. They will be questioned later on. For the moment, we think it most urgent to challenge the concept of "meritocracy." It is hard to demonstrate that the Japanese educational system separates out those with greater or lesser merit on the basis, almost entirely, of college entrance exams. Success there merely shows that, at a relatively young age, certain students were better at memorizing masses of facts and could respond faster to multiple choice questions. That is why the Japanese never refer to "meritocracy" themselves. They have much more appropriate names like the "mock-test education system" through which one acquires academic credentials. This creates, at best, a society based on academic background (*gakureki*) or, at worst, a "low academic level-high educational background society."[21]

(Almost) Time For Reform

It is really amazing that foreign sycophants should be lavishing such praise on the Japanese educational system at the very time that so many Japanese are criticizing it. And this is not just a question of being modest or carping about something that is truly admirable. There are serious defects in the existing system and they have only become more blatant and worrisome over recent years.

Most visible are the lacks in physical plant. Most primary and secondary schools are cramped, poorly constructed, frequently run-down. They are eyesores rather than palaces of learning. They lack modern teaching apparatus, well-equipped laboratories, audio-visual aids, language labs, computer rooms and the like. The worst constraint, however, is that the Ministry of Education has failed to reduce the size of classes, many of which still number 40 or more students compared to 25 or 30 in Western countries. The colleges are even more crowded, private ones taking in as many students as possible to boost revenue. Yet, while the share of the national budget devoted to education is about as high as elsewhere, it is hardly generous and has been cut back rather than expanded.

There has also been some trouble with the teaching staff. This derives partly from the fact that there are not many teachers colleges in Japan and it is not even necessary to attend one to be licensed. In fact, anyone who appears for the test and passes can become a teacher, although few do. Most candidates take the test because they see teaching as a second-best, something to fall back on if they cannot get into a good company or bureaucracy which pays more and offers greater prestige.

Increasingly, according to comments and letters to the editor, teachers are not terribly dedicated. They simply do their job and wait for the vacation. But, even if they were the best teachers in the world, it would not be easy to cope with the overloaded teaching programs and huge classes. There is simply no time for individual attention to either bright pupils or laggards. Moreover, they are stuck with all sorts of administrative tasks which reduce their ability to keep up with the latest developments in their field.

Worse, there has been considerable tension between the teachers' union and the Ministry of Education. Many radical students and leftists went into teaching, either because big companies would not accept them or in the hope of rearing a more humane and liberal generation. Meanwhile, the Ministry has been staffed with some of the most reactionary officials who work under ministers who are occasionally anachronistic holdovers from the wartime period. No wonder there are repeated clashes between the teachers and administrators which certainly do not contribute to harmony or efficiency at school.[22]

What? You never knew that. Nobody bothered mentioning such things when suggesting Japan be the ultimate model. Well, if that were not enough, there has been sniping at the national level because of efforts by rightists in the Liberal Democratic Party to roll back the educational reforms introduced by the American occupation authorities. In particular, they disliked the lack of "moral" training and insufficient respect for "national" values. They also wished to have textbooks express a very peculiar view of reality. And, of course, they wanted to impose more discipline on the teachers. No wonder this was resisted energetically by the Japan Teachers' Union which struggled to preserve the more democratic and liberal heritage.

The biggest stress and strain, however, has come from a completely different source. It arose through the overpowering urge to get into not only any college but the very best, and this by passing the entrance exam. This urge was so strong that it twisted and distorted every aspect of the educational system.

First of all, although designed to be more democratic and do away with prewar elitism, almost spontaneously a new hierarchy of educational institutions arose that resembled the old one. At the top were the state universities, especially the University of Tokyo, with the other major ones just below it and prefectural ones further down. Near the top, but not quite, were the older, more prestigious private colleges. And then the masses of new colleges. If it were possible to make do with any school, there would probably not have been much pressure because there were nearly enough seats to go around. But, with so many aiming for the top, the pressure intensified to unheard-of degrees.

Since the key was passing the entrance exam upon graduation from high school, students gradually shifted their interest to the exam and away from the formal curriculum. If the school they attended did not prepare them adequately for the tests, they went to *juku*. Thus, the *juku*, institutes which sprang up spontaneously and were run on purely commercial lines with no concern whatsoever for the person's overall education, gained over the regular schools. And any school that wanted to keep its students (and their parents) happy had to devote more time to exam preparation. So the schools fell into line with the *juku* and not vice versa.

Finally, with the need to pass these exams, students (and their parents) sought out schools which had a good reputation for getting their wards into the best colleges. Some of them became feeders. Meanwhile, primary schools became feeders to the secondary schools. And even kindergartens were opened which prepared kids for primary school. Of course, to get into them, it was necessary to teach your tot how to pass his first entrance exams. In short, the whole school system was geared to passing entrance exams rather than providing a good, all-around education.

It is not hard to imagine what happened to children who were brought up in this rat race. And the grind of "examination hell" only intensified with the years, requiring ever greater efforts to get into the top schools. Polls showed that students thought of this in terms of "exertion," "mental anguish," and "uncertainty." More and more children developed psychosomatic problems, including headaches, heart troubles and mental disorders. Some tried to escape by refusing to attend classes because they "hated school." Others actually ran away from home. Meanwhile, suicide took a depressing toll among youngsters year after year.[23]

Even more disturbing was that, rather than passively accept, students began to revolt openly. Instances of bad conduct multiplied alarmingly. This involved not only petty misdemeanors like smoking or drinking but serious delinquency and acts of violence against fellow students and teachers. The major scandal was widespread bullying (*ijime*). To the amazement of the public, there was another side to this.

Teachers had also become more aggressive and there were repeated cases of teachers using unwarranted violence against students or participating in bullying.

At this point, the Japanapologists will intercede with comments like, ''it is not as bad as in the United States.'' Maybe it isn't. But it is quite bad enough for Japan and only getting worse. More painful, in certain respects, is that the forms of bullying were actually nastier. According to a survey by the Japan Youth Research Institute, there was somewhat more bullying in the United States than Japan, with 85% of the school teachers noticing this in the former and 74% in the latter. But, in America, this usually involved two groups of students quarreling with one another. In Japan, it was a large group tormenting just one or two weaker fellows. Moreover, while 40% of the U.S. students said they would intervene to stop the bullying, only 20% of the Japanese would do the same while 30% would pretend not to notice it.[24]

For years, the Japanese public had generally approved of the educational system. People had been lulled into complacency by the comforting *tatemae* that the system, for all its faults, was basically a successful one. This was nothing as absurd and outrageous as the Japan as No. 1 version, since the Japanese were never unaware of the *honne*. However, during the 1970s and 1980s, the abuses and aberrations became so painfully evident that the problems could no longer be ignored. Realization of the need for reform, and movements to that end, came from various directions.

The first, and most decisive, was the business community. As noted, private companies had to make up for many of the shortcomings of the school system. This they could do with regard to specific skills that could be taught in-house or at some university. But the lack of imagination and creativity was a more pressing concern as the economy moved ahead. It was no longer possible to remain a copier. Japan had to become an inventor. And enhancing creativity required an overhaul of the educational system. This need was shown by the lack of Nobel Prize winners, most of whom had migrated abroad anyway, and who incisively criticized those aspects which stifled creativity.

Parents were also concerned. They did not like what was happening to their children. According to a poll by the National Federation of Parents and Teachers Associations, parents rejected the present system in which "society places excessive value on academic background." They also condemned abuses like cramming for exams, uniform curricula and heavy stress on the children's future career.[25] In a *Yomiuri Shimbun* poll, only 25% of the respondents expressed satisfaction with the overall educational system while 58% were dissatisfied.[26] But there was little they could do on their own since the only way for their offspring to get ahead was to attend the best schools and rigorously train for exams. The only hope was a thorough reform to change the system fundamentally.

The LDP also talked aimlessly of the need to improve education for years, realizing that there was a growing constituency for this. But it was not until 1984, after Prime Minister Yasuhiro Nakasone took over, that there was a sufficiently dynamic and dedicated leader to do something about the school system. For years already, he had expressed disapproval of the postwar arrangement. Among other things, he regretted the lack of respect for national values and inadequate internationalization. He was also worried about excessive emphasis on educational credentials, uniformity of the curricula, lack of flexibility, school violence and juvenile delinquency. He therefore launched an educational reform that he insisted would be as bold and sweeping as those undertaken by the Meiji oligarchs and the Occupation.

To this end, he appointed a special Ad Hoc Council on Education which met repeatedly and began issuing recommendations. But the reform never came to fruition. The ed-

Nakasone lecturing the younger generation
on educational reform, political ethics
and the like.

Credit: Foreign Press Center/Kyodo

ucational bureaucracy was one of the slowest and stodgiest in the country and got in the way of any radical changes. The teachers' union, which refused to cooperate in the council, opposed most of the proposals and could make them very hard to implement. And the broader public did not push strongly enough. So, when Nakasone stepped down, this particular exercise petered out.

But the problems and abuses did not disappear. They remained and became even worse. It is thus rather odd to claim that Japan's educational system should be a model for others when the Japanese themselves do not approve of so many

aspects and feel the need for reform. In fact, until it is re-
formed, it is not even suitable for Japan. So we would at best
rate it a satisfactory.

NOTES

1. Edwin Reischauer, *The Japanese*, p. 167.
2. See William Cummings, *Education and Equality in Japan*, Benjamin Duke, *The Japanese School*, Richard Lynn, *Educational
   Achievement in Japan*, Ezra Vogel, *Japan As Number One*, Merry
   White, *The Japanese Educational Challenge*.
3. Vogel, *op. cit.*, p. 159.
4. *Ibid*, p. 175.
5. See Nishio Kanji, "Reshaping Education for Today's Needs," *Japan Echo*, November 3, 1984, pp. 17–23.
6. *Japan Times*, January 3, 1985.
7. *New York Times*, July 13, 1983.
8. *Japan Times*, December 13, 1982.
9. *Yomiuri*, Kiryu Column, February 7, 1989.
10. See Lynn, *op. cit.*.
11. *Mainichi*, March 2, 1988.
12. Vogel, *op. cit.*, pp. 164–77.
13. Duke, *op. cit.*, p. xx.
14. *Japan Economic Journal*, September 19, 1987, p. 24.
15. Thomas P. Rohlen, *Japan's High Schools*, p. 316.
16. See Michio Nagai, *Higher Education in Japan*.
17. Duke, *op. cit.*, p. xviii.
18. Stan Gold, "Inside a Japanese University," *Japan Update*, Winter
    1988, p. 3.
19. See Ronald Dore and Mari Sako, *How The Japanese Learn To
    Work*.
20. Duke, *op. cit.*, p. 25.
21. Most of these expressions are widely used in Japan. The last one
    is quoted from former Labor Minister Ishida.
22. Rohlen, *op. cit.*, pp. 210–40.
23. The Japanese media have been so full of this that not even a shallow
    observer could miss it.
24. *Mainichi*, February 15, 1986.
25. *Mainichi*, August 18, 1986.
26. *Yomiuri*, March 19, 1989.

7

Crime
(Integrating The Criminal
Element)

Japanese Criminals As No. 1

Crime. Now, who should we quote? There is such an abundance of eminently quotable quotes. And most of them scrupulously follow Reischauer's dictum: "never, never, never be anything but wildly optimistic about Japan."

One of the first to discover this sector of Japanese superiority was William Clifford, formerly head of the United Nations Crime Prevention Program, who noticed that Japan's crime rate was declining at a time when it was rising in most other countries.[1] But Vogel proselytized it more vigorously, proposing Japan's crime control as another institution to emulate.[2] He seemed particularly pleased that there was none of that libertarian crap and Japanese offenders were not "likely to receive leniency because they are considered to have psychological difficulties or be victims of society or because an able lawyer pursues legal technicalities."[3]

Robert Christopher, the fatuous fact-finder, was most impressed by the high conviction rate and a penal system that strives for "confession, repentance and reform." This is facilitated by social sanctions whereby "the self-esteem of the ordinary Japanese depends upon his identification with the group,'' making ''the withdrawal of group approval a far more powerful deterrent to crime in Japan.'' This not only keeps him on the straight-and-narrow, it convinces those who have slipped not to repeat because ''any Japanese who has once suffered the psychic torments of social disapproval or rejection is unlikely to risk facing that experience again.''[4]

The effectiveness of the police force is praised by David Bayley, who noted that Japanese policemen had much more in-service training and stricter supervision than their American counterparts.[5] David MacEachron was even more lyric: ''police in Japan are generally considered sources of protection, help, guidance, and respect. Public cooperation with the police in Japan is considerably higher than in the United States.''[6] And the result was an extraordinarily low rate of crime. He was at least charitable enough not to throw in that old cliché which is quoted here from Bill Ouchi: ''a woman can walk alone in downtown Tokyo at midnight with no fear of bodily harm.''[7]

That covers most of the basic coordinates of the myth of why Japan is a stunning success in the field of crime control. Alas, as per usual, the situation is grossly overstated and incorrect in many particulars. When the true story is perceived, it is nowhere near as pleasant or flattering. Yet, while some of the following observations may surprise or shock those who only know the apologist version, they are nothing new for anyone who has lived in Japan and read the daily newspaper (which most ''experts'' don't seem to do).

This does not mean that there is no foundation for these positive pronouncements. Judging by the statistics, the crime rate is very low. That is especially true for violent crimes, those which most citizens view with alarm. In 1986, there were only 1.4 homicides, 1.4 rapes and 1.6 robberies per 100,000 inhabitants, which is quite impressive. It is particularly good compared to, you guessed it, the United States, with 8.6, 37.5 and 225.1 respectively.[8] But, compared to European countries or Australia, considerably less violent societies, it was less remarkable. And certainly nothing to rave about when compared to the "socialist" countries. That last parallel, by the way, is not as irrelevant as some readers may feel.

The first question is whether, as its admirers proclaim, Japan has been "solving" the problem of crime as supposedly "proven" by a crime rate that has been falling even while it rose everywhere else. This notion is a flagrant abuse of statistics. While the rate did, indeed, decline after the war for some time, it turned upward again in 1973 and has only leveled off recently. This means that crime is an increasingly serious matter in Japan as elsewhere. It is especially disturbing since the largest increase was found in youth crime and the spread of juvenile delinquency. And drug-related crimes, particularly for stimulants, have risen sharply.

Another quibble is whether one can believe Japan's crime statistics. As H. Takano, the editor of *Insider*, wrote: "such statistics published by the authorities are not necessarily to be trusted, since the nation's law enforcement agencies tend to exaggerate about the substantial achievements made in their policing efforts."[9] This is a fairly widespread opinion. It seems most applicable to drug-related crimes, which are by far the most rapidly growing and threatening. Yet, while the amounts of drugs intercepted expanded massively, the number of arrests did not, with only 20,000 drug users and traffickers arrested in 1986 although it was estimated that as many as 600,000 people took "speed."[10]

There are also certain social hangups that affect the collection of statistics. Victims of crimes, especially robbery and burglary, can expect bothersome snooping which may keep them from complaining. Shoplifting, one of the most pervasive phenomena, is frequently not reported by shopkeepers, especially for juveniles who are let off anyway, to

Ratio of Citizens to Police Officers by Country, 1987

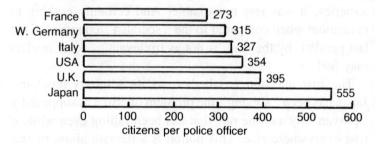

If the Japanese are model, lawabiding citizens,
why do they need so many cops?

Source: White Paper on Police, 1988.
Credit: *Facts and Figures of Japan 1989*, p. 84.

avoid losing face and customers. When it comes to rape, most women find the police interrogation and general attitude too offensive to contemplate. Finally, there is an amazing number of fires, some of which are later confirmed as arson, to hide cases of burglary or murder or used to warn and intimidate home owners. This could strongly induce underreporting of such crimes.

For these and other reasons, various observers have made their own estimate of actual criminal activity. Akira Ishii, on the basis of personal interviews, found levels that were much higher than the official ones, as much as 11 times for burglary, 24 times for shoplifting and 54 times for assault and battery.[11] H. Takano questioned the police estimate that criminal organizations had only collected ¥1 trillion in income in 1985. "Nobody, not even the gangsters themselves, believes the official estimate." He put their take at much closer to ¥7 trillion.[12] If one were to multiply the official crime rates not even by a factor of seven but merely two, three or four, Japan would not look so good.

That, however, is not really what concerns me most. It is

the tendency to stress "violent" crimes and overlook everything else. Obviously, this is very important for ordinary citizens and has become an obsession in the West, where violence is encouraged by traditions of individualism, protest and conflict. But Japan is a very different society, so it may have a different bias.

Among other things, part of the criminal activity is dominated by professional criminals (*yakuza*) who form highly organized gangs or syndicates (*kumi*). There are apparently 90,000 *yakuza* at present, according to the National Police Agency. The largest, Yamaguchi-gumi, numbers some 10,000 members. These gangs exert considerable authority over the membership through a strict hierarchy from the boss (*kumicho*) on down and a sense of loyalty instilled by a code of honor (*jingi*) and rules which cannot be violated without severe punishment. Just like your archetypical salaryman, only more so.[13]

But no one is foolish enough to assume that there are only gangsters engaged in crime. They may be the big units, like your big companies and bureaucracies, but there are numerous smaller units and individuals. There are also plenty of isolated or random crimes. In fact, since the police trace large numbers of crimes to first-timers and youngsters, they are a growing component. With the spread of drug addiction, the peripheral sector can only expand.

What do criminals do? They commit crimes, that's what. After all, that is their trade, that is how they earn a living. Even Vogel had to concede, a bit defensively, that "sometimes the *yakuza* engage in illicit activities."[14] How nasty! Yes, sad to say, many gangsters are engaged in gambling and "entertainment," a lot of this involving prostitution, pornography and other branches of the booming sex industry. Some are racketeers, controlling musical shows, stage shows and even sumo. Others are just toughs and hooligans, who work as bouncers or engage in shakedowns and extortion.

An increasing share of business is derived from drug trafficking. And another emerging sector is smuggling guns into Japan.

Extortion, as mentioned, is one of the major activities. But the Japanese have been incredibly ingenious at finding new wrinkles. Some practice such hackneyed ploys as making local shopkeepers and bar or restaurant proprietors pay protection money. Others known as *seiriya* buy bankrupt companies cheap and then force the creditors to settle even more cheaply, taking a slice for themselves. The *toritateya* collect debts from delinquent debtors, if necessary by harassing them and their family. The *pakuriya* straighten out problems connected with commercial notes. And the *jiageya* have been particularly active recently, buying up small plots of land and consolidating them for larger buildings, alas often doing so despite the resistance of the owners.

Surely, one of the most extraordinary groups is the *sokaiya*, who use their wits instead of force. They buy a few shares of stock in a company, which permits them to attend the annual shareholders meeting and then raise embarrassing questions or disrupt the proceedings. Since a company executive could lose his post for such disturbances, he would gladly pay to avoid them. The other angle is to publish small newsletters which contain scandalous news about companies, and then offer not to distribute them in return for adequate compensation.

Finally, there are the scams, where the Japanese have been outstandingly inventive. Yes, once again standard tricks like selling plots of land that are worthless and for which the seller may not even have the title. Or stocks and securities that are counterfeited. Or membership in bogus clubs. But others have convinced distressed businessmen that they could help them obtain loans, then collected some money up front and disappeared. Two brothers ripped off more than 20,000 people who paid them to find lucrative jobs. Toshi Journal defrauded

10,000 investors out of ￥60 billion by collecting money for stocks it never bought. And Toyota Shoji, through fraudulent sales of gold, swindled some 50,000 customers out of ￥111 billion or more.[15]

From all this, it may appear that if any Japanese sector is truly No. 1, then it is organized crime. And this does not keep amateurs from piling in as well. White collar crime has been growing by leaps and bounds. Most of it is embezzlement, some by your impeccable salarymen. Ramping stocks, spreading rumors to boost prices, and buying on insider tips is quite commonplace among investors.[16] And it would be unwise to assume that even professionals or company executives are totally honest. Tax evasion seems to be a national pastime, especially among farmers, doctors, dentists and lawyers, real estate agents and building contractors. It goes all the way to the top, though, with such prominent companies as Marubeni, Mitsui, Mitsubishi, etc. bilking the government of enormous sums.[17]

Some may feel that this is an acceptable price to pay for a society where there is little violent crime. That is tempting. But it is first necessary to define what is meant by violence. In Japan, no ordinary citizen carries a gun which means that he could easily be intimidated by a gangster with a long sword or sharp knife or merely bulging muscles and a nasty leer. He would already be frightened out of his wits when several of them drive up to his house in a huge car at midnight, shine the lights on his window and make wild threats. This sort of thing has been quite adequate to make debtors flee, leaving their family behind.

That certainly is violence. It is also violence when girls from Southeast Asia are lured to Japan on the pretext of getting an honest, respectable job, and then pressed into prostitution. Or when small landowners are forced to sell. Or when ordinary businessmen are warned that something horrible will happen to their shop or restaurant if they do not pay protection money. Indeed, in many of these cases, one may wonder whether it would not be more merciful to be robbed or mugged once in a while rather than shaken down every month for the rest of your life. . . .

This should be more than enough to cast a shadow on the brilliant picture of Japan as a relatively crime-free paradise.

Crime? What Crime?

To the professionals, even more exemplary than the low crime rate is the high arrest rate. According to the Ministry of Justice, in 1986 almost 74% of the offenders were identified and apprehended. This is even good by Japan's exalted standards. But it is magnificent compared to the United States, with a rate of well under 30%. Here, too, using the American comparison is misleading because the arrest rate is higher in European and other countries. What is actually more intriguing is that virtually all of those who were arrested were ultimately convicted and many of them confessed their crimes (and then apologized).

These statistics look extremely good until you remember that there was some doubt about the actual number of crimes. If there were really, say, two, three or four times as many crimes, this would mean that the arrest rate was only half, a third or a quarter as high. In short, once again, Japan would not compare as favorably against other countries, especially not the "socialist" ones, although it would still be ahead of the bunglers in the U.S.A.

This is very important. Other aspects may be even more significant. For example, anyone who has ever visited the entertainment districts knows that prostitution is rife. While it takes many forms, Turkish baths, girlie shows, hostess bars, *sopu*, etc., it all adds up to the same thing. Yet, there are hardly ever any arrests. This is called a "crime without victims" and the lack of arrests seems less criticizable, to some almost a sign of decent and benign understanding of man's foibles. But prostitution is a crime nonetheless, it is against the law and, by ignoring it and allowing criminals to prosper, the police force is hardly sending society the right signals.

Gambling is also a crime. Another "crime without victims," unless you count the poor devils who lose their shirt in rigged games. But there are few arrests here, too. Extortion and blackmail are clearly crimes, this time with obvious victims. Alas, those paying protection money, hush money, loans at outrageous interest rates and so on are too scared to complain. The same applies to many of those being pressured into selling their land or giving up claims on a bankrupt company.

More intriguing is that, despite a massive crackdown by the police, the *sokaiya* are still in business. They are more discreet, they have found other modus operandi, they often collect their money in private before the general shareholders meeting. And there are thousands of them. For the scams, there are arrests. But how could the police have such a high arrest rate when some confidence men managed to con thousands and tens of thousands of gullible souls before getting caught? Most notably, there has never been a criminal prosecution for insider trading which is a daily occurrence.

Our favorite case, of course, is the "mystery man with 21 faces" (*Kaijin Nijuichimenso*). This daring and devilishly clever gang began a brilliant career in 1984, kidnapping the filthy rich president of Glico confectionary company and demanding ¥1 billion and 100 kilograms of gold in ransom. He was ultimately released. But the group then proceeded to blackmail at least five other food companies, threatening them by poisoning products displayed in grocery stores, and thereby in effect holding the whole nation to ransom. Despite tipoffs to the cops, which were publicized in the national media, the gang was never caught. I told you the criminals were No. 1!

There is one final point, perhaps the most disturbing. Juvenile delinquency of all kinds, involving ever more young people in increasingly violent crimes, has been getting out of hand. This reveals both a weakening of social inhibitions and the inability to deal with this phenomenon. The most troublesome form has been the motorcycle gangs (*bosozoku*) which not only disrupt traffic and cause material damage but also commit prostitution, drug trafficking and murder. Yet the police force, despite repeated efforts, has failed to either control or contain them.

The explanation for Japan's splendid success in the area of crime enforcement, assuming it really exists, is provided by foreigners and natives alike. It involves a tight-knit and homogeneous society where people are supposedly law-abiding by tradition and cultural mores persuade groups to see to it that their members behave. There is a greater need to maintain face in a society where, once having been arrested, it would be harder to get along. There is also the close cooperation between the police and the community, among other things through neighborhood police boxes (*koban*) and voluntary citizens' anti-crime associations.

All of this is true. There is no denying it. And it does contribute to a more lawful society. But it should also be remembered that, in such a tight-knit society with little chance of getting back in, once a person has gone astray he may actually be forced to become a professional criminal because there are no other alternatives. No one who knows would hire him. And, if he has no skills, and no fixed employ, he would already be suspect for more reputable companies. Social pressure then works the other way around: once a criminal, and a gang member, it would be very hard to go straight.

Thus, some of the actual reasons for this supposed success must be looked at more closely. One is that, although the crime rate is low, the number of policemen is fairly large, with two-thirds as many per 1,000 inhabitants as in the United States, where there are substantially more crimes. This means that the police can cover each case more intensively, putting many more cops on the job and thereby enhancing the chances of finding the culprit. It also implies that this huge police force can keep a constant eye on law-abiding citizens, visiting each home periodically to make enquiries that would invade the personal privacy guaranteed in most Western countries.

Once a crime occurs, the suspected culprit—and it must be stressed that this is a person who is still only under suspicion of having committed a crime—will be rigorously questioned, perhaps at length, perhaps under unpleasant circumstances. According to a group of Japanese lawyers, each year 100,000 people are subjected to interrogation that may last for weeks and during which they are denied food and exercise and often cooped up in police cells so small they are nicknamed "bird cages."[18] Meanwhile, they have little access to lawyers and confessions are frequently extracted under duress. No wonder there are so many confessions!

Maybe you didn't think things like that could happen in a "modern," "liberal" country as opposed to a "backward" or "totalitarian" one. But this is a very old tradition in Japan, going back centuries, and it should not be surprising that some vestiges remain. This also explains why there are so many convictions. Knowing that they are quite likely to be convicted, hardened criminals or just ordinary folks who have gotten into trouble will hurriedly admit whatever they feel is necessary to satisfy the police and judges. And they will also express deep regrets and make formal apologies. For then the penalties will be much less severe and they may even get off quite lightly. That this behavior reflects true repentance as opposed to opportunism is very questionable, Mr. Christopher.

The other interesting aspect is that, although there are some

90,000 *yakuza* around, and they are professional criminals practicing trades that should land them in jail, they manage to go about their business freely most of the time. Instead of trying to repress them, or wipe them out, the police are apparently set on the more civilized course of taming them. Thus, files are kept on the gangsters, they are hauled in periodically and sometimes arrested, but the stay in prison is not too long. In return, the gangs are expected to limit their activities in certain areas, like drug trafficking and smuggling weapons. They should also keep unruly, irregular elements who do not belong to their membership in check.

The police authorities are exceedingly sensitive about violent crimes, rape, robbery, murder, the sort of thing that gets into the newspapers and television and makes it look as if they are not doing a good job. On this point, it is possible that the *yakuza* coincide, but for rather different reasons. Since they are left relatively free to engage in prostitution, gambling and other ventures which are terribly lucrative, they don't really need sidelines. And extortion or scams offer regular revenue. So, why get mixed up in violent crimes that often don't bring in much money when you can earn a fairly safe, fairly comfy income within the bounds mutually agreed? And why in the world bother annoying a foreign woman walking around Tokyo at night when that only causes hassle?

Admittedly, things do not always work out as planned and the harmonious cooperation seems to be fraying. On the one hand, there have been cases of policemen going too far, helping criminals escape arrest, warning gangs of raids and accepting bribes or actually becoming criminals on retirement. On the other, the gangs are getting ever deeper into the drug scene and, with the tremendous sums now available, they have been acquiring more guns. They have also been fighting over turf (sorry, market share) more viciously, using these guns. One of the bloodiest incidents occurred in 1985, when the head of the Yamaguchigumi was bumped off and

Japanese policemen protecting *yakuza* at
a slain gang leader's funeral.

Credit: Foreign Press Center/Japan

an internecine battle broke out with a splinter gang, Ichi-wakai. There have since been numerous shootouts in which gang members were killed or wounded and innocent bystanders were also injured.

So, there are ominous blots on the seemingly impeccable record of law enforcement. But they are hardly ever mentioned by the Japanapologists or many of the supposed "experts" so it was necessary to go through what was not a very agreeable exercise. By now, it should be evident that Japan's system is not all that it is cracked up to be.

But I certainly do not want to conclude with the acerbic comments of a rank foreigner. Instead, let me mention that

138

numerous serious and reputable Japanese, including lawyers, social workers and criminologists, are equally disturbed by these manifestations. And so is the average citizen. So consider the views on police and law enforcement reflected in the periodic surveys of the Prime Minister's Office. By 1987, only 56% of the respondents had a good impression of policemen and ever fewer found their performance to be improving. There were complaints of "unkindness" and "rudeness" as well as concern at the number of cops involved in scandals. There was a marked tendency to find that the police were lax in cracking down on gangs and those willing to actively cooperate with the police was on the decline.[19]

From this it should be obvious that the Japanese are not of quite the same opinion as the friends of Japan. Many citizens feel that the crime rate is higher than reported, that the police are not catching enough criminals and are too soft on gangs. They are not so willing to cooperate. And yes, believe it or not, Japanese women would not feel safe walking around certain neighborhoods at night. In short, the public only seems to grant the law enforcement system a satisfactory mark. And we would have to go along with that.

NOTES

1. See William Clifford, *Crime Control in Japan.*
2. Ezra Vogel, *Japan As No. 1*, pp. 204–244.
3. Vogel, *op. cit.,* p. 206.
4. Robert Christopher, *The Japanese Mind*, p. 164.
5. See David Bayley, *Force of Order.*
6. David MacEachron, "Reversing Roles," *Speaking of Japan*, November 1984, p. 12.
7. William Ouchi, *Theory Z*, p. 18.
8. Ministry of Justice, *White Paper on Crime*, annual.
9. *Tokyo Business Today*, October 1986, p. 57.
10. *Wall Street Journal*, December 9, 1987.

11. *Japan Times*, October 16, 1978.
12. *Tokyo Business Today*, ibid.
13. See David Kaplan and Alec Dubro, *Yakuza*.
14. Vogel, *op. cit.,* p. 212.
15. Gleaned from the local press. There are plenty more every day.
16. See Gregory Clark, "Zen and the fine art of market manipulation," *Far Eastern Economic Review*, February 26, 1989, p. 72.
17. This is regularly announced by the National Tax Administration Agency, year after year, with the sums steadily swelling.
18. *The Economist*, September 3, 1988.
19. *Japan Times*, November 29, 1981; *Mainichi*, November 24, 1984; *Yomiuri*, March 28, 1988.

8

Politics
(The Japanese Way)

Politicians: Fronting For The System

Who runs Japan? The politicians, the bureaucrats or the businessmen? That is the eternal question that exercises the minds of the foreign friends of Japan. Normally, one would expect them to pick the politicians since these are the folks who run the government in most other countries. But there are rather few who take that option. One of the most credible is Gerald Curtis, who argues that Japanese politicians have increasingly influenced policy and adapted flexibly to the wishes of the populace.

"Political change in Japan over these past several decades has not come about by bureaucratic fiat or by the imposition of an elite consensus on a submissive public. Rather it has been largely the product of the responsiveness of the political system to shifting public demands, a responsiveness that in turn has been produced by the LDP's determination to return electoral majorities and retain political power."[1]

Most other Western observers do not think as highly of the politicians as a whole. If anything, they are defensive. After all, how can Japan be such a wonderful place if it is run by political hacks? So they rebut any unjust criticism. No, the politicians do not fail to accomplish their tasks in the Diet, say some. No, they are not entirely void of noble impulses, add others. No, they are not that corrupt, insists Reischauer.[2] Or, when they criticize, it is done more gently than for their own country. "The Japanese half-expect their politicians to be corrupt," writes *The Economist*.[3] "Money does indeed grease the political wheel," adds *The Financial Times*, but "it is the price the country has been prepared to pay for a smoothly functioning system."[4]

When it comes to the top leaders, the elite, however the tone changes remarkably. At least at first. For the Japanapologists routinely proclaim the coming of a new dawn. They heralded Kakuei Tanaka, the "computerized bulldozer," who would get the economy going again and dominate the bureaucracy. When he fell ignominiously, they did not have much to say about their former misjudgment. For they were already busy applauding Prime Minister Miki, "Mr. Clean," who would clean up politics and restore integrity. Alas, he got nothing done. So the sycophants were happy to have Fukuda and Ohira, men of the party apparatus, who knew how to make the machinery turn. These were solid and mature leaders, soon to be repudiated. When Zenko Suzuki, whose views nobody ever grasped, appeared, they were momentarily nonplussed but eventually glorified his nebulous philosophy of *wa* (harmony).

The darling of the academics and media, however, was Yasuhiro Nakasone. Here was an activist, a man who knew what he wanted, someone who was open, an internationalist, even charismatic. Finally, a leader who appealed to Westerners. But he did not appeal as much to Japanese. So, without further ado, the Japan claque dumped Yasu and clambered on the Takeshita bandwagon. He was more attuned to domestic concerns, he knew how to work things out behind the scenes (*nemawashi* and all that), he was a consensus-builder. This, according to *The Wall Street Journal*, made him the "right man for the times."[5] It did not disturb starry-eyed

The most flagrant *tatemae*: unity and harmony
in the Liberal Democratic Party.

Credit: Foreign Press Center/Kyodo

gaijin that the Japanese press was grumbling about "a lack
of policies," "expressionless face and gloomy character,"
"constantly low popularity," "a country bumpkin whose
internatioinal recognition is zero," and "scandals about
money always surround him."[6]

When Takeshita fell, the foreign journalists turned on him.
He had been foolhardy to impose the very tax reform they
had earlier applauded. He had pushed the Japanese too far.
Surely, Sosuke Uno, the only relatively clean politician (who
was not too old and decrepit) the LDP could muster, would
be a good chap. Before they could praise him too lavishly,
he turned out to be a rather clumsy womanizer. At least they

could save face by claiming the girl was a *geisha*. And now we have Kaifu. Will he turn out as well as the Japan claque hopes? Who cares? If not him, then another. There will be plenty more prime ministers coming down the pike and one of them is bound to have the right stuff.

Despite these periodic displays of enthusiasm, none of which lasted very long, it turns out that there were adequate reasons not to get carried away by the possibilities of Japan's politicians. They are a pretty sorry lot.

First of all, these are rarely individuals who have risen from the masses and become champions of the people, which is admittedly a *tatemae* in any society. In Japan, it is particularly inappropriate today. More and more politicians are simply the children, or spouses or in-laws of older politicians who inherited their seat. Or they are former secretaries, who ran the constituency in practice. Or they are former bureaucrats, or former party officials, or former trade unionists, or former Soka Gakkai activists, who were coopted by the party.

Hardly any of them have specific political ideas. Hardly any of them have proposals. If they did, it is highly unlikely that they would have been accepted into the party. And it would be incredibly difficult for them to implement such ideas or proposals because most of the parties are not interested in change. Oddly enough, this no longer applies only to the Liberal Democrats whose desire to maintain the status quo is eminently practical. The Communists, Socialists and Komeito are wedded to programs that are so amorphous and archaic that they no longer correspond to current realities. If one of their members should suddenly espouse visionary proposals, he would only create embarrassment.

Anyway, most politicians are kept far too busy with petty tasks to do much about actual legislation. One chore is to keep the local constituents happy by providing whatever favors they request, whether jobs, or entry to schools, or suitable presence at a wedding or burial. The most important function is to bring something home from the grab bag and distribute largesse. Pork barrel politics are pretty much the name of the game. And it is much easier if one is a member of the ruling party and has been around long enough to obtain a ministerial post.

The key is thus to get reelected time and again. For that, good local connections greased by favors is helpful. But money is even more decisive. And that comes from business interests one can support. While rendering service is perfectly legitimate, it is sometimes hard not to go a bit further. Thus, the biggest headache has been corruption and the scandals they bring not only to the LDP but other parties as well. Fortunately for them, only a small portion ever come to public notice or are so bad that the culprits would have to resign. And then they would be campaigning for reelection soon after, just to prove that they had been absolved by the people.

Still, enough scandals have arisen to keep the country embroiled in one or another almost permanently. Only a few of the major ones are mentioned here. In 1948, the Showa Denko scandal brought down the cabinet. There was massive bribery in the shipbuilding industry in 1953, which implicated LDP Secretary General Sato. Embarrassing, but not enough to keep him from becoming prime minister. In 1965-66, there was a series of bribery scandals, including one involving then Prime Minister Sato. Kakuei Tanaka was so deeply involved in ''money politics'' that he had to step down, this even before the Lockheed affair emerged. During the 1970s, there was massive bribery of the Marcos regime by Japanese companies, and some of this money reportedly got into Japanese hands as well. But that putative scandal was hushed up. And similar misdoing in Korea and Indonesia never even came to light. Soon after, the international telecommunications monopoly KDD got into trouble for distributing gifts to influential Diet members. More recently, we have the Recruit scandal, about which more will be said.[7]

This is pretty heavy corruption, surely enough to make the comments of Reischauer slightly absurd. It is not only that major scandals have occurred. There were so many minor ones that there was always something overshadowing the political scene. Moreover, everyone knew that this was only a tiny part of the total corruption, just the "tip of the iceberg" as they say. Equally serious is that the scandals involved not just a small number of wayward politicians, and lower-ranking ones at that. No, as we have seen, they implicated ministers, prime ministers and sometimes dozens of Diet members. That is why Japanese political scientists speak of "structural corruption," an assessment that appeared on target to Robert M. Orr, Jr., one of the few foreigners who knows Japanese politics well.[8]

What are the chances of ending corruption? Not very good. This sort of thing has been around not only since the war, it goes much further back, beyond the Meiji era, beyond the modern period. It can be traced to reciprocal gift-giving, and regularly is by foreign academics. But it is more purposeful than that. And the goal is not only to fill politicians' campaign chests so they can win the next election, a line trusting foreign journalists often fall for. A lot goes into their own pockets. Politicians, as every Japanese knows, are fairly well off and could not possibly afford their lifestyle solely on the basis of honest income.

No wonder no one expects the latest efforts at political reform to be any more effective than earlier ones. Money is the lifeblood of politics and politicians are not going to engage in dangerous surgery. Just a few token resignations, a few orders to the ministries, a bit of contrition, and then wait until the scandal is forgotten. Nothing much will change. As Professor Masayuki Fukuoka of Tokyo's Komazawa University said, people admit that "trying to have ethics in Japan is like trying to buy fish at a greengrocer.'' He therefore developed the Japanese Rules of Morality, which might be borne in mind by gullible *gaijin*: "If it doesn't come out, it is OK. If it comes out, blame it on an aide. If that doesn't work, say everyone does it. That always works.''[9]

No wonder the Japanese half-expect their politicians to be corrupt. But they do not pass this off as a cultural quirk or a minor misdemeanor, like the foreign academics and journalists. They are deeply unhappy about it. That has been shown by every survey on the subject. And the views can be pretty bitter when expressed in personal conversations. They rate their politicians miserably low with regard to competence, integrity, effort, etc. But they rarely go so far as to vote the bums out which means that the politicians stay and every now and then stray.

This is not quite the end of the story. Even if the politicians are not genuinely concerned about political causes, know less about national policies than small-time, pork-barrel politics, and are occasionally venal and dishonest, they do have a job to do. Their job is to legislate, namely to draw up and adopt laws and have them put into effect. To judge by over forty years of postwar experience, that job is not really done by them. The bureaucrats appear to handle not only the details but many of the principal issues as well.

There is presently a trend among American political scientists, certainly more so than Japanese ones, to claim that this view is outdated and incorrect. The Liberal Democratic Party has been around long enough to assume most of the legislative functions. And basic decisions are taken by informal groupings in specific fields. They are the so-called "tribes" or *zoku*. That may be another manifestation of hope springing eternal. It takes much more than good intentions to become true legislators. Parliamentarians must have drafting skills, they must have research staff, they must understand the workings of the legal system, they must—above all—have some control over implementation.

In practice, the politicians really only provide the basic mood or context for legislation, expressing what they feel the people want (and may be judged differently by the bureaucracy). But they do not possess the ability to put this into legislation that could work and, for that, they are still thrown back on the bureaucrats. More serious, they never know how laws will be applied, for this is entirely in the hands of the bureaucrats. Even LDP bosses and *zoku* chieftains mainly act as lobbyists for special interests or to promote some few political concerns.

This inability to take control was proven most convincingly by Prime Minister Nakasone. Here was a rare leader with policies and a program, one who tried to get around the bureaucracy by setting up special committees. One who was actually in power for five years, very long by Japanese standards. His goals included administrative reform, tax reform, educational reform, boosting defense spending, bringing politics to the people, opening the market to imports, and various other things. None of them were actually accomplished.

It is argued that Takeshita achieved more through patient, behind-the-scenes negotiation. But his great "successes" were also dubious. He did not push through the "Maekawa plan." First of all, no plan ever existed. True, domestic demand increased. But that was because Takeshita could spend all the money Nakasone saved. As for the tax reform, that was a pretty soggy one to begin with, fixing a very low level of value added tax with so many loopholes that much of it could be avoided. In the end, the reform still proved unpalatable and had to be diluted.

If the prime minister could not accomplish much, how could more be expected of ministers? After all, most only held their portfolio for a year or two until it was the next guy's turn. The bureaucrats knew this and never paid too much attention to their titular head who could hardly impose the party line, let alone his own policies. At best, he could put up a show of knowing what he was doing (if the bureaucrats coached him) and leave office without any serious embarrassment. Without controlling the ministries, however, it was quite impossible to effectively "run" the country.

Perhaps that is not so bad, the sceptics will say. If the politicians are ignorant and venal, and don't have strong ideas to begin with, they should probably not be in charge. That does make a certain convoluted sense. Only then you are not talking about democracy but something very different.

Bureaucrats: Making Things Run

If that is what Japan's politicians are like, then certainly there would be cause to worry about the safety of the ship of state. But never fear! The bureaucrats will rescue the nation! That, at any rate, seems to be the message from the overwhelming majority of foreign observers. Just look at how the renowned London *Economist* explained the situation to its readers:

"While Japan's economy and society have adapted to the modern world, its political system has remained feudal. Its Liberal Democratic Party government exists to distribute wealth, patronage and power and its faction leaders share some of the characteristics of the ancient, dynastic warlords. Fortunately Japan has competent bureaucrats. While their political masters are preoccupied with grubbing for money, power and influence, the bureaucrats run the country."[10]

Isn't that nice. It is certainly comforting. Especially when we hear so many nice things about them from foreign academics. Ezra Vogel reassures us that the people who really run the ministries and make key decisions are permanent bureaucrats rather than politicians. Indeed, should the politicians try to interfere, the bureaucrats may denounce this attempt to challenge their jurisdictional authority.[11] Chalmers

Johnson, who has studied the balance of power most closely, sums it up very succinctly: "Although it is influenced by pressure groups and political claimants, the elite bureaucracy of Japan makes major decisions, drafts virtually all legislation, controls the national budget, and is the source of all major policy innovations in the system."[12]

Such an usurpation would be perilous if it were not that, according to the bureaucratophiles, these are most exceptional people. Johnson speaks of "a powerful, talented, and prestige-laden economic bureaucracy."[13] Vogel lauds their education, the source of legitimacy in his Japan. "Leading bureaucrats invariably have attended the best universities," like Tokyo University, and more specifically, its Law Faculty. They are extremely dedicated.[14] It is therefore not surprising that they are respected and obeyed by the politicians, businessmen and general public. As for Robert Christopher, he dubs them the "prime guardians" and "watchdogs" of the national interest.[15]

Are there any failings or drawbacks? Not much reference to that. Of course, there is some inefficiency, sloth, perhaps occasional arrogance. Corruption and influence peddling? Yes. But not very much. For Vogel, "guarding the guardians" is not a serious problem. Johnson, who knows the bureaucrats better, is not so sure. He concedes that cases of corruption among higher officials have occurred. He would doubtlessly grant that even more has been going on at lower levels. But that is not the real threat anyway. What must be avoided is "a pattern of cooperation between the government and big business that may have unintended consequences." This could arise from hand-in-glove relationships created by employment of retired bureaucrats.[16]

We do not entirely disagree with these comments. They have a degree of validity. It's the same old story. They are just too rosy and overblown, presenting a view that only those who believe in the tooth fairy could accept unreservedly.

It seems pretty clear that the bureaucrats take up the slack left by the politicians in the legislative process. They do draft the laws, admittedly after consultation with the politicians, businessmen and other sectors that would be affected. They even help the ministers defend this legislation in the Diet. Then they proceed to put it into effect. Here there is even less interference from above. And they are reasonably effective at it.

What is most disturbing, however, is that frequently it is not the law that rules in Japan. Japanese legislation is notoriously vague with gaping holes you could drive a truck through. That is not accidental. It was done on purpose. The bureaucrats want to leave themselves plenty of leeway to interpret the laws as they see fit, when and if they see fit. And, to find out exactly what the law means, the rest of the Japanese population has to curry favor with the bureaucrats so that it may be interpreted or filled in suitably through administrative guidance (*gyosei shido*).

This is a grievous breach of the fundamental principle of the rule of law and leaves ample room for all sorts of abuses. Most evident is arrogance, since the bureaucrats have so much power and mere citizens must bow and scrape to get things that may be theirs by right. Perhaps even more serious is that bureaucrats can use their power to shape laws and administrative actions in their own interest. I am not thinking of petty cheating so much as massive obstructionism blocking any reforms which might reduce their authority or prestige, including administrative reform, educational reform, agricultural reform and virtually every major political initiative that did not appeal to them.

Worse than this is that they regularly act in the interest of their specific clientele as opposed to the public in general. MITI does its best for the industrialists, especially big companies; Finance for the bankers and brokers; Agriculture looks after the farmers (not the consumers); Construction generates

work for the contractors; Health does what it can for pharmaceutical companies and physicians (not their patients); and
so on. There is no ministry whose mandate it is to care for
the people as a whole and thus no bureaucrats are willing to
put the nation first. "Prime guardian of the national interest"
my eye!

Then, of course, there are abuses of a more vulgar nature
which have inevitably crept in. There is, indeed, influence
peddling and corruption. After all, to get the bureaucrats to
make the right decisions, companies would not hesitate to
treat them lavishly, in the customary manner, with fine meals
and generous presents. Top officials were also involved in
the KDD, Recruit and other scandals. But the most effective
reward is to offer a cushy job on retirement. Johnson was
right. The practice of *amakudari* (descent from heaven) is
the primary source of abuses. Yet, it is not only tolerated
within very wide bounds, this form of "revolving door" has
been institutionalized. Bureaucrats expect such a job when
they retire and companies fight to get the best, for they know
that these employees will bring back more government contracts.

Aside from this, there is still the question of effectiveness
and efficiency of the Japanese bureaucracy. In most cases, it
is just assumed. Johnson doesn't bother much with that subject and Vogel did not look into the practical implications
even for his case histories. This is also glossed over by other
academics and it is exceedingly hard to find literature on the
failures. So, while admitting that there have been great successes, let me just mention enough cock-ups and white
elephants to let curious readers know that they do exist.

First of all, the immaculate MITI. The Ministry of International Trade and Industry has been instrumental in fostering
numerous sectors. But, as we noted, it also promoted some
which should have been avoided, like aluminum and non-
ferrous metals. It lavished more effort and funds than justified

on others, like steel and petrochemicals. It failed to accomplish its goals for alternative sources of energy, including nuclear. And it would have been wiser to run down certain sectors faster, surely coal and simpler textiles. The silliest flop, however, was the bright idea of establishing settlements abroad where aged Japanese could retire.

The Ministry of Finance is run by what the committed bureaucratophiles term "the elite of the elite." During the 1950s and 1960s, it seemed to earn that title by balancing budgets without even raising taxes. That act didn't work in the 1970s and 1980s, and Japan ran up whopping deficits that were worse than most OECD countries. Even today, it has a huge national debt that eats up almost 25% of the annual budget due to interest payments. MOF also found that its regulation of banking, securities, insurance and so on was a bit of an anachronism. As these powers go, it is being cut down to normal size.

The Economic Planning Agency never really engaged in planning; it did not have the authority, the budget or the expertise for that. But it was the nation's economic forecaster. This gained it some renown in the 1950s and 1960s, when growth usually exceeded targets. During the 1970s and 1980s, when growth fell short of targets, it was less popular. Still, as we pointed out elsewhere, both exceeding forecasts and not attaining them are errors, even if the former is more agreeable than the latter.[17]

The Ministry of Transport, you will remember, went on a monumental shipbuilding binge as of the 1950s. And it would have earned the nation's undying gratitude if only it had stopped in time. But it kept pumping money in too long, and the shipyards expanded too far, leaving a sorry financial mess. The same thing happened, with variations, to another pet project, the world-famous express railway system. The *shinkansen* lines were extraordinary. They were also very expensive. And they cut into the traffic of existing lines. What with one thing and another, the Japan National Railway's total debt was ¥41 trillion when it closed down.

The Ministry of Construction. Well, it built the world's longest tunnel, the Seikan Tunnel from Honshu to Hokkaido. But this took so long that, by the time it was finished, no one knew what to do with it. MOC also built the world's longest bridge, the Seto Bridge to Shikoku. But the tolls were so exorbitant that traffic was low and it was soon in the red. Red ink and white elephants. How touching. The Japanese colors.

We have already said enough about education to realize that the ministry has made one or two mistakes. The Ministry of Justice might also take a look at some aspects of its law enforcement and criminal justice systems. Health and welfare will be dealt with later. Defense. Admittedly, the budget is low. But the country could readily be invaded if it were not protected by the American military presence and nuclear umbrella. The Ministry of Post and Telecommunications. This is one I could never figure out. What possible explanation can there be for charging more to make a telephone call or mail a letter abroad than to receive them from exactly the same country?

How could this happen? Vogel already told you. The elite bureaucrats are the finest fruit of the educational system. They spent most of their youth learning facts by rote memory until they passed the exam. Then they studied law of all things. They are accomplished pen pushers and paper shufflers with little practical experience, business acumen or technical knowhow. Just try to find an economist at EPA, an engineer at MITI or an architect at Construction. I wish you luck. Even if they are fast learners, as some are, they are rotated every three years so that they never become proficient at anything but administration.

As you can see, after ten years in Japan, I am more of a bureaucratophobe than a bureaucratophile. And I am in good company. Rather than bore you with my own sob stories, let me quote from one of many irate letters to the editor, this sent in by an anonymous housewife.

"In the work section of the waiting room for applicants, two women employees were laughing loudly at a TV comedy show. . . . Isn't it incredible that public servants are watching TV during their working hours? . . . I arrived just after 4 p.m. only to see the 'workers' cleaning up their desks, chatting in groups or absorbed in travel agency pamphlets. They were obviously just killing time and waiting for 5 p.m., quitting time, to roll around. Since our taxes pay their salaries, I was so dismayed at the scene. In this sense, I must say our taxes are wasted."[18]

I'll vouch for this. I have seen the same thing time and again. But I am cheating a little. These are not the bureaucrats Vogel, Johnson, Reischauer and the others write about. They are only interested in the career bureaucrats, the elite. Alas, 99% of the bureaucrats are quite ordinary ones, just like those Anonymous-san complained about. And it should be the task of the career bureaucrats to see to it that they are doing their work.

As for the career bureaucrats, they do not fare much better at the hands of Japanese writers. According to Albert M. Craig, "Japanese historians tend to view the modern Japanese bureaucrat as the willing tool of all of the villains of history from the absolutist leaders of the early Meiji to the undemocratic party leaders of the Taisho, the militarists of the thirties, and the conservative party politicians of today. . . . Even more critical of bureaucracy than the writing of postwar historians is a second large literature written by ex-bureaucrats and newspaper reporters to expose the foibles, failings, formalism, and frustrations of bureaucratic life in Japan."[19]

So, once again, it is the foreign admirers who praise an institution that is regularly criticized by the locals. Odd that Vogel doesn't know that. This quote was taken from the first page of a book he edited in his younger, iconoclastic days. And we may just as well end with Craig's conclusion which we think is fair and shows that foreign academics can be balanced and objective when they make an effort.

"Japanese bureaucracy is not the model of efficiency that some who talk of Japan, Incorporated, would have, nor is it the neutral body pursuing national interests that the bureaucrats themselves often describe. But neither is it the jumble of dysfunctions portrayed in the writings of the critics. Japanese officials work long hours when necessary; in terms of any comparative standard they are honest; and they accomplish most of the tasks set for them with a reasonable competence."[20]

Businessmen: Pulling The Strings

The Japanapologists don't have much to say about business circles when it comes to politics, if not to insist that they really are not as important as claimed. Indeed, to hear them tell it, you would think that businessmen were just little poodles who follow obediently behind the all-powerful bureaucrats. The journalists are not quite as naive as the academics, and they realize the business community is very influential, but occasionally they succumb to the idea that things have changed, that the politicians and bureaucrats actually run the government. The writing was supposedly on the wall when the charismatic Yasuhiro Nakasone came to power. More recently, it was announced that big business had its "wings clipped."[21]

Nonetheless, business has played a crucial, and often dominant, role ever since party politics began in the 19th century. This tradition carried over after the war and, if anything, has been reinforced with time. Whereas the early postwar leaders really were quite dynamic, and knew what they wanted and how to get it, more recent politicians have been much weaker and amenable to control and guidance. The bureaucrats, who could lord it over managers when their companies were fragile and dependent on state support, no longer have much to offer. By now, business leaders clearly have the upper hand.

In judging just how effective the business community is all you have to do is consider most of the legislation and policy decisions that have been adopted over the past decades. In nearly all cases, they favor business interests and, in most cases, they were discreetly or more noticeably inspired by business groups.

Many of these measures were related to the economy and affected business directly. There was, for example, the process of industrial policy in which businessmen, rather than bureaucrats, worked out the concrete programs, were involved in them, sent key researchers, and obtained concrete benefits. Once they no longer needed as much assistance from the government, they blocked MITI's attempt to impose its will. Companies were the primary beneficiary of protectionism and managers whispered into the ears of officials which tariffs, quotas and NTBs would do the most good. When it became necessary to dismantle some of the barriers, they whispered into receptive ears which should go first and, of course, urged all possible delay.

Nothing bothers corporate executives more than having to pay taxes, and they exerted pressure to keep rates as low as possible. When they did not succeed, they engaged in tax evasion like everybody else. Now they are on the offensive, having inspired the plank in tax reform of lowering corporate taxes. The biggest program during the Nakasone era was administrative reform, and he cooperated so closely with business that he sometimes looked like the poodle of the business lobby. This reform, by the way, was directed against the bureaucrats who were unable to prevent it (although they did hamper its progress).

But business circles have meddled in other, more general

areas as well. Naturally, they did what they could to keep the Ministry of Labor from supporting workers and got it to follow business' lead on things like minimum wages, regulation of part-time and home work, supervision of factory safety laws, and so on. Certain companies have militated for increased defense expenditures. The private sector already urged educational reform well before Nakasone's arrival. And they fought the farm lobby. Finally, business associations have always played a preponderant role in foreign policy, something quite unique in modern countries. They, more than anyone, decided where development aid should go, which countries were potential partners and should be wooed by the foreign minister, and then left the ministry with the ignoble task of smoothing over any trade conflicts or investment shock they incited.

Admittedly, business did not always win, not in the sense of getting all it wanted. But it would be plain silly to regard this as a "defeat," as the foreign press periodically does. For example, when thick smog covered Tokyo and vicious pollution diseases erupted, it was impossible to block legislation on pollution or the creation of an Environmental Agency. But the restrictions were kept within bounds, and gradually weakened, while the EA was muzzled. In the end, the law for equal employment of women was passed, but it was stalled for years, shorne of any sanctions, and women actually had to surrender earlier gains. More recently, under foreign pressure, the Japanese market has been opened somewhat. But businessmen could be pleased that they had postponed that day so long.

Naturally, there were times when the business community was divided. Yet, that alone did not signify that business had lost its clout or had its wings clipped. This applies particularly to the switch from fiscal restraint, budgetary control and administrative reform under Nakasone to pump priming and economic stimulation through public works under Takeshita.

That was, indeed, an about-face. But from one business-backed policy to another. It is simply that the more established companies trying to reduce taxes were outmanoeuvered by the construction companies hungry for work. These latter, by the way, were the principal backers of Takeshita.

While most of the literature and reporting deals with the national level, it is at the local level that businessmen are most effective. There are towns and districts where a large company has sufficient clout that its wishes are promptly heeded. After all, it is the major provider of jobs, the major source of tax revenue, and the major purchaser of local goods and services. Anyone who thinks this is not enough to give it a decisive say in local politics is hopelessly naive. The company will thus influence tax rates, expenditures, location of infrastructure, land and zoning regulations, acquisition of licenses and permits and sundry matters that are far more important than what happens in Tokyo.

To achieve its aims, the business community works through a number of organizations. The Federation of Economic Organizations (Keidanren) is the voice of big business. The Japan Chamber of Commerce and Industry includes smaller firms as well. The Committee for Economic Development (Keizai Doyukai) consists of more dynamic, supposedly enlightened business leaders. The Japan Federation of Employers Associations (Nikkeiren) acts on behalf of business in labor relations. While the membership is not strictly the same, there are innumerable links between these bodies and, despite occasional friction or disagreements, they are all working to impose the views of business.[22]

This can be done in various ways. The most evident is funding of the Liberal Democratic Party. This is all the more essential in that the LDP does not really have much popular support and needs enormous amounts of money to win frequent election campaigns. Naturally, companies back not only the LDP but its factions, especially those of the current

Puppets and puppeteer: Nakasone,
Suzuki and Keidanren's Doko presenting
administrative reform.

Credit: Foreign Press Center/Kyodo

prime minister and potential successors. They also bankroll specific politicians in a position to do something out of the ordinary for them. By the way, business also allocates funds to middle-of-the-road and moderate Socialist parties like Komeito and the Democratic Socialist Party.

The business community does not usually intervene directly in the electoral process. But individual leaders make their views perfectly clear as to which parties and policies they endorse and sometimes also which ones they regard as a grave threat. They may urge their employees to vote for specific candidates, a suggestion that is heeded quite frequently, especially in rural areas where it is easier to ascertain how people voted.

Control over the bureaucrats is obtained through sumptuous wining and dining, periodic gifts and, above all, the practice of *amakudari* which has already been referred to. Lest there be any misunderstanding, this is not just a kindly gesture toward the able bureaucrats who have striven so diligently for the nation. Companies pick those officials who can help them (and have perhaps already helped them) because they served in the right ministry and still have contacts there. Banks therefore receive ex-bureaucrats from Finance, airlines from Transport, contractors from Construction, armament makers from Defense, pharmaceutical companies from Health, and so on.

Most of this is more or less above-board. Various laws have been adopted to regulate political funding but everyone knows they are regularly bypassed. Still, that is grudgingly tolerated. The same applies to the "revolving door" for bureaucrats. Everyone knows it leads to influence peddling and also that the measures adopted to contain abuses are inadequate. But that is also part of the acceptable rules by which one may play. While no one claims this compromise is good the Japanese have become accustomed to it and rarely get excited when critics point out that this really is "structural corruption."

Yet, despite the amazingly broad range of legitimate or tolerated channels that should provide more than enough leeway, there are still flagrant violations of the rules. This happens all the time with regard to public works contracts, where contractors bribe officials for inside information and local politicians for sending work their way. There are kickbacks for placing orders with specific suppliers. And inspectors have their palms greased for not reporting infringements of fire, work safety or environmental regulations. Much of this is minor. Still, as mentioned, there have been some major scandals as well.

One of the biggest of late involved the Recruit Group. Its

chairman, Hiromasa Ezoe, widely regarded as one of Japan's most dynamic businessmen, distributed over a million unlisted shares among 76 people. Once these shares were placed on the market, it was possible to sell and reap very substantial gains, estimated at ¥5 billion in total. The whole operation was very discreet and indirect in that hardly anyone was actually bribed; the lucky ones bought shares and simply took profits. At most, this could be regarded as a favor. But it irked the public which saw it as much more.

The first question was who had received such "favors." That was not so easy to trace since, in many cases, shares did not go straight to the beneficiary but a secretary, spouse or relative. Among those favored were over a dozen top LDP leaders, including past, present and possible future prime ministers Nakasone, Takeshita, Abe, Miyazawa and Watanabe. There were also former ministers of education and labor. Plus several career bureaucrats, executives of Nippon Telegraph & Telephone, local politicians, a newspaper editor, political analyst and some opposition Dietmen.

Even more revealing is why the favors were granted, i.e. in return for which other favors. It was perfectly obvious that this fit into a rational plan. Recruit's main line of business is as an employment agency, and one recipient was in charge of the relevant section of the Labor Ministry. Another line is publications, thus the officials from Education. It also has a real estate branch which was involved in a land deal with a local official. Recently, Recruit diversified into communications, an effort greatly facilitated by special help from NTT. As for the LDP big shots, more than specific services they could provide a generally conducive atmosphere and recognition. And perhaps more. Who knows?

From this it should be obvious that businessmen are not manipulated by the bureaucrats and politicians but, to the contrary, pull the strings. This fact may not have registered with foreign observers yet. But the Japanese are certainly aware of how things happen and why. And, in every survey on the subject, they pick the business community as the real power broker. Once again, not very democratic, although definitely part of the Japanese way.

People: Accepting But Not Approving

When the Japanapologists describe the political system they refer to all the major actors at length except one—the people. The people are almost a residual, what is left over. Or they are an object, moved about like pawns by the others. But they are almost never active participants who determine the nation's policies, select its leaders and see that their will be done. For this does not seem to be their role in practice nor in the writer's ideal world.

This attitude was betrayed by Vogel, who conceded that LDP leaders picked the prime minister from among themselves and deemed it a positive feature. At least this way, "the Japanese do not risk the election of a top official who has charismatic appeal but is unable to work effectively in the central government."[23] Then the bureaucrats would draw up policy, have it adopted by the Diet, and proceed to direct the country. Since the latter were such fine, upstanding chaps, they could presumably be trusted and it was not really necessary to worry about "guarding the guardians."

Where did ordinary citizens fit into this process? Well, there were deliberative councils which could present their views. And there were the various lobbies and "multipurpose" groups (villages, towns, companies, professional associations). They could defend their members' interests. Thus, once these intermediaries had been heard, the bureaucrats could make decisions with little concern for "idiosyncratic objections" from Dietmen. And, having been prepared by the best minds in the country, "the outcome appears not as something a narrow group of bureaucrats decided but something 'we Japanese' decided.''[24]

Unfortunately, as everyone—including Ez Vogel—knows, the deliberative councils are appointed by the bureaucrats or politicians and include hand-picked members who are expected, on the whole and in due course, to reflect views from above and not below. Especially since most do not have any particular constituency which has instructed them on what to propose or could recall them. As for the lobbies and other special-interest groups, they present the views not of the "people" but specific segments thereof. They are far more likely to skew decisions in their own favor than seek a common position.

So, in explaining the excellence of Japanese politics, Vogel falls back on the bizarre concept of "fair share." Unlike the United States, where the winner supposedly takes the whole pie, the Japanese will apportion it in such a way that everyone receives a piece. Or, if this is impossible one time, next time the disadvantaged party has a claim to a larger share.[25] There is no clear explanation of how, but it can be assumed that an equitable division will be arranged among the multipurpose groups.

While this is a very appealing formula, there are some minor drawbacks. One is that there is no law or custom that guarantees fair shares. Another is that there is no machinery to attain them. A third is that there is no impartial body to ensure that everyone receives a fair share while each of the contestants is mainly concerned with getting the largest slice possible. The fatal flaw, however, is that things simply do not work this way in practice.

Japanese decisions, despite the urge for surface harmony, are very hard fought. Each group is convinced of its rights and under pressure from members to defend them to the hilt. In practice, compromises are hard to achieve and neutral parties trusted by all concerned are few and far between. So the rule of winner take all usually prevails. I have yet to hear of an LDP Dietman who stepped down graciously to leave his seat to someone he felt was better qualified. Or of a ministry that gave part of its budget to another whose activities were more important. Or a company which refused a contract because a competitor could do a cheaper job.

Quite to the contrary, in Japan more than elsewhere, the spoils go to the strongest group or, if they are divisible, then in exact proportion to the strength of the various contestants. Thus, if the LDP amends draft legislation to take into account Opposition proposals, it is only because the Opposition is in a position to block the debates or make the prime minister look silly. If small enterprises get an agency to cater to their needs, it is much smaller and less well funded than the bureaucracies that assist the stronger, better connected big companies. If the farmers obtain rice subsidies, it is not because they are part of Japan's cultural heritage but that they have disproportionately large political clout.

Fair shares are only available for groups that are well-organized, actively promote their interests, and elect the right politicians.

Thus, the farmers get a fair share (although fair hardly seems the right word). So do small retailers. So do doctors and dentists. But others get a miserly portion or nothing at all because, no matter how numerous, they are not well organized, do not agitate enough or only have Opposition backing. That includes labor, not only the various trade unions but more so unorganized labor, the general public as consumers or victims of environmental destruction, most of the racial and social minorities, women, youngsters, the aged and disaffected. That's a hell of a lot of people!

The very idea that Japan's leaders are concerned about granting a "fair share" is disproven by repeated actions. Serious cases of pollution broke out during the 1960s and were stubbornly ignored by the authorities, those who protested were criticized and discredited, and it took years for the victims to get any compensation. Villages and urban districts were disrupted by infrastructure projects or factory construction and little was done to meet their needs. In one of the most notable, the struggle over Narita airport, the opponents' bitterest complaint was that the government refused to "hear" them. The government also refused to hear antinuclear activists, student radicals, women seeking equality, consumers urging cheaper and safer products and so on.[26]

Quite to the contrary, the government followed a policy that was effective, but little more. The standard approach of the LDP (and more so, the bureaucracy) has not varied. First, try to ignore any protest movement. Then, if it makes too much noise, isolate and discredit it. If it remains strong and attracts further attention, offer limited concessions, more along the lines of a sop than substantive change. This can be done easily and at no cost to the party through the national budget. Later, if it has actually gathered a following, try to control it. If this is impossible, at least coopt some of the leaders so the movement will lose its vigor.

The plight of the "losers" in this society, and they are legion, does not seem to interest the Japanapologists. They are patently more interested in the "elite," those whom they deem capable and worthy of directing the government and administration. And not only that. They prefer the elite to the people, masses or whatever you want to call them in every sector. Political parties over ordinary voters, career bureaucrats over ordinary citizens, company executives over ordinary workers, professors over students, the educated over the benighted, parents over children, and so on. That is why they find Japan such an admirable society. It is "meritocratic."

How then can they present the Japanese system as a model for democracy as well? Rather than concede that you can have "meritocracy" or you can have "democracy," but not both, they want Japan to be the perfect society. As good as and even better than places like the United States or Europe. "If the term 'democracy' is used to signify the expression of diverse interests in the political arena and the capacity of the government to satisfy these interests, it could be argued that Japan is now a more effective democracy than America."[27] This quote from Vogel. Now try Reischauer. "The Japanese political system . . . appears to measure up quite well as an effective system of democratic rule, not notably inferior to those of the West and perhaps stronger in some respects."[28]

How they can draw such conclusions is hard to understand. If democracy means rule "of the people, by the people and for the people," then what passes for democracy in Japan certainly does not qualify. At best, it is rule of the people by a dominant party and elite bureaucracy, for the businessmen and other pressure groups. Ordinary people play a very minor role. It is probably their own fault, since they could have accomplished more if they tried harder. But acquiescence is not quite the same thing as self-determination.

At this point, our foreign friends have again clearly parted company with the Japanese people. As we already noted, few of them think highly of the politicians, bureaucrats or businessmen. And they are not happy with the political system in general. This echoes from every opinion poll or open discussion on the subject. Here are just a few of the latest. According to the annual survey of the Prime Minister's Office, fully 64% of the respondents believed that public opinion was not reflected in politics. And a *Yomiuri Shimbun* poll found as many as 83% voicing discontent with present-day politics.[29]

Another kind of poll is even more revealing. It tracks the "support" or "approval" rates of the various governments. These appear quite frequently and usually follow the same trajectory. First, when a new leader is proclaimed by the LDP, he is fairly well received and enjoys a brief honeymoon with the public. From then on, it's all downhill with few exceptions. The low points for recent prime ministers were 19% for Tanaka, 26% for Miki, 19% for Fukuda, 21% for Ohira, 29% for Suzuki, 26% for Nakasone and an incredible 4% for Takeshita. Uno might have beat that on the downside if he were ever taken seriously. But the voters' judgment was clearly expressed in the disastrous Upper House election of July 1989. Alas, it does not seem that the voters liked Opposition politicians much more.[30]

It is indeed odd that the Japanapologists do not consult public opinion polls more often. It is even stranger that they regularly neglect the views of their counterparts and the press. Most Japanese academics strongly criticize the businessmen, bureaucrats and politicians, with few actively backing the LDP. And the press, as the "experts" would know if they read it, condemns specific cases of incompetence and corruption and more generally political and bureaucratic mismanagement. But the foreign friends apparently live in their own little bubble, quoting one another and discarding anything that runs contrary to the theme of Japan as No. 1.

Still, for anyone who actually follows the political scene, it would be unthinkable to give Japan a high grade. Of course, it is not as bad as the Third World. But it has not climbed into the circle of truly democratic countries either.

NOTES

1. See Gerald L. Curtis, *The Japanese Way of Politics*, p. 243.
2. Edwin O. Reischauer, *The Japanese*, p. 309–10.
3. *The Economist*, September 24, 1988, p. 21.
4. *Financial Times*, December 29, 1988.
5. *Wall Street Journal*, July 12, 1988, p. 28.
6. *Tokyo Business Today*, December 1987, p. 16.
7. These cases are referred to more extensively in Woronoff, *Politics The Japanese Way*.

8. *Tokyo Business Today*, November 1988, p. 25.
9. *Wall Street Journal*, December 27, 1988, p. 1.
10. *The Economist*, September 24, 1988.
11. Ezra Vogel, *Japan As No. 1*, pp. 54 & 67.
12. Chalmers Johnson, *MITI And The Japanese Miracle*, p. 21.
13. Johnson, *op. cit.*, p. 21.
14. Vogel, *op. cit.*, pp. 55–6.
15. Robert Christopher, *The Japanese Mind*, p. 230.
16. Johnson, *op. cit.*, pp. 68–9.
17. Woronoff, *The Japan Syndrome*, pp. 120–4.
18. *Mainichi*, October 26, 1988.
19. Albert M. Craig, "Functional and Dysfunctional Aspects of Government Bureaucracy," in Ezra Vogel (ed.), *Modern Japanese Organization And Decision-Making*, p. 3.
20. Craig, *op. cit.*, p. 32.
21. *Far Eastern Economic Review*, June 11, 1987, p. 90.
22. For more on business organizations and political action, see Woronoff, *Politics The Japanese Way*, pp. 150–174.
23. Vogel, *op. cit.*, p. 64.
24. *Ibid.*, p. 90.
25. *Ibid.*, pp. 117–8.
26. For more on grass-roots opposition and activism, see David E. Apter, *Against The State*, Kurt Steiner (ed.), *Political Opposition and Local Politics in Japan*, and Gavan McCormack (ed.), *Democracy In Contemporary Japan*.
27. Vogel, *op. cit.*, p. 97.
28. Reischauer, *op. cit.*, p. 327.
29. *Yomiuri*, June 13 & May 4, 1989.
30. *Yomiuri*, 23 June, 4 May & 6 May, 1989.

9

Society
(Discordant Harmonies)

Solidarity Outward, Not Inward

When I first lived in Japan, the *tatemae* I believed in most
firmly was that of great unity and solidarity among the Japanese people. After all, it is presented as the most self-evident
of facts in virtually all the books on Japan and you can hardly
find anyone who denies it (and is not a crank or a Commie).
Just see what Forbis said. "No other major nation has such
a homogeneity of face, skin, and hair color. From this flows
the Japanese sense of nationhood and unity—and perhaps
also the sense that any individual's first loyalty is to his nation,
not to his individual welfare."[1] Or Christopher: "Far more
than the citizens of most collectivized societies, Japanese are
dominated by a sense of responsibility to the various groups
to which they belong—their country, their company and so
on."[2] And Prime Minister Nakasone spoke of a "spontaneous
community" with a monoracial/monolithic nature (*tanitsu
minzoku kokka*).

Yet, the longer I stayed, the more apparent it became that
there was something awry. By now I would staunchly question the veracity of this portion of the conventional wisdom,
no matter how incredulous others may be. To understand
why, it is crucial to remember that there is more than one

form of solidarity and, while certain manifestations may be very strong, others can be quite weak. Moreover, the strong ones, if sufficiently visible, can hide the weak from view and create a misleading impression of overall solidarity.

There is no doubt that the sense of national identity is powerful, that is, the Japanese versus the others. This derives from ancient concepts of the nation as a sacred entity and even deeper cultural lines drawn between *uchi* (inside) and *soto* (outside). It is helped along by the relative geographic isolation of Japan which, in bygone days, contributed to a physical separation that was only exacerbated by extended periods of closure to the outside world. It is still hardly breached by token foreign visitors or Japanese tourists and businessmen who go abroad.

The heightened sense of one nation is strengthened by the mistaken notion, but one which is amazingly prevalent, that the Japanese are a distinct and homogeneous race. Remember Nakasone's comments. Still, there is ample evidence that many of their ancestors came from Korea and China while others probably originated in Southeast Asia. Ever since those far-off days, there have been considerable admixtures with the immigration of Chinese and Koreans a millennium ago and then, in very different form, as forced laborers during the Pacific War. Now there is some intermarriage with other peoples.

But the biggest flaw in the claim to homogeneity is the existence of indigenous minorities. One is the Ainu, who inhabited vast stretches of Honshu until they were thrown back to Hokkaido by the invading "Japanese" and almost decimated since. The survivors are presently (mis)treated as anthropological curiosities and tourist attractions. In Okinawa, to the south, the native population was of quite a different race. Finally, although this is not a racial distinction, the former outcastes or *eta*, who engaged in "unclean" tasks, were isolated in clearly marked communities and are still discriminated against as *burakumin*.

For a while after the war, it looked as if nationalism—so harshly criticized as a cause of great suffering—was abating. Now, however, cultural currents are pushing the Japanese in the opposite direction. Not content to be separate from other races, merely different from the rest, there is an irrepressible urge to appear unique. Few peoples have ever taken the idea of uniqueness to the same lengths as the Japanese, and none today. For there is an outpouring of books, articles and lectures to convince the Japanese just how much they are distinct and, most often, superior. As Jared Taylor, who grew up in Japan and knows the country very well, noted:

"When the Japanese talk about their island nation and their homogeneous population—and they talk about them a lot—it seems to me that they are not trying so much to explain Japanese behavior as to cite justifications for it. They are imbued with the notion that for better or worse, they are different. When they make contact with the outside world, they seem to be looking for confirmation of their uniqueness rather than for its denial. There is a pervasive, exclusive notion of 'we Japanese' that draws a firm line between 'we' and 'they.' "[3]

Inevitably, this sort of thinking, and the behavior that must arise from it, reinforce national solidarity versus outsiders. Whether it is good is another question. Certainly, for foreigners, it is unpleasant. For the Japanese themselves, it is perhaps exalting to feel different and better. But that only widens the breach and encourages them to accentuate characteristics that should otherwise be moderated.

Equally obvious is the strength of solidarity within Japanese groups. This results from hierarchical structures and vertical links, which are exceptionally vigorous and enduring in Japan as compared to other societies. This was pointed out most effectively by Chie Nakane.

"What is most important is that in Japan a group inevitably and eventually develops the vertical type of organizational structure. Further, an organizational structure based on the vertical principle appears more pronouncedly in well-established, large institutions with a higher degree of prestige. . . . the stronger the functioning of the group, the more likely it is that its human relations have been built along these lines."[4]

Such structures and links exist in virtually every group or institution: company, bureaucracy, school, university department, political party, religion or *yakuza* gangs. It even pervades what elsewhere are informal groupings like college clubs or hobby classes (judo, kendo, flower arrangement, etc.) and even radical movements which claim they want to overthrow the existing order. In Japan, such groups can hardly be escaped and it is extremely difficult and perilous not to belong to one.

Within each group, the internal cohesion is constantly reinforced by common goals, meetings and activities, indoctrination sessions and also joint relaxation. Tremendous demands are placed on the members' loyalty and anyone not going along with the group's decisions would come under relentless pressure. Opting out is no easier in practice. For members will continue visiting the defector and even urge his friends and family to get him to return. Perhaps the best reason for not defecting, and this keeps many dissatisfied members in, is that it is extremely hard to move to any other group whose own internal cohesion keeps it from absorbing outsiders.

There is thus no doubt that national solidarity and group solidarity are exceedingly strong. But these are not the only forms of solidarity. There must also be positive and regular relations within the nation from group to group. And that kind of solidarity, one which is rather widespread abroad, is sadly lacking in Japan. There are few horizontal links between different groups and also different categories of Japanese, such as men and women, young and old, rich and poor.

Examples of mediocre relationships, which can range from indifference to antagonism, are too numerous for me to mention more than a sampling. (By the way, this is all commonly known and fully documented.) Big companies are harsh rivals, fighting over market share pitilessly. In so doing, they care little about what happens to outside suppliers or lesser subcontractors. Within the company, white-collar and blue-collar workers have few contacts or much in common. The same goes for male and female workers. Trade unions, the traditional source of worker solidarity, are badly splintered and not only along ideological lines. Within each company, there may be a different union for each plant, and the union does not worry about the fate of part-timers or subcontractors' workers.

The relations between political parties are extremely limited. Talk of cooperation, even a coalition, has gone on for decades with little real cooperation materializing in the opposition camp. Within the ruling party, supposedly one single party, the factions are constantly intriguing against each other. The only things they can unite on are to stay in power and to see that no faction hangs on to power for long. To hear it told, university faculty meetings are endless griping sessions in which cooperation from department to department is rare and joint activities with other universities almost nonexistent. We already know how *yakuza* gangs treat one another. But apparently schools of flower arrangement are no less drastic.

So, while unity and harmony remain the goal (and appear as the *tatemae*), friction and factionalism are the reality. The bitter *honne* of everyday life is continual quarreling and jockeying for position of factions (*habatsu*). They emerge almost spontaneously due to the penchant for small groups and the tendency of more dynamic leaders to attract disciples and followers. They only merge when one manages to dominate

176

the others or in order to repel common adversaries, this latter alliance quickly disintegrating once the pressure is off. Such factions can be found in virtually all institutions and, as soon as they grow too much, they tend to splinter.[5]

Aside from this, and despite all the talk of nation and group, the Japanese are not joiners in the sense understood abroad. They do not become members of a broad range of organizations, whether deeply involved or merely to express interest or sympathy. There are few youth movements like the Boy Scouts or Girl Guides, there is not even much of a little league for baseball or neighborhood soccer teams. There are not many voluntary associations for causes like aid to developing countries, eradication of some contagious disease or preservation of historic monuments. There are not many environmentalists, no equivalent of the Sierra Club, and certainly no Green Party. Despite the way consumers are cheated by domestic manufacturers, distributors and farmers, there is no true consumers' movement. Nor is there any "grey power" for the aged.

With regard to those outside of their primary groups, there is rarely more than benign neglect. As intimated, "true" Japanese, whoever they may be, show little concern about the poor treatment of Ainu, *burakumin* or Koreans. Nor do the rich display much commiseration for the poor. There are dreadfully few charitable organizations, most of them sponsored by the small Christian community. As for politicians, they not only do not care about the interests of the "people" as a whole, they do not even bother speaking to them except at election time.

Even more extraordinary is the lack of cooperation or contact between men and women. Men are preoccupied by the serious tasks of life, holding down a job, staying at the office for countless hours. Women should look after the home, the kids' education and make things pretty and comfy for their hubby. Men have so far shown little understanding that their

177

wives or daughters might want a career instead. And they resist the rise of women in their own company, bureaucracy, party, club, etc. There has been a women's lib movement of sorts. But it gained little backing from men. Even stranger is that husbands and wives rarely go out together and even young men and women, who would be dating or courting anywhere else, hardly mix. That really is unique!

Relations between Japanese of different ages are stymied by other distinctions. The rule of seniority still prevails and the young must bow and kowtow to the old. Young, by the way, does not mean by several years or decades but one single year. A person who was born a year later or, more often, entered a formal group a year later, is a junior (*kohai*), one who joined a year earlier is a senior (*sempai*), and only those who joined at the same time are relative equals (*doryo*). Relations between them are regulated hierarchically which makes the structures colder and stiffer than necessary.

Language is what makes these gaps and distinctions, which obviously exist elsewhere, more rigid and unbridgeable. It is impossible to speak to anyone in Japanese without knowing that person's station in life, whether senior, junior or equal, whether superior or subordinate, whether from a larger or smaller company or organization plus whether male or female. For there are specific linguistic forms and whole expressions that must be used depending on which category you are in and which category the person you are speaking to is in. Naturally, the younger, lower, and females speak up to the older, higher and males, who speak down to them in return.[6]

The most extraordinary example of this social constipation is the Japanese cocktail party where people from different backgrounds are invited. Those who know someone else stick to them. Those who don't would not dream of just walking up and introducing themselves. They could not even start since they do not know if the other person is higher or lower and thus which language to use. They must be introduced by some go-between. If none exists, they stand in a corner munching on canapés or *sushi* and perhaps chatting with a hostess to whom they know they can speak as an inferior and who is there so they are not entirely alone and bored.

No wonder horizontal or lateral solidarity, which often flourishes in other societies, has remained stunted and under-developed in Japan. It stood no real chance because it was crushed under the weight of national identity and group ego-ism, because the primary group would not tolerate rivalry from secondary groups and informal associations, because tradition and linguistic barriers got in the way. Yet, without it, nationalism remains hollow and group loyalty only makes it harder for all Japanese, of all categories, to work together. That is why I think Japanese unity and solidarity are greatly overrated.

Wait, Mr. Woronoff. Didn't you forget something? What about consensus? Everybody knows Japan has a consensual society.

Well, what about consensus? For years, if not decades, there has been a consensus in Japan that something had to be done to improve, upgrade or reform the school system, electoral system, party politics, women's rights, human rights, and racial discrimination, the fiscal deficit, social se-curity and welfare, government administration, agriculture, defense and taxation, and so on. Yet, so far there have been rather few notable initiatives and even fewer actual accom-plishments. And this while more conflictual societies like America, Britain and the Soviet Union under Reagan, Thatcher and Gorbachev were making radical changes. In Japan, the only consensus seems to be immobilism and drift.

I think consensus has also been overrated. So, next time they tell you Japan has a consensual society, ask them just which consensus they mean and what concrete action it has resulted in!

Gender, Generation And Other Gaps

Normally, one would expect those praising Japan's society to make a big fuss about the ideal Japanese family. After all, that is the basic social cell, the most important institution in any society. And it is also the one where flowery *tatemae* seems to be the habitual presentation. The happy family, the united couple, mom and dad busy bringing up the kids to be wholesome, upstanding citizens, and all that jazz. But the family hardly figures in even the extensive writings of Reischauer and is not proposed as a model by Vogel or anyone else.

There are good reasons for this. If you admire Japan, or pretend to do so, then certainly the less said about it the better. For the Japanese family is decaying and crumbling at an alarming speed. Only some of that can be traced to "modernization" which affects all societies through phenomena such as the trends toward nuclear families and urbanization. This, too, has been reshaping the Japanese family as the nuclear family replaces the multi-generation and extended family. Naturally, it is doing so more pervasively in the cities. But also in the countryside, with more farmers, fishermen or miners seeking seasonal jobs elsewhere, the family core is shrinking.[7]

The real worry, however, is that even this core is splitting under the pressures of Japanese society. The swelling ranks of salaried and seasonal workers are drawn away from the family by the employers' insistence on hard work, long hours and loyalty. The result is that most fathers get up early, make a long commute to the office or factory, and spend a lengthy day there. Alas, they do not head home after that, like fathers elsewhere. They stay on for overtime, or go out with colleagues, or just wait to avoid the rush hour. In addition, many are sent abroad or transferred to distant offices for years at a stretch without their family.

The outcome is that Japanese fathers spend less time with their family than in most advanced or developing countries, this amply documented by various international surveys as well as personal observation. Worse, they seem to have less to do with their families even when at home, devoting most of their free time to sleeping, relaxing or watching television. They do not go out often with the family, play with the kids or engage in other homey activities. They are, by and large, absent mentally even when they are present physically. And they seem to be happiest when relieved of such family "duties" to return to work.

Thus, the mother has become the principal support of the family, something she can only accomplish partially because of Japanese culture. Naturally, she can and must run the household, do the shopping, cooking, housekeeping and so on. She can also look after the family budget. But it would seem that her main task is to take command of the children's education, devoting endless time and effort to preparing the kids for college exams. In so doing, she may become the "educational mother" (*kyoiku mama*) or more redoubtable "mother monster" (*mamagon*) who dominates and perhaps crushes their personality.

But there are some things a mother simply cannot do. She cannot become a suitable role model for a son, who must learn to behave like a man, or help a daughter learn how to relate to men. This is frustrated by the sharp distinction between male and female roles and further enforced by linguistic constraints, with boys having to learn men's language from a man and girls having to learn how to use women's language in discourse with men. The consequence has been mounting confusion and frustration as the children try to sort things out and usually only learn their place after being inducted into a company.

While mothers could devote themselves entirely to the children once upon a time, when Japan was actually much poorer,

Flower arrangement. Now, that's
a fitting pastime for women.

Credit: Matsushita Electric

it seems that with affluence they have been forced more than
ever into the labor market. By now there are as many house-
wives working as remaining at home. This means that millions of children do not even have a mother's regular care
and return home after school to look after themselves. These
batches of "latch-key" children are in ever greater difficulty
both as concerns education and assimilation of Japanese culture, although it may be a blessing in disguise that they are
no longer devoured by their mother.

The impact of these trends on the family has been pretty
devastating, although not always visible due to the Japanese
urge to smooth things over, cover up defects and present a
happy face to the outside world. This partially explains why

divorce has not become widespread, a point seized upon by the Japanapologists. Look, they say, Japan's divorce rate is much lower than the United States. But it has risen appreciably from where it was before and it compares less well to European or other Asian rates.

Moreover, divorce is not usually a feasible solution. Most women do not hold a decent job, they possess relatively little personal wealth, and they could not get by financially on the stingy alimony (if any). So, they frequently decide to stay on, living physically with their husband but distancing themselves emotionally. While there is no divorce in the legal sense, there is clearly a divorce within the family and this has become an increasingly familiar phenomenon called *kateinai rikon*.[8]

While this tends to work as long as the husband is employed and bringing in a regular salary, the relationship undergoes severe strain when he retires. Then he hangs around the house, doing little useful and just getting in the way. He is, in women's parlance, a ''cockroach'' who invades his wife's domain, a ''heap of bulk garbage'' which should be thrown out or ''unlabeled canned goods,'' having lost his identity.[9]

Relations have, on the whole, not been much better between the generations. According to Japanese mores, those who are younger must talk up to, and show considerable deference to, those who are older or seniors. But the family experience has not provided a suitable atmosphere. The father was away too often and rather than someone they honor or care for he may be almost a stranger and treating him with respect is an imposition. Mother has been around, but she was so overbearing they had to resist or be crushed. And, anyway, she is just a woman which is not much within the social hierarchy. This means that most children have grown up without training in how to relate to elders within the traditional Japanese framework.

This has to be inculcated later in life. It first becomes the task of the teacher, along with actual education and preparation for exams. Eventually it is taken over by the employer who spends as much time on instilling the proper attitude toward superiors as more practical matters. But this cannot be done as effectively at a later age and remains rather artificial. While juniors do learn the linguistic forms, adopt a proper demeanor and bow in the regulation manner to seniors, their heart is not in it. If anything, it irks and annoys them (although they do insist that their juniors speak up to them, bow suitably, and don't express any distaste for such formalities).

From this, it must be obvious that, although one may get along well enough with seniors and juniors, the best relationships are established with relative equals. Namely, those of roughly the same age or who joined the work unit in the same year. With them, it is possible to use more informal language and engage in more relaxed conversations. Naturally, they also have more in common. This creates exceptionally strong bonds within each age class. And, since age classes are so narrow, it subdivides generations very minutely and actually hastens generational change while magnifying the gaps with the others.

For historic reasons, generational change has also been more sweeping in Japan than elsewhere. This could hardly be avoided when one considers the dramatic economic and political transformations. The prewar and wartime generations were brought up in a fiercely nationalistic, strictly disciplined and harshly totalitarian system. They lived through the period of intensive mobilization for the Pacific War and then the bitter combat on foreign soil or the grueling efforts to keep the economic machine running at home. They underwent incredible hardship, deprivation and selflessness for a cause that suddenly collapsed.

What greater differences could possibly exist with the succeeding generations? These were children who grew up in peacetime and for whom war was soon not even a memory. From year to year, as the economy expanded, there was more comfort and affluence, especially for the kids who were often spoiled silly by their parents. They lived in a more democratic country, one which permitted greater individual choice and freedom, and where the strictures and restrictions of earlier generations made ever less sense. No wonder new goals were sought.

The first postwar generations were rather tame, to judge by the names used to describe them. There was the "my home" generation which hoped to get away from work more frequently. Next the "new family" generation which wanted to create closer and warmer relations between men and women, parents and children. Briefly, during the early 1960s, there were radical students who sought political and ideological change, but they were not quite typical of broader circles. Then came a relatively spiritless generation, one with less backbone but certainly preferred by the authorities.[10]

After this, generations seemed to come thick and fast. One was called "crystal" after a book that advocated an easy-going, materialistic and somewhat amoral lifestyle. Others adopted their own fads and fashions, including the *takenoko-zoku* who dyed their hair and did weird dances in Harajuku. And now we have the *shin jinrui* or "new human race," one that has clearly rejected the "old human race" (*kyu jinrui*). But this is not the end. Younger children are creating the *shin shin jinrui* ("new new race") and *dai san jinrui* ("third human race").

What is striking about the generation gap in Japan, as opposed to other countries, is that there has been so little open rebellion. There was some during the immediate postwar years, of a social nature, then in the early 1960s, of a political and ideological nature, as well as the rise of motorcycle gangs (*bosozoku*). But, by and large, the demands and behavior have been quite conservative. Who could complain about wanting more home life or better family relations or even, if one is not too stodgy, cutting loose on weekends as long as you are back at work or school on Monday. The more recent "races" are also fairly well-behaved and do not create a disturbance.

But all of this is deceptive. In Japan, open revolt seems doomed to failure. Hidden revolt is not. In fact, it is extremely easy because of the distinction between *tatemae* and *honne*. As long as you say the right things, go through the right motions, and don't stand out, you can pretty well get away with it. It is possible to hold on to your job without making exceptional efforts if you accept that you may be promoted less rapidly and never reach the top. Thus, it is possible for the superstructure to remain intact even while the essential pillars are being eroded underneath. And it will not collapse as long as there are still enough dedicated souls to hold it up.

How long such individuals remain is open to question. For the generational trends have been in directions that are distinctly opposed to traditional values. This is noticeable from personal observation. There is definitely more individualism in the younger age classes, more insistence on the right to go one's own way and more taste for a comfortable, materially rich life. This contrasts sharply with older classes which are much more group-oriented, willing to subordinate their goals to those of the company, nation or some higher entity, and willing to accept any necessary sacrifice and privation.

For those who spurn the anecdotal, there are polls and surveys which have repeatedly and consistently confirmed such observations. One comes from the Ministry of Education, which meters changes in young people's values. Over the years, the following goals have slipped markedly: to live a clean, honest life and to work for the benefit of society. Two others have just held steady, but attract few youngsters: to achieve personal prestige and to work for personal wealth. The biggest increases were scored by: to live a leisurely life and to attain personal pleasure. This last goal is now expressed by over half of the respondents.[11]

While one might expect some loosening in the broader social realm, where discipline and sanctions are harder to impose, it is most striking to find similar trends even in matters regarding the company. Further surveys reveal that attitudes are clearly changing. One, by the Prime Minister's Office, indicates that less and less young workers are willing to sacrifice personal life for the sake of the company. Another, by the Labor Ministry, indicates that more and more workers want to change jobs.[12] And yet others add that ever fewer expect to be promoted to the top or even want to make the effort to become an executive.

These are manifestly warning signs. Japan cannot continue to exist and perform as it has in the past if the family keeps eroding and each coming generation is more "me" oriented than the last. Yet, there appears to be little recognition of the threat or efforts to salvage the family and bridge the generation gaps. This is what brings our overall grade down to an unsatisfactory.

Meritocracy Or Schoolocracy

Well, dear readers, since this is a book on Japan it is only appropriate that we pause briefly for a multiple choice quiz. Please indicate the correct answer. Japan's society is: A) based on wealth, B) based on birth, C) based on merit. I cannot but assume that all of you, quick as a flash, picked C as the right answer. The Japanapologists have been assiduous on this point and their indoctrination has been highly effective. Nowadays, it is almost impossible to read about Japanese society without coming across a reference to "meritocracy." We already quoted Reischauer on that under education. Ron Dore goes even further and claims that "the

Japanese system is one of the most single-mindedly merito-cratic in the world.''[13]

The writers rarely bother proving the point. It is probably assumed proven by dint of ceaseless repetition. Indeed, few enough even bother explaining what they mean by meritocrat-ic. I guess it signifies a class structure based on educational attainment with equal opportunity provided for all. You know, something like the delightful vision conjured up by Frank Gibney.

"In many ways, Japan is a true meritocracy. One can move up, if one obeys the rules, and get quite far through sheer competence. The railroad motorman's son from far-off Akita prefecture who excels in the exams and enters Tokyo Uni-versity will find himself, by that very fact, elevated to a pre-eminence in the Japanese community that his family might not otherwise have achieved for generations. He will be ac-cepted into a government office or large corporation on the basis of his school affiliation (as long as he does well in the corporation's testing process) and handled as a member of the elite. But he is an elitist the way the Chinese mandarins were elitists, by right of scholarship and merit (plus possibly some help from a few acquaintances). But he does not think of himself as part of an elite social class. And, unlike people who climb from humble circumstances in America, he rarely turns his back on his antecedents. Family is family. Akita is still home. And, after all, everybody is Japanese.''[14]

This sounds too good to be true. It is. When you start picking at it, most of the strands of reasoning unravel. As we already mentioned in the education section, the system in no way guarantees "merit." It only ensures that, upon grad-uating from high school, the person concerned was able to pass the university entrance exams. This was done largely on the basis of rote memory and untiring practice with mock tests. To call this meritocracy is certainly a misnomer.

It could better be understood as a schoolocracy. It is a

system whereby children start training for college entrance exams at an early age, frequently only three or four nowadays. They are primed to pass tests for acceptance in one of the better kindergartens, which prepare their kids for primary school. Then a better primary school, which prepares them for high school or, if you are lucky, can guarantee placement through a feeder system. The "good" high schools then concentrate on getting students into "good" colleges. Just in case, serious students also attend cram courses.

If all this were accessible to every family, then one could perhaps speak of equal opportunity. But it is not. Specialized kindergartens are very expensive, the primary and secondary schools which provide the best preparation, and are often direct feeders to the next higher level, may be private and even more costly. Sending your kid to *juku* can run into a small fortune. If he flunks the first exams, he may have to be supported as a *ronin* for another year or two until he does pass. Finally, if all else fails, money can buy a place in one of the lesser colleges that serve as diploma mills.

That is why kids from outer prefectures like Akita, and kids from poorer or even modestly endowed families, and kids whose parents did not go to college before them, are finding it harder and harder to climb the educational ladder. This inauspicious trend is already perfectly evident. Although the state universities were intended for such children, and therefore charge lower tuition fees, by now more of the seats are taken by the offspring of middle and upper class families. Private colleges are even more dominated by the well-off.

When it comes to entering a good company, the test helps, of course. But strangely enough it is much easier to pass if you come from the right university. And, it is a known fact that most successful candidates are already chosen before the test, not after. More important is contacts, which can be college chums or your parents and relatives. Company executives are adept at using the "back door" to get their children into the same or an affiliated company. Once in, connections (*kone*) are essential for promotions and work assignments, with the old-school tie counting for as much as ability or drive.

Sorry, the answer to our question was not C. Let us try another. Japan's society is egalitarian. Yes or No. Did you pick Yes? I wouldn't be surprised if you did. After all, the books on Japan are full of references to an egalitarian society. They even prove it with really solid statistical evidence: the Gini coefficient. This shows the percentage of the population in each quintile (20%) of income. While income is not equally distributed (it isn't anywhere), it is more evenly spread in Japan than elsewhere.

The catch here is that the Gini coefficient only measures income distribution. It does not consider other sources of earnings or assets. Thus, the fairly even distribution can be traced to fairly equal salaries among the ubiquitous salary-men or perhaps small farmers. But it does not take into account sales of land, capital gains on stocks and bonds, or inheritances. And these are becoming the main sources of wealth.

Actually, over recent years, the only way to get rich was not to work for a salary but to profit from the stupendous rise in the value of securities and land. While wages were growing a few percent a year, hardly enough to keep up with inflation, other assets were soaring. As everyone knows, stock and land prices were climbing at spectacular rates that left everything else far behind. So, while your salarymen were not exactly getting poorer, your holders of securities and land (often the same chaps) were getting immensely rich.

We might also recall that, along with ordinary salarymen, there are genuine capitalists. The sort of people we mentioned before who founded and still run companies. They have been prospering because they own stock in those companies. They have also been prospering because they collect fabulous salaries. Even ordinary company executives, those with no ownership rights but who hold high posts, have been getting along quite nicely. That is not only due to income but perks of all sorts, which are very generous in Japan. They include housing subsidies, cheap loans for mortgages, free car often with chauffeur, ability to stay at company rest houses, priority access to company clinics and hospitals, etc. (Just like the "socialist" system.) So don't be fooled by statistics that show a small income spread from ordinary workers to top executives. They are meaningless if they do not consider the perks.

Meanwhile, a lot of well-to-do folks have been aging and passing away. They have put aside enough to leave their one or two children huge amounts of cash, land and other assets. The value of inheritances has been increasing at much more than the rate of inflation, actually by double-digit figures from year to year. So there are a large number of Japanese who were born with a silver spoon in their mouth.

The result has been an explosion of dollar millionaires and billionaires. Japan actually ranks higher in the *Forbes* listing than any other foreign country on a per capita basis. Indeed, there are roughly as many Japanese billionaires proportionately as American billionaires. The truly amazing aspect is that all this wealth has been accumulated only over the past four decades since the war whereas it often took generations and even centuries for Europeans or Americans to amass similar wealth. The other, equally striking point is that more Japanese became rich through land and/or stock speculation than by creating and running a company, which certainly benefits society more.[15]

The rise of the new rich (*nyuu ritchi*) does not automatically cause the emergence of poor or miserable elements of society. But it should be enough to make observers look more closely than they usually do. For then they will notice more inequality in that direction as well.

When you examine income distribution within a company, it will not appear so great aside from the fact that women and blue-collar workers are earning considerably less than male white-collar employees. However, if you consider income inequality between different types of companies, the gap is remarkable. Employees of smaller firms systematically earn less than those of larger ones, although they put in more hours and have less perks and social benefits. The range from the largest to the smallest companies can be five-to-one. Beneath the employees of the small companies, there are still many part-timers, seasonal workers, day laborers, home workers and the like, many of them not even making the minimum wage and with almost no social benefits. And soon they will be joined by the unfortunate aged who have gone through their limited savings, don't have a family to fall back on, and get pitifully little welfare.

Admittedly, a foreigner may not notice such things. After all, they are a bit abstract unless you suffer from inequality personally, and this is rarely the case for the friends of Japan. Perhaps they also assume that since most Japanese look alike they also live alike. Japanese amongst themselves, however, are extremely good at differentiating. They know who is earning more and who is earning less and they know where they rank. While the then more limited inequality may have been tolerated in earlier years, it is now a subject of criticism in the media and complaint in private conversations. It is clearly reflected in public opinion polls. When the Prime Minister's Office asked what they thought of income differentials, 75% replied that they were unequal or unfair.[16]

One last question: Japan's society is classless. Yes or No. By now you will probably not trust me. But then you may remember that none other than Edwin O. Reischauer claimed "it's virtually a classless society."[17] Robert C. Wood explained that poverty had been done away with. And Robert Christopher, he of the Pulitzer Prize, insisted that there were no Beautiful People. If that is insufficient, you are bound to think of the most widespread cliché of all, Japan as a middle class society. Japan as a society in which, year after year, as much as 90% of the people asked defined themselves as middle class. And these are official statistics collected by the Prime Minister's Office.[18] That should be proof enough.

Well, if there are any statistics that qualify as the world's worst, these are probably it. They are based not on the sort of questionnaire one would normally expect, namely to pick among three alternatives: lower class, middle class, upper class. Rather, the respondents can choose lower class, lower middle class, middle middle class, upper middle class and upper class. There are three middle class responses which, with a purely random selection, should result in 60% in that category.[19] Considering that the Japanese don't really like to stand out and the poor can opt for lower middle class while the rich pick upper middle class, it is quite natural to get something like 90%. So this figure is completely useless as a means of measuring middle class consciousness. Still, it is revealing that for years the middle has been eroding as more respondents concede they are upper or lower class.

The reality, as just noted, is that there are more and more rich and more and more poor. That suggests the emergence of classes in material terms. But class formation involves more than simply earning much or little, possessing more or less wealth. It is also a societal phenomenon whereby certain categories rise or fall on the social scale and tend to pass this status on to their children.

That process is now occurring in Japan. And the chief instrument is none other than the educational system, which the Japanapologists claim to be the great leveler, the source of an enviable meritocracy. This is done by families easing the passage of their children to higher levels by helping them attend the right schools and cram more. And that is only part of the story. The other, perhaps more significant aspect is that it is the very schools that determine one's status.

We mentioned that it was necessary to attend "good" schools. We did not define them. The Japanese do not either. It is almost impossible to find any objective criteria for the supposed excellence of "good" schools. Certainly, there is no guarantee that you learn more. They are usually just schools which have been around longer, have a nobler tradition, were founded by some great man, or benefit from other equally subjective evaluations. Yet, everyone knows which ones rank where. Tokyo and Kyoto are at the top, those in smaller cities or outer prefectures are further down, top private colleges like Keio and Waseda head the private schools and precede some state ones, lesser ones follow along. The "good" high schools, primary schools, kindergartens and so on are simply those which place more of their students in the above.

If there is some objective reason for attending "good" schools, then it is definitely because they manage to get their students into "good" jobs. Once again, not necessarily jobs in the most creative, profitable or dynamic companies but those which have been around longer, have a larger staff and enjoy greater prestige. These companies regularly draw their new employees from the same schools year after year, probably for no other reasons than that they have done so in the past and present employees feel more comfortable dealing with their own kind.

Using school as the basis for the emerging class structure has another aspect. This one related to the degree of schooling attained. Systematically, those who managed to graduate from a college, no matter how mediocre or how poorly they did there, belong to the upper echelon. They will be recruited as white-collar employees with chances of promotion to the top. Those who merely graduated from high school, no matter how clever or diligent, will be hired as blue-collar workers or in service trades. Their chances of climbing high are severely restricted.

That is what makes all the talk of company comradery, i.e. the boss working in the same office, using the same canteen, wearing the same uniform, etc. so silly. Management and labor are always separated by the social gulf that the former are university grads and the rank-and-file just high school grads plus, obviously, the fact that subordinates have to talk up to superiors and, indeed, any older workers in a seniority-based system. They are also increasingly separated by physical distance. Most head offices are now located in glitzy buildings in Tokyo while the factories are off somewhere in the sticks, perhaps hundreds of miles away.

True, periodically the boss does visit the factory, usually to commemorate some festive occasion like the anniversary or production of the millionth widget. He will then don the company uniform, like everyone else, but the workers know who he is because they've seen his picture, he is surrounded by a bunch of flunkies and, anyway, they have been forewarned. He may even eat in the same canteen that day. Otherwise, he is off in Tokyo, in a well-appointed office on top of a skyscraper, mixing with his own kind and taking meals in fancy restaurants.

The pecking order having been settled, and Japanese tending to stick to their own group, it is not surprising that upper class children meet and marry upper class children. And there has been a discernible mingling among the offspring of top politicians, top bureaucrats, top company executives and the scions of those who simply happen to be rich. Lower class children mix with their own kind. College graduates would not deign marry high school graduates and the latter would rarely aspire to this. Not surprisingly, the children of college graduates go on to college and then continue upward. Children of high school graduates would dearly like to do the same, but their parents may not have the money. So many of them fall back.

In short, Japan is a class society, where entry is gained through an elite school system and maintained through birth and wealth. It is anything but what the foreign admirers claim. There is an elite, there are "beautiful people," there are also poor people, and Confucianism still keeps women and youngsters in their place. The Japanapologists could have realized this if they only bothered looking at the facts instead of advancing theories. Or, if they actually were studious, they might have uncovered the strongest social principle at work in Japanese society, namely hierarchy. It was very nicely stated by Jared Taylor.

"All societies establish hierarchies. In few societies, however, are they so widespread or important as in Japan. For the Japanese, rank is so finely determined that equality is rare—everyone and everything are at least slightly above or below the nearest apparent equal. Family members, workmates, schools, companies, even nations and races all have their places. Hierarchy is inseparable from orderliness; a group is not properly organized unless its members are ranked."[20]

The urge for hierarchy is incredibly tenacious in Japan. As I have repeatedly noted, no sooner is one hierarchy undone (by the Meiji Restoration, Pacific War, Occupation, death of a company founder or faction leader) than the Japanese almost spontaneously and unconsciously begin creating another. So, four decades after the last major disruption, they have had plenty of time to rank society again. This deep urge has systematically undermined the more rational and conscious wishes to attain such goals as equality and merit. For which reason, neither the Japanese nor I would rate the established society more than unsatisfactory.[21]

NOTES

1. William Forbis, *Japan Today*, p. 9.
2. Robert Christopher, *The Japanese Mind*, p. 51.
3. Jared Taylor, *Shadows of the Rising Sun*, p. 36.
4. Chie Nakane, *Japanese Society*, pp. 65–6.
5. For factions in general, and political factionalism, see Jon Woron-off, *Japan: The Coming Social Crisis* and *Politics, The Japanese Way*.
6. For an excellent description of linguistic and other distinctions, see Taylor, *op. cit.*, pp. 47–50.
7. For more on the family, see Woronoff, *Japan: The Coming Social Crisis*, pp. 60–108.
8. "Till Divorce Do They Part," *Japananalysis*, December 1985, p. 10.
9. See Cherry Kitteredge, *Womansword: What Japanese Words Say About Women*, Tokyo, Kodansha International, 1987.
10. For more on generational changes, see Woronoff, *op. cit.*
11. See "The New Generation," *Japan Update*, Spring 1986, pp. 6–10.
12. Basic Survey of the Employment Structure, Tokyo, Ministry of Labor, annual.
13. Ronald Dore, *Taking Japan Seriously*, p. 204.
14. Frank Gibney, *Japan: The Fragile Superpower*, p. 79.
15. *Forbes* July 26, 1988, pp. 91–147.
16. Public Opinion Survey on Society and State, Prime Minister's Office, May 1988.
17. *Washington Post*, October 26, 1985.
18. Public Opinion Survey on National Life, Prime Minister's Office, annual.
19. I am indebted to Earl Kinmonth for this insight.
20. Taylor, *op. cit.*, p. 43.
21. For a good and authoritative Japanese view, see Tadashi Fukutake, *Japanese Society Today*.

10

Internationalization
(Time To Join The World)

Leadership Or Followership

Newspaper! Newspaper! Get your newspaper here! Read all about it!! FUKUDA LAUNCHES NEW ERA OF JAPANESE FOREIGN POLICY. JAPAN OFFERS ASEAN $10 BILLION. JAPAN OFFERS CHINA $10 BILLION. Read all about it! OHIRA LAUNCHES NEW ERA OF JAPANESE FOREIGN POLICY. DEPENDENCE ON AMERICA REPLACED BY OMNIDIRECTIONAL DIPLOMACY. Read all about it!! SUZUKI LAUNCHES NEW ERA OF JAPANESE FOREIGN POLICY. PEACE AND HARMONY FOR THE WORLD. Read all about it!! NAKASONE LAUNCHES NEW ERA OF JAPANESE FOREIGN POLICY. JAPAN TO TAKE ITS RIGHTFUL PLACE AMONG NATIONS. JAPAN TO BE LEADER, NOT FOLLOWER. JAPAN BOOSTS MILITARY STRENGTH. Read all about it!! TAKESHITA LAUNCHES NEW ERA OF JAPANESE FOREIGN POLICY. JAPAN BECOMES BIGGEST AID DONOR. JAPAN UPSTAGES UNITED STATES IN WORLD FORUMS. Read all about it!! KAIFU . . .

Yes, get your daily newspaper, and get your weekly news magazine, and watch television and listen to the radio. But don't assume this will necessarily help you understand what

198

is going on. The more Japan has become newsworthy, the more the media realize that a flashy Japan headline or rousing Japan story will sell copies and attract viewers, the less certain it is that the news they present is worthy of being taken seriously. That appears to be the conclusion of most members of the public I meet. They don't quite know what the truth is; but they do know that it is unlikely to be what the headlines suggest.

In trying to make Japan's international relations coherent and intelligible, it is impossible not to start by rectifying some of the misperceptions spread by the media. This means deflating the stories they have blown out of all proportion, seeking some degree of continuity, putting things in their proper context, looking at the fine print in policy statements and, above all, seeing how much is actually accomplished and whether words ever turn into deeds.

Japan has long taken a kindly and benevolent position toward the plight of the international community and each successive prime minister has expressed his personal commitment. One of the finer bits of rhetoric was uttered by Prime Minister Noboru Takeshita in keeping with his *furusato* ("spiritual heartland") concept. He told the Diet, on November 28, 1987, a date not long remembered, that Japan would extend aid commensurate with its strength to developing countries, cooperate with the United Nations and make a positive contribution to the solution of international disputes. "By having sympathy for people who are suffering from hunger and disputes, and having tenderness that can feel their pain, I think we can really feel that the earth is a *furusato* for all mankind."[1]

And it has done some things of note. For example, Japan has steadily increased its foreign aid to developing countries. There is no question but that the amounts provided have grown from year to year. It is, however, a bit much to claim that it is making an exceptional effort, let alone becoming the world's aid hero. Yet, the media continually bombard us with "news" to that effect. Thus, each major offer was played up strongly, $10 billion to ASEAN, $10 billion to China, and assorted billions to other places. Each increase in Japan's official development assistance (ODA) was greeted rapturously. And, when Nakasone prepared his 1985 aid offensive, this was heralded as a "Marshall Plan."

Now, let us stand back a bit. Japan did offer $10 billion to ASEAN. But it was not $10 billion at one go but over a period of five years, being $2 billion a year. Not quite as newsworthy. And the money would only be disbursed once agreement had been reached with the recipients on the exact use. Even less newsworthy. And this "offer" was not a grant but a loan that had to be paid back with interest. Hardly worth mentioning. Furthermore, most of the money was eventually paid to Japanese suppliers of equipment for the project. So what?

This has been the standard routine. The Japanese make a grandiose gesture. The media build it up even more. And then they fail to check what has become of it, only to awaken with a start when the next grandiose—and newsworthy—gesture is made. So, what has become of Japan's Marshall Plan? Well, this was never a plan as such, just a few ideas as to how Japan might make a contribution and get other aid donors, especially the United States, off its back. There were no concrete arrangements and no budget was adopted. The plan was simply forgotten when Nakasone had other urgent matters to deal with and it became defunct when he left office.

Fortunately, there is more continuity for the regular aid budget which has been growing steadily until Japan really did become the world's biggest donor. For this, Japan deserves unreserved congratulations. Still, there was no reason to swallow its own claims of "doubling" ODA three times over the past years. This would, if taken literally, mean that it would be disbursing eight times more yen in 1993 than when the first "doubling" began in 1978. A look at the figures shows this to be dramatically incorrect. What actually did happen was that Japan doubled the average level for a preceding period, which was already smaller. It doubled not in yen but in dollars whose value was more than cut in half. And it did not disburse all the aid it offered.

Admittedly, through this doubling, redoubling and reredoubling Japan did become the top donor, passing the United States which had formerly held the lead. But that was in global terms and one should always beware of globalizing. That it comes before France, Germany and Great Britain is not surprising; it is more than twice their size. Yet, in per capita terms, Japan is still a laggard. It has given one of the smallest shares of GNP for decades and it does not expect to reach the average level until 1993.

What it has not yet accomplished in aid, the Japanese authorities claim has been achieved through investment. Its companies have invested heavily throughout the world, in the Americas, Europe, Africa and especially Asia. In so doing, Japan has increased its net external assets tremendously, making it a contender for the No. 1 position. But it is hard to accept the argument that this somehow compensates for the still mediocre aid record. None of these investments was made out of kindness or charity, they were not intended to create a happy *furusato* but a Japanese appendage, one that should generate profits.[2]

More significant would have been to open Japan's market wide to imports from all nations, advanced and developing. You know, trade not aid. This was, of course, promised repeatedly. And each new prime minister claimed that the goal had already been achieved, that Japan was "the world's most open market." Yet, evidence to the contrary continued to mount and further market-opening initiatives were adopted.

There have been over a hundred so far. Yet, the market is still hard to penetrate.

The process of opening the Japanese market, alas, was not advanced by the foreign media. Most journalists proved amazingly gullible. They were willing to swallow the line that the market was really open and foreign businessmen (in particular, their own) were just not making sufficient efforts. If anyone was not making sufficient efforts, it was the journalists. Nothing could have been easier than to document the maze of non-tariff barriers that proliferated in virtually every sector. Or to show how much red tape was imposed by the bureaucracy. Instead, time after time, it was foreign diplomatic pressure that made the Japanese concede the existence of NTBs, administrative restrictions and distribution controls the press had largely missed.

If the media goofed on trade and aid, it did a much worse job on defense. To judge by what I read, this could only have been the work of a reporter with a split personality or a team of two, one manic, the other depressive. The stories seem to turn in an endless circle. First, it is reported that Japan's budget is one of the lowest in the world in per capita terms, it is not living up to the commitments to its allies, and the United States should be sick and tired of this free ride. Then, after enough pressure, Japan announces not a small but a big build-up. No time for applause, the story line reverses completely. Japan has the world's third largest military budget in global terms, it would be dangerous for this to increase, it would frighten Asian countries out of their wits. Eventually, it is noticed that the build-up was not so big. And we are back at the beginning of the cycle.

In order to sort things out, it is necessary to distinguish between per capita and global efforts, just as with aid. By now, Japan has the world's third biggest economy, it has a large population and the yen is strong. It is therefore not surprising that, in global terms, it should have such a big budget, especially when measured in dollars. By using ever shrinking dollars, it is also possible to "prove" that there has been a tremendous escalation in expenditures. In yen terms, the situation is quite different. The increases have not been so massive, just a bit ahead of inflation. In per capita terms, things are turned upside down. Japan incurs one of the world's smallest expenditures at 1% of gross national product (or 1.5%, depending on how it is calculated). That amounts to about a third of the NATO level, a quarter of the United States and a tenth of the Soviet Union.[3]

This makes the manic's case much less solid than the depressive's. Japan's military budget, while high, is not very much when you consider the large population, heavily concentrated in cities and industrial centers, that has to be protected. It is not very much when you consider that the Soviet Union is nearby and has accumulated far more troops and material. Moreover, Japan is located in the proximity of serious zones of tension between the Koreas, the Soviet Union and China, the Philippines and Indochina, and far away from its sources of oil and raw materials. In short, if anything, its defense effort is inadequate and it would have been forced to do much more if not for the American nuclear umbrella and security treaty.

But, the potential! Japan's economy is so strong it could vastly swell its expenditures and become a threat to everyone in sight!! Thus, responds the manic. Yes, the potential is there. Japan could acquire more weapons and it could enlist more soldiers. But potential is nothing without will and the government has repeatedly shown that it does not want to raise the priority. In fact, if anything, it has fought hard and used every possible trick over the past four decades not to do more. The only exception, and one that proved the rule, was Nakasone. He wanted to boost Japan's profile and expand the budget well beyond 1%. He had five years to do it. But he failed. And there is no other putative prime minister around who is likely to try again.

This would not keep Japan from upgrading its peaceful, diplomatic activities. And the media have treated us to all sorts of hallucinating visions. In fact, every time a Japanese prime minister or foreign minister made an upbeat policy statement, this was promptly turned into a bona fide initiative. It "proved" that Japan was finally taking its rightful place in world forums and becoming a leader rather than a follower, thereby showing up the Americans (in American media), British (in British media), French (in French media) and so on.

Here is just a partial listing. More can be found in your favorite newspaper or magazine. Fukuda was enhancing Japan's role in Southeast Asia and China. Ohira was throwing off the American yoke and developing an imaginative omnidirectional strategy. Nakasone spawned so many initiatives it was hard to keep track. At the United Nations. In the Middle East. In Indochina. In Afghanistan. In the Philippines. Finance Minister Miyazawa proposed a rival plan to solve the Third World debt crisis. Even such an unlikely chap as Noburu Takeshita was heralded by the *Far Eastern Economic Review* for "leading his country on to the international stage" and making Japan "the rising world star."[4]

The only drawbacks were . . . in most cases, there was no initiative in any real sense, namely one that had a carefully worked out plan, that could draw on the necessary financial and manpower resources, that was solidly backed by the government and foreign ministry, and that had any followthrough beyond the often limited tenure of the originator. In fact, it was rarely more than a vague promise, a hope, a good intention dreamed up for a speech or press conference by some well-meaning politician. Or it was concocted, purely and simply, by the press to fill empty space. If you look for

Principles! What principles? We're only
interested in buying oil.

Credit: Foreign Press Center/Kyodo

initiatives that actually had concrete results, you will have a
lot of trouble finding them.

The conclusion, one we would have hesitated to set down
before, is that Japan has rather little foreign policy of any
sort. Its international presence is severely limited and certainly not commensurate with its population, economic
strength or political potential. It is still an economic giant
and a political midget, just as it has been since the war.
Obviously, there have been changes and improvements. Japan's influence has been growing. But it is not quite ready
to use its clout, flex its muscles, stand up and be counted,
or any other nice journalistic phrase.

The Closed-Country Syndrome

"Internationalization, Mr. Woronoff. Can you give us a lecture on internationalization?" I've visited sixty countries in my lifetime and never, except in Japan, have I been asked to talk to people about internationalization (*kokusaika*). How does one become part of the international community? improve relations with the rest of the world? feel that one is tied to that world and not dangling outside? Not only me, the Japanese will ask anyone who looks sufficiently foreign to explain to them more about this intriguing subject.

They also talk and write interminably about the need for *kokusaika*. You can easily find a quote a day. Nakasone punctuated every speech with an appeal for greater internationalization. Takeshita pushed it more gently. Businessmen also try to raise consciousness. According to Takashi Ishihara, Chairman of Keizai Doyukai, "future policies will need to be based on an international viewpoint and be aggressively designed to contribute to the well-being of the entire world." Takashi Hosomi, former Chairman of the Overseas Economic Cooperation Fund, issued a stirring challenge: "Now that the country has grown into a major economic and political power, Japan can no longer afford to live in a fairy tale realm. It has to boldly step into the world arena and make positive proposals for the maintenance of peace and security throughout the world."

Probably, the Japanese do need lessons on internationalization. They talk about it. They dream about it. They think it is the right direction to go. But they never seem to get there. To date, they have done such an uncommonly poor job of it that *kokusaika* remains a slogan or buzzword. There are many reasons for this failure.

Japanese external policy was severely hampered by a refusal to devote precious manpower and money to the task. While the economic ministries were reinforced and their programs amply funded, the Ministry of Foreign Affairs was neglected. It still is neglected. It has a staff that is a quarter the size of the U.S. establishment and half that of countries half Japan's size, like France and Great Britain. Even today, the diplomatic corps does not attract the best candidates or offer as much prestige as MITI and MOF. Worse, whenever an economic issue is at stake, diplomats are overshadowed, second-guessed and overruled by officials from MITI, MOF and even Agriculture.

This is quite easy to understand. While the foreign ministry of most countries deals with a broad range of activities, many of them diplomatic and political, the only issues Japan was interested in were economic. It wanted to have ready access to sources of raw materials, it sought to export more goods to more places, and it had to help Japanese investors when they got in trouble. Unlike Europe and America, where trade followed the flag, Japan's flag followed trade.

This can be seen from the slow and disjointed manner in which Japan expanded its international presence. It did not rush out and open embassies in every important capital or ones it felt some affinity for. It went from country to country, following in the footsteps of the businessmen who set up offices, factories or mines there. When there were enough commercial transactions to justify diplomatic recognition, that came. And, if there was enough trade and the country was not really compatible, say China or the Soviet bloc, trade relations soothed any ideological qualms. No wonder even its prime minister could be referred to with some disdain as a "transistor salesman."

For the longest time, the only relations that mattered were with the United States. Nearly all other relations were a function of this. And policy followed Washington's lead very closely. Only in recent years has Tokyo attempted to work out its own position which, given the traditional relations and the pro-American lobby in the foreign ministry, does not really stray very far. To call it omnidirectional was a big exaggeration and that fiction has since been discarded. The higher priority and bigger profile given to external relations under Nakasone were also toned down. Japan is still a follower.[5]

By now, of course, Japan has established diplomatic relations with most countries and become a member of the universal organizations. But it is not part of the smaller, tighter ones that actually do something. It is not part of the world alliances, although it has a bilateral relationship with the United States. It is not part of any economic arrangement like the European Community or African and Latin American common markets. It is not part of any regional association such as exist in the Americas, Africa and Europe but not Asia. That is not because of bad wartime memories alone, they were as bitter between France and Germany which now cooperate closely. It is that Japan has shunned deeper relations with any country and hardly regards itself as Asian, preferring loose advanced country "clubs" like the OECD and Group of Seven.

This means that Japan still cuts an exceptionally solitary figure in the world community. It only has close relations with the United States but they are periodically subject to strain. And the United States has special relations with many other countries. For the rest, its contacts are mainly economic, largely of a commercial and pecuniary nature, which do not generate any particular warmth or affection for Japan. If anything, since they are often tilted in Japan's favor, they actually create stresses and strains. So, while it has very few enemies at present, Japan also has rather few friends. This was seen most visibly when it ran for a seat on the Security Council and could not rally support. In a peaceful and prosperous era, this does not really matter. Under other circumstances, Japan could feel uncomfortable.

Surely, now that Japan has a mature economy, a sizable

military establishment, investments all around the world and could run its own diplomacy and set its own priorities, one would expect radical change. Indeed, the expectation is so great that it is often projected by the media. Thus, the many stories about Japanese initiatives and Japanese leaders speaking out. But the urge still comes more from outside than inside. It is foreigners who want Japan to play a bigger role, not the Japanese themselves. And that's the rub.

A dynamic foreign policy, a prominent international presence, occasionally taking the lead are not a function of size or wealth but ability and will. Countries as small as Singapore or as backward as Egypt have cast a larger international shadow than Japan. Japan either does not know how to do more, which would explain the many appeals for foreigners to lecture on internationalization. Or it does not want to commit the financial and manpower resources, which is my sneaking suspicion.

More than forty years after the war, Japan still does not have leaders who are especially interested in playing a visible role or capable of assuming one were it thrust on them. Nakasone was again the exception that proved the rule. The only Japanese prime minister ever to speak English, to have shown much curiosity about what was going on elsewhere, to have a grand design for Japan. Yet, his international fling, even while applauded abroad, did not go down terribly well with the Japanese people. They seemed quite happy to come under a more cautious and insular Takeshita.

Leaders in a different mold could only emerge from a culture which embraces internationalization. Yet, lecture after lecture have failed to arouse any such desire amongst ordinary citizens. Relatively few travel abroad in any meaningful sense. After all, you cannot regard sex tours to Southeast Asia, honeymoons in Hawaii or shopping expeditions to Paris as a genuine international experience. More sadly, the successive contingents of businessmen working abroad have increasingly severed themselves from the countries they live in, isolating themselves in Japanese ghettos, eating in Japanese restaurants, sending their kids to Japanese schools and hurrying back to the home office where the promotions are.

The only true hope resides in what are called "returnees." These are Japanese children who lived abroad with their parents and who, with luck, actually went to foreign schools and mixed with foreign kids. They have experienced another culture and could transmit their experiences. Alas, they are not wanted. The returnees apparently disrupt the humdrum routine of the schools, don't fit in with more thoroughly Japanese children, and have to be put in special classes. Even companies which could use their abilities often restrict them to the PR or international division.

This means that the much touted efforts to create *kokusaijin* or "international people," something Japan alone has to strive for, are doomed to relative failure. Without such "international people," alas, there is not much hope for internationalization. Indeed, Japan is already in a very peculiar and embarrassing position. It only has a handful of trusted figures capable of mixing in international circles, men like Saburo Okita, Nobuhiko Ushiba and Naohiro Amaya. They show up at every international gathering and if they were not available, or should they pass away, it would not even be possible to fill Japan's seat.

Meanwhile, there are mounting trends that go in the complete opposite direction. One is for the Japanese to stress not their commonness but their uniqueness. This is pressed by a vast literature (*Nihonjin-ron*) on the special characteristics and calling of the Japanese people. "Separate but equal" is not terribly good. But separate and superior is considerably worse. Alas, the basic message of these books is not that Japan should get in line but that it go to the head of the line or stand aside. While Japaneseness is exalted, foreignness is criticized or belittled.[6]

Fortunately, these are still only trends. But, if they are not reversed, the result would be a hierarchization of international relations with Japan on the top rung. It used to place itself well below the United States, but any residual awe is rapidly disappearing as America fails to solve its economic problems. Only because it is a first-rate military power has it not entirely fallen from grace. The European countries come further down because they have not done as well economically and are not as strong militarily. The Soviet Union, for all its military might, is too backward economically to be respected. Further down is the Third World, first the more hopeful places like Korea or Taiwan, then the Godforsaken ones, the vast majority.

This is obviously the wrong direction for Japan to move in. Ever since the war there have been broad currents toward equality in the international community. This is not rigorously logical, since differences do exist. But no country can hope to be integrated in today's world without deeper acceptance of the principle of equality. This means that such attitudes in Japan would only make internationalization harder.

Rather than a new opening, Japan is probably heading for a new closure. Not a physical one this time. It depends too much on foreign trade, investment and military support. But a mental one, as people look inward more and try to ignore the outside world as best they can. Is this more Woronoffian pessimism? No. Lots of Japanese are also concerned. Here is what Professor Eiichi Shindo of Tsukuba University wrote: "Internationalism is a phony fad. Instead of cultural diversity, prosperity has created a closed society increasingly out of step with the rest of the world."[7]

The U.S. Connection

From what has been said so far, it might be concluded that Japan only rated an inferior with regard to foreign policy.

But this does not take into account its one big success, a success sufficiently ample to compensate for any number of failures. That is the special relationship with Washington which, although no more special than that of Canada or Western Europe, has been exploited more ably by the Japanese.

This is seen most clearly in defense. While the United States has security treaties with many nations, the one with Japan is unique. Unlike the others, which obligate the parties to come to one another's aid, the U.S.-Japan Security Treaty only commits the United States. Japan does not have to defend America. This makes it a rather strange, one-sided arrangement that is very inferior to the NATO Alliance. Yet, in return for this non-commitment, the United States stations troops on Japanese soil, keeps numerous warships in the vicinity and provides a nuclear umbrella.

What is Japan's counterpart? It has rearmed and set up a Self-Defense Force and it has sort of promised to block the straits and protect its sealanes for 1,000 miles. It also makes the right noises at the right time. But its follow-through has been grossly inadequate. With one of the lowest per capita defense expenditures, it does not really maintain enough troops, ships or planes to protect the home islands from a serious enemy attack. And its other vital missions may just be wishful thinking. Exactly what it would do in the case of hostilities involving the United States elsewhere in the world is pure conjecture. This makes Japan a rather sorry ally (if one can use the term). But it still enjoys as much support as the best.

When it comes to foreign policy, Japan's scope has obviously been affected by the U.S. connection. It has usually toed the line, making Washington's friends its friends and Washington's enemies its enemies. But this was no problem. The American sphere was much larger and richer than the Soviet bloc and those were the countries it wanted to deal with anyway. In so doing, Tokyo could benefit from the positive relations that emerged under the Pax Americana and avoid getting entangled in the nasty ones, which were America's business.

What really matters to Japan is that it have access to export markets and raw materials as well as the possibility of investing abroad. That has been provided by its American friends again. It is the United States which opened its domestic market wide to Japanese products and only restricted them when imports claimed too large a market share. The U.S. also helped restore the economies of the wartorn nations and created a congenial environment for international commerce by launching organizations to promote trade and financial liberalization, like GATT and IMF. Then it spearheaded campaigns to aid the developing countries. Japan did participate in these movements, and it did liberate its trade and currency and give aid. But it always lagged behind, getting more than it gave in round after round.

Seen from the Japanese viewpoint, this was a wonderful achievement. Japan has as complete defense protection as could be expected at moderate cost. It became part of the international community without making great efforts or sacrifices. It exported quite freely while keeping its own market fairly closed. And it was not overly generous in foreign aid. In short, this was not a free ride but certainly a cheap one.

Of course, while there were gains in monetary terms, there were notional losses. Japan could not freely determine its defense, foreign policy, trade or aid posture. But it did not really mind. The decision had been taken at an early stage that these were secondary while economic growth was primary, the highest and almost sole priority of government after government.

Moreover, Tokyo did enjoy some leeway. As noted, it could decide whether, how and when to help its allies. It was able to stall with tariff reductions and keep non-tariff barriers even longer. During the Korea and Vietnam Wars, its support was not exactly unstinting. And as trade with the People's Republic of China, Soviet Union and East bloc became attractive, it went ahead despite American misgivings, merely covering its tracks by working through smaller, dummy companies rather than major corporations.

How was Japan able to accomplish this? Probably because it did limit its other efforts and concentrate on the essentials, economic development and the U.S. connection. By letting the United States take the lead elsewhere, it earned Brownie points for trade. By towing the American line, it gained a reputation as a consistent and reliable friend.

But it was more than that. The Japanese got to know the Americans much better than others. In particular, they saw through two crucial *tatemae*. One is that of openness, frankness, laying your cards on the table and like rhetoric. This only resulted in eternal conflicts and clashes with the European allies that played by the same rules as the Americans and were embroiled in one controversy after another, although, in the end, the Europeans were better allies, better trading partners, more generous aid donors and so on.

Tokyo was too smart to contradict Washington. In fact, whenever a problem arose, Japanese politicians took a very low posture, apologized profusely for any misunderstanding and sent a minister or prime minister scurrying off to Washington. Then negotiations ensued to "immediately" overcome the problem. This flattered the American ego immensely. It was perhaps not noticed that the negotiations dragged on for weeks, months and years. All this while, the status quo was maintained. Finally, when American patience was exhausted, there were threatening noises and pounding on the table. The Japanese duly apologized for delay. And the charade continued until finally a decision was reached that placated Washington. It was again not noticed that the decision was slow to be implemented, watered down and circumvented in various ways until the next conflict erupted.[8]

214

This has proven to be a very effective tactic. Saying "no" to Washington is risky and counterproductive. Saying "yes" and then doing what you want is more graceful and successful. Moreover, even if you do ultimately give in, the time gained by stalling and delaying is precious. It means that billions of dollars are saved on defense expenditures until perhaps there is another detente and you can get off the hook again. For aid, it is the same thing. You postpone heavy costs. For trade, it is even more crucial. There is both time to sell more exports and to keep out imports while establishing a productive base abroad and tying up the distribution network at home.

The other American *tatemae* is that relations should be conducted on a people-to-people basis. The Japanese and American peoples should be friends, not just the leaders. That is, alas, rather impractical and terribly expensive. Huge amounts of money or costly goodwill gestures are needed to make an impression on 120 million Japanese. If Tokyo were to try the same thing, it would have to please 240 million Americans. It was considerably more expedient and cost-effective to use the customary Japanese tactics of buttering up and buying off only those individuals who count such as influential politicians, diplomats and more broadly the opinion-shapers.

There are various ways of doing this. Some quite cheap. It is merely necessary to feed the egos of American leaders. That was easily done by sending missions off to Washington, giving those who came to Tokyo very handsome treatment, and talking to them as friends and allies rather than trouble-makers. Nothing was better than giving in, conceding that Japan was wrong and would do whatever was suggested. The leaders felt they had actually achieved something and could go back home and proudly proclaim their triumph. That it was a rather petty and hollow triumph was only perceived much later. While all Japanese used these tricks, none exceeded the mastery of Nakasone who kept the fearsome Ronald Reagan at bay for years with his inimitable Ron-Yasu routine.

Alas, not everything came so cheaply. The Japanese have been pumping millions of dollars a year into lobbying activities of all sorts, some to defuse specific trade conflicts, others to create a generally congenial atmosphere. By now, they are the biggest lobbyists after Israel. But there is a decisive difference: Israel needs American backing against its Arab enemies; Japan wants to influence American opinion with regard to conflicts with American companies or the government. Yet, it has apparently done quite well in this quest, having the sanctions against Toshiba watered down, getting a better hearing on specific complaints, and especially removing the more offensive aspects of the 1988 trade law.

Lobbyists, however, are not the best defenders of Japan's cause. They are hired guns. They are clearly biased in its favor. So their motives and statements are regularly questioned and they may not be as effective. In addition, the more money is spent on lobbying, the more Americans ask why it is that their supposed friend and ally has to do so much of this. Far more is gained by working through seemingly neutral and reputable intermediaries.

Surprisingly enough, Japan's biggest boosters have been American ambassadors. Once upon a time, and even today for most postings, the ambassador was a professional diplomat or someone who contributed to the president's election campaign. For Tokyo, Japan specialists have been selected, people who apparently know all about Japan and also, in most cases, have a favorable view. Edwin O. Reischauer was the first in this line and the most significant recently was Mike Mansfield. They saw it as their task to foster amity between the two nations, to build bridges and also to prevent hostility and antagonism. Thus, they became spokesmen for Japanese views in Washington and, indeed, throughout the country.

Back in Tokyo, they often resisted pressure to make Japan comply with unpleasant American wishes.

The most dramatic gesture was made by Reischauer, who actively lobbied for the return of Okinawa to Japan, a return that should be a noble gesture rather than a counterpart for something else. Thus, Japan got Okinawa, Reischauer earned a formidable reputation as a foreign friend, and the United States got nothing, not even minor commercial concessions in existing trade conflicts.[9] Mike Mansfield has interminably repeated the same simplistic message: Japan is America's best ally; Japan is America's best trading partner.[10] And he did more than just help verbally, he ran interference for the Japanese government by inhibiting efforts of the State Department, Department of Commerce, U.S. Trade Representative, Pentagon, White House and especially Congress to press for faster, more drastic action.

No wonder the Japanese loved Reischauer and Mansfield and did not want them to leave. They "understood" Japan and defended it from foreign barbarians who did not. Unfortunately, as Ian Buruma pointed out, an eagerness to defend Japan "may not be quite the right frame of mind for a man with the brief to represent American interests in a tough and competitive world."[11] The result often was that Japan appeared to have two ambassadors, a Japanese and an American one, while the United States did not have any. This could only undermine its position and generate ugly friction when, as had to happen, the ambassador was overruled or contradicted by the president or Congress.

More serious has been the softening up of the whole diplomatic service. Young officials posted to Tokyo or holding down the Japan desk in Washington knew that they were more likely to have a smooth and gratifying career by being receptive to Japanese wishes than by firmly espousing American ones. Moreover, initiatives that could create unpleasantness for the ambassador, because he would have to make

Ambassador Mansfield bravely standing up
for American interests.

Credit: Foreign Press Center/Kyodo

strong demands on his Japanese counterparts, were toned
down or postponed until he left. Meanwhile, Tokyo had no
trouble in sending tough and unbending diplomats or trade
negotiators to Washington where they worked steadfastly and
stubbornly to promote Japan's interests.

But American diplomats were not the only ones rooting
for Japan. There were cabinet members (and sometimes the
President). There were also governors, senators and Con-
gressmen of states seeking to obtain Japanese investment.
Even the hope, often subsequently disappointed, of getting
a factory to locate in their electoral district was enough to
make them very good friends. And friends in Congress could
be extremely useful when broader questions regarding Japan
were raised. Friends in the state and local administration could

be even more crucial for matters of land, construction, labor, licenses and so on.

What is more remarkable is that the Japanese have been so successful in recruiting among government departments with which they have had rather poor relations. The U.S. Trade Representative and his staff have regularly been after the Japanese, urging them to free the domestic market and prying open one sector after the other. Yet, after retiring from the USTR, many officials have become lobbyists or spokesmen for Japanese companies. Almost overnight, they changed sides. This is a flagrant example of American *amakudari* and it can only be feared that this reward has been for not being as tough as they might have been. More insidious is that present staff of the USTR know that they will also do better by making the Japanese friends not foes, even if this means softpeddling American interests.

The biggest thrust, however, has been to infiltrate intellectual circles. Academia proved a push-over. There were more and more academics clamoring to defend Japan against unjust pressure or unfair restrictions. In doing so, although professing their own, brilliantly conceived views, they adhered to the Japanese line very closely with regard to trade, aid, defense and other issues. Washington-based think tanks, which are really PR operations for favored causes, also pitched in. The most active were in the free trade lobby, decrying every American attempt to block Japan's entry to the U.S. market while remaining impervious to Japan's even more blatant efforts at keeping its own market closed.

The supposedly objective spokesmen proved highly effective in influencing public opinion. They were interviewed and quoted by television, radio and the press. They provided input for the fact-finding efforts of Congress, the Pentagon and CIA. They became advisors of presidents and politicians. Some eventually moved into the government and a few were actually appointed ambassador to Tokyo. There has probably never been a larger, more influential group acting in the interests of a foreign state than the myriad "friends" of Japan.

Thus, Japan was able to turn what had once been a lopsided relationship in which it was the junior partner into one where it got away with more than any other country. In short, it suckered Uncle Sam. That is an achievement, but not a very great one since it has been done so often. And there was still friction with the American populace. Meanwhile, Tokyo failed to make very many friends elsewhere and its clout was limited. Perhaps the others were more zealous in pursuing their own interests, or they have a smaller fifth column, or Japan simply could not concentrate as much effort on them. Whatever the reasons, even with this American "success," it would be appropriate to rate Japan an unsatisfactory for foreign policy and internationalization.

NOTES

1. See assorted speeches of assorted prime ministers, including this one by Prime Minister Takeshita of November 28, 1987.
2. For more on aid and investment, see Jon Woronoff, *Japan's Commercial Empire* and *World Trade War*.
3. See Woronoff, *Politics, The Japanese Way*, pp. 357–66.
4. *Far Eastern Economic Review*, August 25, 1988, p. 20.
5. For more on foreign policy, see Woronoff, *op. cit.*, pp. 341–378.
6. See Peter N. Dale, *The Myth of Japanese Uniqueness*, and Ross Mouer & Yoshio Sugimoto (eds.), *Images of Japanese Society*.
7. Eiichi Shindo, "Japan Must Shed Old Ways," *Asahi Shimbui*, January 8, 1989.
8. For numerous examples, see Clyde V. Prestowitz, *Trading Places*.
9. For Reischauer's version of his contribution to the bilateral relationship, see Edwin Reischauer, *My Life Between Japan and America*.
10. Consult the various, almost unchanging speeches of Ambassador Mansfield.
11. *Far Eastern Economic Review*, December 11, 1986, p. 62.

11

Quality Of Life
(If You Can Call That Quality)

The "Rich" Japanese

1988 was a historic year for Japan. In that year, its per capita gross national product became the largest in the world, passing the United States, Scandinavia and the rest of Europe, and leaving the developing countries far behind. The figure was $19,547 per person.

It was also the year the outside world discovered, or was told, that Japan is rich beyond compare. None other than the special correspondent of *The Economist* hurried back and breathlessly informed us: "The Japanese are increasingly showing that they are like you and me. Except they have more money." To be certain nobody missed the point, he added: "The Japanese have also been spending because they feel rich. However, appalling the land-price inflation in other respects, it gave people the wherewithal to buy all kinds of things."[1] This was corroborated by *Forbes* in an article entitled "Enjoy! Enjoy!"

"Japan is entering a golden age. After sweating and sacrificing to rebuild their economy and supply themselves with modern life's basics, middle-class Japanese are now beginning to indulge themselves in life's luxuries, from mink coats and BMWs to precious metals and jewelry."[2]

Has Japan entered a golden age? Or have the foreign media gotten carried away again? Anyone who approaches the figures rationally would have to choose the second alternative. Indeed, it is scandalous that anyone could write about Japan without pointing out the vital flaws in the statistics.

Once again, the figures are presented in dollars, dollars which had lost half their value relative to the yen over the preceding years. This is what permitted Japan to leap ahead in the GNP sweepstakes. So, it is absurd to argue that the Japanese, whose individual wealth had only increased moderately over the period, were vastly richer just because the new exchange rate was more favorable.

Digging somewhat deeper, we encounter the oldest fallacy of economics, generally known as the "veil of money." Monetary terms are very poor at expressing actual value in any real sense. Money is only worth what it buys. And, in Japan, money does not buy very much. That is because prices are so high. This should be obvious to anyone who has ever had a coffee at a Japanese hotel or taken a taxi to the airport. Since that must include foreign journalists and academics, it is hard to grasp why they did not put two and two together and draw the appropriate conclusions. So let us help them.

According to figures from the Economic Planning Agency, Bank of Japan, Bank of Tokyo, Tokai Bank and anyone else who bothers to check, virtually everything in Japan is expensive. Compared to the United States, food in general costs twice as much. Delicacies like beef may run five times the price, but even the staple rice costs four times the international rate. Utilities, mail and telephone are costly and gas runs much higher. Every form of transport (taxi, bus, train and plane) is dear. And so are most services. Housing, the most important item, costs twice as much for something half as good. The only articles that are close to the U.S. level are clothing and footwear as well as made-in-Japan consumer goods, although even then you could probably get them cheaper at an American discount store.

The most blatant example of high costs and the heavy yen bloating nominal value applies to land. The EPA recently calculated that the value of all the land in Japan was four times that of all the land in the United States. Since the latter is 25 times larger, this means that the price of land is now one hundred times as high. In short, Japan is theoretically worth the United States and Europe put together while the bit of land surrounding the emperor's palace is worth all of California.[3]

Such considerations have led Japanese specialists to conclude that the price level in Japan is about 2.5 times that of the United States. This means, according to such authoritative commentators as Hiroshi Takeuchi, chief economist of the Long-Term Credit Bank of Japan, and Eishiro Saito, chairman of Keidanren, that Japan's per capita gross national product should only be about $7,000.[4] Somewhat less extreme results were achieved by comparing domestic purchasing power. The OECD and Britain's Central Statistical Office found Japan to be 50% more expensive while the Union Bank of Switzerland estimated that the cost of living in Tokyo was twice that of New York.[5]

Whatever studies you look at, Japan comes out much more poorly than nominal figures would indicate. I think it could safely be ranked at about half the American level. That would put it well behind Sweden and Germany and a bit ahead of Great Britain. It would be closest to France and Italy, countries Japan does not normally compare itself to. If one adds quality of life, as opposed to mere money, then certainly the Japanese would not even be up to the level of Singapore which officially only generates a quarter as much per capita GNP.

After stripping away the "veil of money" and rectifying the exchange rate distortions, the Japanese are hardly rich.

And they most certainly are not "stinking rich," as *The Economist* claimed.[6] In fact, it is even questionable to label them middle class when one considers living standards. This is what makes the claim of 90% to middle-class status so grotesque and also dubious. Countless Japanese have refuted this claim, including Kimihiro Masamura of Senshu University. "Japan's middle class is not really middle-class by anyone else's standards, and it will probably never be rich by international standards," he said. In fact, "Japan's middle class is lower-class."[7]

Any hope of middle-class lifestyles or affluent living are dissipated by the two largest items in the average family's budget. Food takes up 27% and the mortgage on the house another 16%, which is very high. There is not much left over after that and savings for old age, an absolute necessity. Thus, most Japanese are happy if they can buy food and clothing, meet mortgage payments, cover the kids' education and enjoy some little luxury every now and then.

No, the Japanese are not rich as a whole. That has not been achieved by their economy. It has merely made them somewhat richer than they were before. Average real earnings were rising by almost 5% a year during the first three postwar decades. That does deliver a modest improvement, although not as much as may appear. For these statistics are based on the official inflation rate, one that hardly reflects rising costs. If you include the recent uptick in land and housing costs, much of these gains would be wiped out.

Why then this impression of wealth, which is very real and almost overpowering in parts of Tokyo? One reason, quite simply, is that Tokyo has concentrated an ever greater share of the national wealth. It is increasingly the only place to live if you have money and, indeed, hard to live in if you do not. It is therefore full of department stores, boutiques, hotels, restaurants, etc., etc. But it is in no way typical of Japan. Any trip to the outer prefectures will show people living more modestly, even if many farmers are now better off. And an even shorter trip to the outer districts will show that the ordinary Tokyoite is equally far from affluent. These are excursions I would strongly recommend to starry-eyed journalists among others.

Of course, there are now some rich people who do buy mink coats and BMWs. They are primarily the *nyuu ritchi* who have profited from land speculation and the booming stock market. They can afford virtually anything and, no matter what curious ideas one may have about Japanese being humble or frugal, they do not hesitate to spend on a lavish scale and let everyone else know they have "arrived." Much of the visible wealth is their doing.

Ordinary folks, however, are not big spenders. Office workers, shop assistants, teachers, civil servants, normal farmers, factory workers and the like are only earning a bit more than before. They could not possibly go on a spending binge. But they do contribute, for a rather different reason. Now that home ownership is too costly, they have a lot of cash available and apparently console themselves with occasional luxuries, a trip abroad, nice clothing, some jewelry. These are not the rich but what advertising company Hakuhodo called the *akirame-ritchi*, those who have given up on being rich but still have to boost their morale and maintain the pretense of comfortable living.

An impression of greater affluence is also generated by the profusion of gadgets. Ownership of consumer durables has reached unprecedented levels. Virtually every family possesses a color television, refrigerator, washing machine, vacuum cleaner and camera. Most have a passenger car, stereo, air conditioner and microwave oven. A growing minority has a piano, CD player or personal computer. And you can scarcely find a girl in the streets without a Dior scarf or Gucci handbag.

But even that is a bit illusory. Japanese TVs, refrigerators and vacuum cleaners are very small, washing machines only use cold water, air conditioning and heating are not central and throughout the house but by individual units in one room or another. Passenger cars are smaller and there are fewer of them per capita (only half the U.S. level). The fashion goods are frequently made in Japan. And the average dwelling is half as large, more distant from the city center, and less well built. More serious, increasing numbers of families can no longer afford their own home, and no quantity of consumer gadgets or fashion articles will console them for that.

So far we have spoken of the new rich and the not-so-rich. But we must not forget the other end of the social ladder. First you have what the Japanese themselves call the "new poor" (*nyuu puua*). These are people who find it impossible to maintain the lifestyle to which they had become accustomed in earlier years. Most of them are supposedly middle-class families but ones which cannot afford to buy an apartment and have to rent a mediocre one. They may have to scrimp on food, clothing and entertainment. They do not quite know where the money will come from to round out the month. But at least they get by.

The same cannot be said of the truly poor. There are also lots of them. They live in more remote prefectures, farm marginal land, try to fish depleted waters, were fired by the town's only factory or mine when it closed down. They may become day laborers, residing in misery districts like Kanda. There are also numerous aged, with inadequate pensions or none. Many are homeless (*furosha*) and some live from begging or scavenging. It is impossible not to see them, they inhabit the subway and train stations or sleep on park benches. But the Western media still manage to overlook them and the academics do not find them worthy of mention, let alone serious study. Like the three monkeys, the friends of Japan see no evil, hear no evil and speak no evil.

Thus, anyone who claims that the Japanese as a whole are

well-to-do, rich, or stinking rich is exaggerating so grossly that he should have his eyes checked and his poetic license withdrawn. Even the Japanese, who usually strive to give outsiders a good impression, cannot muster the courage to mouth such *tatemae*. They realize all too well that their living standards are mediocre compared to many foreign countries even if they are still better than in the Third World or the early postwar period. Moreover, most of them regard the coming years with foreboding. That much has been confirmed by repeated official surveys.

So, if you ask the Japanese whether they feel rich, you are more likely to get comments like those of Hiroshi Takeuchi of the Long-Term Credit Bank, who concludes that it is "misleading to say that we are now the richest people in the world."[8] Or Eiichi Shindo of Tsukuba University, who comments: "Japan Inc. may pride itself on being No. 1 but our vaunted affluence is more glitter than substance . . . working people are tightening their belts and resigning themselves to substandard housing and urban amenities."[9] For more of the same, just ask your Japanese friends.

This brings us back to the key question, one I have asked again and again without getting any sensible answer. What is the purpose to working, producing, exporting if not to enhance the living standard of the Japanese people? As long as Japan remains a rich country with poor people, something I complained about a decade ago, its economy deserves a much lower evaluation than it commonly receives. For this particular aspect, namely (in)ability to generate wealth, I think even a mark of inferior is overly generous.

All Work And No Play

It is already unpleasant enough to have a standard of living that falls well below American and European levels. It is even worse when that substandard standard is only attained by working considerably longer than Americans and Europeans. Indeed, the Japanese put in such long hours that they often seem to be in a completely different league. This has won the Japanese the nickname of "workaholics," one they are no longer so happy to bear.

To compare the respective inputs, the best measure is the number of hours worked a year. Japan is the only advanced country which remains above the 2,000 hour level, with over 2,100 hours a year at present. In the United States and Britain, the level is around 1,900 and, for France and Germany, under 1,700. This means the Japanese work about 400 hours more each year than the latter which adds up to ten 40-hour weeks. That they can cram it into a 52-week year is sure proof of Japanese ingenuity.[10]

But even these figures may understate the amount of work expected of the Japanese. They only include scheduled work hours and overtime clocked in. There is plenty more. Factory workers are supposed to come early and set up their equipment before hours and then stay on after closing time to tidy up. Most don't take their full lunch or coffee breaks. If somebody goofs up on the assembly line, or the prescribed quantity of work is not completed in the allotted time for some other reason, they may "voluntarily" stay to finish the job. Aside from the quality control meetings, many put in additional hours working on projects and coming up with suggestions.

Salarymen put in even more extra time although, as I hinted, not all these hours are well used. They have to arrive long before starting time, cut their lunch break short (or have it in the office), and then stay in after hours, only part of this as official overtime. They must develop new work-related skills, like bookkeeping, foreign languages or computer use on their own time. Then comes the socializing, which is hardly voluntary. Managers have to go for a drink with other managers or invite their subordinates, who have little choice

229

but to accept. Only part of this is socializing, the rest ends up being a discussion of company business. Even the occasional excursions, New Year's bash, and so on, are quasi-compulsory and work-related.

If you were to add it all up, certainly the Japanese salaryman would be working another ten weeks more than some foreign counterparts. Then he may do something they would never even contemplate, namely give half of his meager summer vacation back to the company. This brings the actual summer holidays down to about seven days in manufacturing and five days elsewhere. Not quite a solid week in most cases, since few employees take it all in one go. He may also work on Saturday (and Sunday), even when it is not formally required or supposedly forbidden.

While working hard and showing devotion have their merits, it is finally sinking in that this may just be too much. It is gradually being conceded that Japan should reduce the amount of work and provide more free time. One cause for this unprecedented rethink is that the workers themselves have increasingly shown that they want more leisure, especially younger ones. Few would be so bold as to demand extra time off, let alone take what has been granted to them. But every public opinion poll and survey in years has indicated a desire for more leisure even if it hurts income, with over half opting for that in surveys by the Prime Minister's Office and Japan Productivity Center.[11]

It has also become painfully evident that too much work can be a bad thing—for the workers and the companies. There has been an alarming surge in the incidence of physical ailments and social abuses which can be traced directly to excessive work. A recent study by the Labor Ministry revealed that over 80% of salaried workers suffer from stress, experiencing bodily pains and fatigue or psychological troubles.[12] More and more of them need treatment. Meanwhile, alcoholism has been spreading throughout society, with drinking no longer just a social activity but a means of escape. And there have been more suicides than ever among adult males.

Those most afflicted are the managers. This phenomenon was described by *BusinessWeek* in an article I am pleased to quote, there being so few media attempts at uncovering the truth.

"The myth has it that Japanese executives are consummate team players, happily working their lives away for the good of their companies. The reality is far different. Japanese executives are among the most harried, insecure, and frustrated in the world. Despite unprecedented prosperity, stress is exacting a heavy toll from many of Japan's white collar workers. Now the country faces slower growth, and that prospect has sharply heightened stress on the job. The upshot could be higher rates of absenteeism, alcoholism, and even suicide among the most talented and dedicated employees in Japan."[13]

The strongest impetus, however, has come from abroad. Foreigners do not regard Japanese work practices as amusing or admirable; they feel that it is impossible to compete against people who work that fanatically and still maintain a civilized lifestyle. Either they become workaholics, too, or the Japanese have to relax a bit. More than just complaining, Western spokesmen have made it clear that it is regarded as unfair competition and that, if need be, measures will be taken to block Japanese products until the message gets through.

Thus, the process of consensus building which began with the younger generations, and was finally assimilated by the trade unions, has reached higher levels. In 1980, Prime Minister Ohira unveiled his "ideas for developing the nation toward the 21st century," which included a generalization of the five-day week. The Labor Ministry adopted a formal goal of reducing working hours and ministers personally requested

Main Priorities in Life

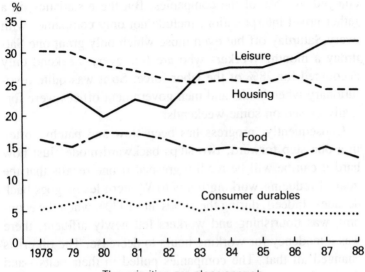

The priorities are clear enough.
But how can you achieve them?

Source: Public Opinion Survey on Life of
the Nation, Prime Minister's Office, 1988.
Credit: *Facts and Figures of Japan 1989*, p. 103.

company presidents to cooperate. Even MITI set up a leisure development section and the Social Policy Council approved a "Leisure Constitution."[14] Meanwhile a semi-governmental think tank, the Leisure Development Center, boldly predicted that annual working hours would fall to 1,500 by the year 2000.[15]

Alas, it takes more than positive sentiments and well-intentioned rhetoric to accomplish such formidable tasks. Particularly when many company executives and the key business organizations, including Nikkeiren, resist the move. So new legislation and administrative guidance had to be adopted. One measure was to reduce the statutory 48-hour working week to a 40-hour week, like most other advanced countries. Even higher priority was attached to making the five-day week

232

universal. Presently, according to Japanese statistics, it is enjoyed by 75% of the companies. But these statistics, in a rather novel interpretation, include not only companies with every Saturday off but even those which only grant one Saturday a month. Workers who are free every weekend only accounted for 28% of the labor force. So it was quite revolutionary when banks and then government offices were formally closed on some weekends.

Consequently, progress has been slow and patchy, often in a one step forward, two steps backward mode. Just how hard it can be will be readily grasped if one recalls that the goal of reducing working hours to Western levels goes back decades. Indeed, during the 1960s and 1970s, when the economy was flourishing and workers felt newly affluent, there was a tendency for working hours to decrease. The oil crisis changed all that. The companies pulled in their belts—and those of their employees—and demanded longer hours to overcome the crisis. Since wages were stagnant and costs rose, employees complied because they needed more income. And the gap with the West was not closed during the 1980s because of the *endaka* or high yen crisis. In fact, it has only gotten larger of late.

Even if the laws and regulations hold, and the official number of hours worked decreases, it is far from certain that the total input will be reduced. For one, the law which shortened the working week made it much easier to impose more overtime. This is tacitly accepted by those workers who put wages ahead of leisure. Too many Japanese simply do not feel they can get by on their ordinary salary and the only solution is to do more overtime or get a second job. In addition, many Japanese also find that leisure is too expensive; they simply do not have the money to enjoy it and thus the extra free time is wasted.

But the biggest constraint is not eagerness to work, or even the need for more money, but what is loosely called company "loyalty." As indicated, most employees already give back half their summer vacation and put in extra hours in the evening or on weekends. This is not "voluntary" in any real sense. They are under pressure from management to work longer. When nearly everyone succumbs, those who refuse only stand out and are regarded as "egoists" by their colleagues who have to carry their share as well. Such shirkers, who do not put the company first, also have trouble getting promoted and end up with smaller wage increments. Until this pressure ends, the laws and regulations will be systematically circumvented.

Resistance is particularly noticeable at the lower end of the dual economy. Big companies can, by and large, afford to give their own employees more free time. But, since the work must be done, they impose greater burdens than ever on their suppliers and subcontractors, which have to pitch in. Hard up for money, they do not quibble, nor do their regular employees, nor do part-timers in general for whom the concept of a workweek is pretty nebulous anyway. The worst abuses here derive from just-in-time supply. When a factory expects a load of parts first thing Monday, that has to be produced and delivered over the weekend if necessary.

So, the rat race goes on. In good years, with production rising, workers have to put in more time to keep up with orders. In bad years, with sales slumping, personnel is cut back and the remaining staff has to work even harder to make up and a bit more to compensate for stagnant earnings. There have been no years, except in the early 1970s, when wages were going up and hours down. Thus, we can safely assume that the Japanese will remain workaholics well into the 21st century. Even if they do reduce working hours somewhat the gap with other advanced countries should remain as the West decreases hours yet further. That Japan remains No. 1 in sweating labor is not really to its credit.

To Make Life Worth Living

"The best things in life are free," or so the old song goes. But most Japanese are not aware of this. They lead a life in which it is almost impossible to get those "best things" for any amount of money. And that is the saddest aspect of Japan, because many of them were very widespread, accessible and cheap, if not free, before the mad dash to modernization. With each passing year, however, they have moved further out of reach.

Take such a simple thing as a boy and girl going for a walk in the park and saying sweet nothings while they look up at the moon, which is what that song was written about. Due to social pressure, emanating less from the family than the company, that sort of treat is exceedingly rare. The boy is expected to show his devotion to the company by staying late at work and then perhaps retiring to a drinking establishment with male colleagues. If he were to say, "sorry, I have a date," he would be ostracized. Even if he said, "sorry, I want to see my wife and kids," his chances of promotion would diminish. Likewise for the girl.

If they could make adequate excuses, and not do it too often, of course they might be able to meet. But dating between employees of the same company is a no-no, as there could be awkward complications. And meeting someone in another company, or among friends, or at a club, is not so easy when you have to spend most of your time in company activities. That may explain why so many Japanese youngsters cannot even find a spouse without help from their family, a traditional match-maker (*nakodo*) or, let us not forget, a superior at work who may introduce likely young men to likely young women already screened by the company.

Where would they go walking? Probably not in a park. There are few enough parks in Japan. When open, they are terribly crowded, and many close in the evening or the benches are occupied by hobos and bag ladies. In any big city, it would take an hour, or two or more to get out to something resembling countryside. So most meetings are arranged in town and consist of wandering around the shopping or entertainment districts. This means, by definition, an expensive date.

But, let us not spend too much time on frivolous matters. The intense crowding, ruthless urbanization and incessant social pressure have deprived the Japanese of much more. We already mentioned family life, with the father frequently away from home. When he is home, most of his time is spent recovering from the fatigue of work. If he wanted to get away with the family, where would they go? Few playgrounds, fewer parks, not many resorts and a weekend bungalow is exceedingly rare. Many neighborhoods don't even have cinemas and the "family" restaurants can only be afforded now and then.

Personal life has suffered as well. It is quite difficult to get away from it all and engage in whatever one regards as most important, be it friendship, sports, culture or philosophy. Religion, which Japanese nurtured for centuries, has been reduced to occasional visits to the temple on festive occasions, almost sight-seeing for many nowadays, and accomplishing certain rites. While most are supposedly both Buddhist and Shintoist according to the official statistics, public opinion polls show that only 20% believe in any religion, the lowest figure East or West.[16] What, if anything, young people believe in of a spiritual (rather than material) nature is a bit of a mystery.

The most obvious casualty is nature. This is particularly unfortunate because the Japanese, by all accounts, were more attached to nature than virtually any other people. Yet, in only about a century, untold millions have been cut off. The cities and towns are so densely built up that little greenery remains and in many places there is not a tree or flower aside from the plastic ones merchants use to decorate their shops. While older folks may make an effort to return to the distant countryside, whole generations of youngsters have grown up without the slightest idea of what nature is and do not seek it. If anything, they feel uncomfortable in all that emptiness and hurry back to urban pleasures.

Thus, leisure revolves around commercial activities, most of them exceptionally expensive in Japan. Sports is one example. In a densely urbanized region, it is hard to provide enough facilities and the cost of land and construction pushes the price-tag yet higher. Thus, Japan only has about 500 tennis courts and 1,500 golf courses for the millions of players. And it is necessary to pay exorbitant fees and wait extensive periods to use the facilities. The average cost of joining a golf club is ¥5 million or more than the average salaryman earns in a year. It can take a week's wait to spend an hour on a municipal tennis court. That is why so many "sportsmen" carry on these activities in driving ranges or tennis practice areas which are tiny spaces surrounded by netting somewhere closer to town.

Of course, not everything is expensive. You can go fishing. Naturally, not in a mountain stream or along the seashore, but in Tokyo. Rice paddies have been turned into "fishing ponds," stocked with carp which can be fished at ¥600 an hour. Unfortunately, the fish taste so bad that no one eats them and most turn them in for coupons to engage in more fishing. Yet, even this sort of farce is accepted as the only substitute for the real thing by Japanese avid for relaxation.

These comments are useful as a prelude to the statistics of the Leisure Development Center, the government's think tank on the subject, which churns out the most fantastic figures. Thirty million people engage in jogging, 26 million in baseball, 20 million in fishing, 14 million in tennis, 13 million in golf, and so on. It would seem that the whole population is out there enjoying themselves like mad, making Japan the

Pachinko—Japan's foremost contribution
to modern culture.

Credit: Foreign Press Center/Kyodo

most leisure-oriented society in the world. It is not mentioned
that these statistics do not correspond to those issued by the
proprietors of such establishments or that the fishing may be
in a rice-paddy pond and the golf only twice a year on a
fairway. As for the jogging, the only time I have seen many
salarymen running is when they rush for the commuter trains.

Cost has also handicapped cultural activities. There are
relatively few concerts, ballets or plays and it is only possible
to see the opera when the Met or Vienna Opera come for a
visit. There are not many exhibitions of painting or sculpture.
And even traditional arts and crafts or *kabuki* and Noh are
far from widely disseminated. That is not surprising when

you consider that Japan has rather few theaters, concert halls, art galleries or museums. Some traditional arts are patronized by the state but everything else has to pay its way, including the art exhibits in downtown department stores. More serious, however, is that lacking a receptive public and depressed by an atmosphere that stifles creativity and originality, many of Japan's best musicians, conductors, painters, sculptors, ballerinas and so on have gone abroad.

What is more surprising than for high-cost, high-class culture to suffer is that even the most popular of art forms, cinema has been undergoing a dreary decline. There are only about 2,000 movie theatres in the country and the average person sees one film a year, usually foreign. This in the land of Akira Kurosawa and Nagisa Oshima, both of whom now need foreign backers since the indigenous industry only wants sure-fire money-makers, most of them pot boilers with, according to Dan Furst, three basic scenarios: "handsome *yakuza* (gangster) beats up a girlfriend or two in anger, then compromises the honor of his gang; a naive *burikko* (cutie pie), separated from her schoolfriends while on holiday, ends up with smiling Adonis; wayward husband has fling with sexy girls then returns to his forgiving wife and kids."[17]

No wonder so many Japanese fall back on watching television as by far their principal leisure activity. According to NHK, the national broadcasting system, the average Japanese spends three hours a weekday and four hours on Sunday viewing the boob tube. The figure is actually higher for women and children than men, whose weekend is often spent sleeping off their fatigue. Despite modest efforts by NHK, the quality of television is rather mediocre. It is packed with soap operas, quiz shows, cartoons, *yakuza* and *ninja* movies, and the like. Its stars are called *tarento*, although talent is one thing most lack. There are hardly any current events or political programs, rare interviews with prominent figures, and a modicum of culture (some opera or *kabuki*).

The next biggest activity, according to NHK, is reading. For men, much of this takes place while commuting. So one should not expect too much as regards quality. While the circulation of newspapers has remained stable, that of general magazines sunk, and sales of serious books plummeted, comics have proliferated wildly. Over a billion of these *manga* are sold each year. They probably account for half the "reading" in Japan, to judge by the dog-eared copies to be found in any coffee shop. With good literature driven out by bad, it is hard to understand how Vogel could possibly praise the standard of literacy and "sophistication" of the reading public.[18]

What about travel? We are stuffed with reports on how much the Japanese travel nowadays and have perhaps been trampled by a herd of Japanese tourists while in Honolulu or Paris. Yes, they do travel more. But not so much when you consider how many Japanese there are. Some eight million went abroad last year which, while large in one sense, only represents 7% of the population. Seen another way, each Japanese goes abroad once every fifteen years. That is a less impressive figure. Moreover, while travel supposedly broadens the horizon, group travel in packaged tours Japanese-style does not.

So, are the Japanese happy as Vogel, Reischauer and others intimated? Are they "the largest body of contented people in the world," as the Japan Society's MacEachron proclaimed? Not that you would notice from their behavior. Not that you would notice from the comments they make on their lifestyle. Not that you would notice from less anecdotal sources like polls and surveys. NHK, in comparing international attitudes, found 91% of the Americans satisfied with their lifestyle but only 66% of the Japanese. *The Sunday Times* of London, in a broader study of 16 countries, placed the Japanese among the least satisfied with their lives.[19] The Prime Minister's Office, in an annual survey, has recorded a long-term trend

240

for the Japanese to be increasingly worried about the future.[20]

But there is no need to belabor this point. The Japanese know that they cannot have many things that are readily available to so many other people, including plenty who do not earn a quarter as much. They are disappointed and disturbed. And they don't even bother trying to put a happy face on it. They have just learned to live with a rather crummy lifestyle and there is no great expectation that this will change soon. Thus, for quality of life, Japan should continue receiving very inferior grades.

Indeed, on this particular, most Japanapologists agree. Not through what they say, of course, but what they do. No matter how much they urge others to "learn from Japan," they personally prefer admiring Japan from a distance, platonically as it were, rather than become part of that society. They would not dream of living in Japan like Japanese. When they come, they live like *gaijin*, which is vastly better. No rabbit hutches for them, no 60-hour weeks, no giving up their weekends and vacations, no sacrificing pleasure for work, no repressing their personality. If anything, they behave more like *gaijin* and enjoy the prerogatives which they know many Japanese would like to, but cannot, share.

But don't let my interminable Cassandra-like griping get you down. Never fear. If Japan has not risen to the challenge thus far, there is no reason to suspect that it will not do so in the future. Indeed, the Japanapologists ceaselessly remind us, the society is constantly transforming itself and there are new prowesses to be expected at any moment. This means it is petty and futile to bother with any present defects, in short order they will disappear only to be replaced by another metamorphosis. This was announced, among others, by the editor of *The International*, back from a quickie trip to Tokyo.

"Japan is entering a period of profound change. . . . Put simply, Japan is about to sit back and enjoy. It may sound uncharacteristic but all the signs are there. . . . The Japanese have decided that they want to take their place in civilized world society. They want to swap material wealth for social wealth and that means longer holidays, shorter working hours, better housing, increased leisure facilities and more overseas travel.''[21]

NOTES

1. *The Economist*, August 13, 1988, pp. 27–8.
2. *Forbes*, January 25, 1988, p. 36.
3. National Economic Accounting Report, Economic Planning Agency, 1988.
4. *Japan Economic Journal*, July 4, 1987, p. 7 and *Speaking of Japan*, November 1988, p. 17.
5. *The Economist*, December 24, 1988, p. 49 and *Financial Times*, August 23, 1988.
6. *The Economist*, December 24, 1988, p. 48.
7. *BusinessWeek*, September 12, 1988, p. 50.
8. *Japan Economic Journal*, July 4, 1987, p. 7.
9. *Asian Wall Street Journal*, May 24, 1987.
10. *Wages and Hours of Work*, Japan Institute of Labor, and *Monthly Labor Surveys*, Ministry of Labor.
11. *Japan Times*, November 24, 1986, and *Yomiuri*, June 19, 1989.
12. *Yomiuri*, November 28, 1988.
13. *BusinessWeek*, April 7, 1986, p. 52.
14. *Yomiuri*, April 21, 1989.
15. *Japan Economic Journal*, May 7, 1985.
16. *Japan Times*, July 21, 1982.
17. *Far Eastern Economic Review*, August 25, 1988, p. 34.
18. Vogel, *Japan As Number One*, pp. 158 & 162.
19. *Look Japan*, April 10, 1984 and *Japan Times*, March 14, 1983.
20. Public Opinion Survey on National Life, Prime Minister's Office, annual.
21. *The International*, December 1988, p. 3.

12

Amenities
(Be It Ever So Humble)

Life In A Rabbit Hutch

A decade ago, there was almost a scandal when the European
Community included in one of its briefing papers a reference
to the Japanese as "workaholics living in rabbit hutches."
Naturally, all kindly and sympathetic foreigners thought one
just doesn't say things like that. It is necessary to be gentle
and diplomatic in revealing Japan's weaknesses. But there
was no scandal. The Japanese liked the expression, found it
rather apt and have since repeatedly referred to their dwellings
as "rabbit hutches."[1]

In this one sector, there is no *tatemae*. Housing is not only
so bad, it is so visibly bad that there would be no point in
telling fibs to one another or even foreigners. The only way
of saving face is not to invite any but relatives and intimates
home, and especially to avoid having superiors or foreigners
over, so that the shame can be kept in the family. To that
shame is now being added a growing sense of frustration
because, as opposed to long hours or modest incomes which
seem to be improving, the trends for housing have largely
been negative.

It is hard to imagine how a Japanese lives if you have not
lived in the same sort of digs yourself. Even the official

Bemused politicians visiting an ordinary
family's rabbit hutch.

Credit: Foreign Press Center/Kyodo

figures, depressing as they are, only paint a pale picture. According to the Construction Ministry, the average floor area is 81 square meters. But this includes much larger units in the countryside as well as cramped quarters in the city. It varies from about 112 square meters for the average private house or condominium to 45 square meters for rental units. This compares with an average size of 94 square meters in Germany and 135 square meters in the United States.[2]

Size is not the only thing. There is also the question of quality. Japanese homes are not that well built. Every trick is used to have thinner walls and shallower basements (if any) to save on wood and concrete. The work is often done in a hurry or by subcontractors earning starvation wages, so it can be quite shoddy on occasion. Even the Construction Ministry seemed dismayed by the response to its survey on housing quality, when seven out of ten condo occupants complained of noise and one out of three owners of detached houses, mainly wooden-made, said there were leaks in the roof. Even more had defective doors and windows, wall paint peeling off and corrosion of the balcony. And this only a year or two after they moved in.[3]

There is also the matter of amenities. While 94% have tap water, only 58% have flush toilets and 44% are connected to sewage facilities. Hardly any have central heating, let alone air-conditioning. The houses and buildings are surrounded by small bits of land, hardly what one would call a lawn and perhaps only a meter or so to the road. Rather than a "garden," it is more likely to be turned into a "parking space." The only thing that is imposing are the pretentious names: Akasaka Mansion, Aoyama Heights, Chofu Palace, Sato Gardens, Miyamoto Chalet, etc.

Then, of course, there is the distance from the city center, something that is very important since the outer suburbs are increasingly inhabited by salarymen who have to report to work five (or six) days a week. Time was when the average commute was only an hour each way. Now it has risen to an hour-and-a-half, going on two for some living around Tokyo. Commuting, by the way, does not mean driving your car into town, a luxury hardly anybody can afford. No, you take a local train, connect with an express train, transfer to a subway and then perhaps walk ten minutes to the office. In those conveyances, you are lucky if you can sit and people are packed together so densely that many foreigners simply could not take it.

Your neighborhood, if the expression can be used, is usually just the district round about a subway or train station. It is crisscrossed by highways and superhighways, with cars, buses, trucks and trains making an incredible racket that the

houses cannot shut out. Not far from the station are some
dilapidated ma-and-pa shops, perhaps a superstore, the pachinko parlor and crummy restaurants and bars. Interspersed
among the homes and apartment buildings are "farms" and
factories, some still belching out smoke and fumes. If you
are lucky, there is a school not too far away and maybe a
tiny park or playground for the kids. None of these comments
comes from my imagination, I know these places all too well.

And who lives in such homes? Usually a whole family,
sometimes even a two-generation family, since young people
still do not go out on their own much and it is increasingly
necessary to look after grandma and grandpa. With fewer
residential units per 1,000 population, naturally these "rabbit
hutches" hold more inhabitants than Western dwellings. They
become particularly crowded when fitted out with the standard
equipment and gadgets, refrigerator, rice cooker, TV set and
so on. More and more have rugs over the *tatami* mats and
beds instead of *futon*, which only adds to the clutter. It is
almost unbearable when everybody is at home, which may
explain why the father is so often absent and not really missed.
Since there are not actually "rooms" in the ordinary sense
but living spaces separated by sliding paper walls, privacy is
the biggest—and rarest—luxury of all.

Remember, we are talking about the average Japanese in-
habiting the average unit. There are plenty more who cannot
afford even this. Many are stuck in "one-room mansions"
whose number is growing rapidly. Or they are the humble
owners of even scruffier houses, some of which look more
like barracks, and could not even be used to lodge migrant
workers in Europe. Or they dwell right along the highways
and railway lines where the noise is deafening. Or, and I am
not certain if it is much more merciful, they live further out
and commute two or three hours each way.

The rich? Yes, the rich do live better. But they still don't
manage the lifestyle of the rich anywhere else. They may

have a detached house with a somewhat larger lawn or garden, a regular place to park the car, but hardly the sort of grounds their counterparts possess in Europe and America. They may not even have a one-car garage, let alone a two-car garage. Only a small minority boast a (tiny) swimming pool. In town, they dwell closer to the center and have more spacious quarters. But nothing to rave about.

What does this cost? The average Tokyo house will run you ¥85 million (four-fifths of this for the land). A condominium within ten kilometers of the emperor's palace costs ¥65 million; one in the outer prefectures, ¥40 million.[4] A nice, but hardly extraordinary, home in Denenchofu, the "Beverly Hills" of Tokyo, goes for almost ¥3 trillion. To get a feel for the numbers, you can probably take any unit in Europe, America, or most of the Third World, and multiply the cost by at least four and perhaps eight or ten to know what it would cost in Japan. Thus, your cheaper condo costs as much as a lovely apartment in many capital cities and the luxury home could be traded in for a Park Avenue penthouse, an English mansion or a French chateau. Perhaps this explains the pretentious names.

The big hitch at present is that the average Japanese can no longer afford the average Japanese home. This was announced, not by the trade unions or Socialists but the very official Economic Planning Agency in its 1988 Report on Regional Economy. The mathematics are clear. The average house in Tokyo costs ¥85 million. Since it could not be bought outright by the average salaryman, it would have to be mortgaged. Then, for the next twenty years, the owner would have to pay a sum larger than his disposable income. Clearly impossible. It is generally assumed that a worker can afford to pay about five times his annual income. The house, at 16 times his annual income, is obviously too pricey. The condo near town, at 11 times, is also beyond reach. He might just make it with the more distant condo at 7 times his annual income.[5]

Yet, even then, he would have to get a mortgage. If he were extremely lucky, he might get part of it from the state-run Housing Loan Corporation. For the rest, he would need very good collateral, or a guarantee from his parents, or even better, the company he works for if it is well known. Then he could spend the rest of his working life paying 30% to 50% of his take-home pay. If he were still not able to swing it, the bank might let him arrange a two-generation mortgage whereby his children would be bound to continue payments.

If one thing is certain about the average Japanese, then it is that he wants to own his own house or condo. This is reflected overwhelmingly by every survey. There is no higher priority. Alas, it is painfully evident that more and more Japanese will have to live in rental units, none too nice, none too cheap. The chances of fulfilling their dream have grown slimmer with each passing year.

How could this happen? Quite simply. The government's top priority was economic development and it was geared to helping the companies and managers. Housing had a much lower priority, sometimes none at all. The field was largely neglected aside from a modest home loan agency and some rather mediocre public housing (*danchi*). The rest was entrusted in the private sector, largely unregulated and uncontrolled, which made an incredible mess of it. While there were far too many mistakes and problems to include them all, a number are worthwhile looking at.

First of all, amenities. They are scanty. As mentioned, only 44% of the inhabited areas are equipped with sewage against as much as 90% in Germany and Britain. Only two square meters of park space compared to 20 or 30 abroad. Less than one kilometer of expressway per vehicle versus three and four times that in Europe and America. Indeed, many neighborhoods don't even have sidewalks, simply a line painted along the roadway to keep cars and pedestrians apart.[6] The reason is that the public authorities did not provide the funds or organize the necessary infrastructural works. Also, by not planning ahead and buying the land early, they let costs get out of hand.

Other things were not even botched due to cost but sheer neglect or stupidity. Japan is densely populated. In every other country, this had led to laws encouraging the construction of high-rise buildings within the cities. Not so in Tokyo, Osaka, Kyoto, etc. There are small, private homes stretching as far as the eye can see and only now disrupted by some towering structures that ruin the landscape and crowd neighborhoods ill-equipped to receive them. That was not an accident. Zoning laws permitted the waste of land and housing regulations inhibited the creation of unified, high-rise districts.

I mentioned the odd hodge-podge of buildings in the typical neighborhood. Actually, this includes even parts of the downtown area and the upper-class suburbs. It was caused by sloppy zoning codes which, although in theory, providing for separate residential, commercial and industrial zones, made most of them "mixed." So, in most places, you can put up a house or apartment building, a store, or a factory. Indeed, you can even buy a house and turn it into a grocery store, or noodle shop, or all-night bar with *karaoke* singing. In front of your house, you can install a *sake* vending machine. And there is nothing much your neighbors can do about it.

Construction costs, by the way, are exorbitant. As was already noted, the industry is incredibly fragmented and labor-intensive. This naturally boosts prices. The fact that builders collude on who gets which job and charge pretty much what they want only makes things worse. Lack of prefabrication and large-scale projects adds to this. But the government has not intervened much to bring costs down. Rather, the bureaucrats maintain all sorts of archaic standards and certifications that get in the way of greater efficiency and lower costs.

Obviously, the biggest curse is the high cost of land. It is extremely important because the cost of housing is inflated by land costs which account for 50% to 80% of the total. This is already an old problem. Land prices have been rising steadily during the postwar period and went into a dizzying spiral twice. First, in the early 1970s, when Prime Minister Tanaka launched his "remodelling" plan. Then in the mid-1980s, when the worst speculative binge occurred. In 1987 alone, land prices rose 77% in Tokyo and 22% for Japan as a whole at a time of supposedly zero inflation. This brought the total increase in land prices since 1955 to about 45-fold.

Japanese authorities, and naive foreigners, sometimes attribute this astounding rise to living in a small, mountainous country with too little room. That *tatemae* is part of the reason perhaps, but a minor part. Tight, crowded countries like Holland, Belgium, Switzerland, Singapore and even Hong Kong have done better. The real cause (the *honne*) is that Japanese land policy has been disastrous. Rather than promote broader distribution of the population, it stimulated concentration by supporting the development of Tokyo as not only the nation's capital, but its commercial, financial, educational and cultural center. This while many remote coastal and mountain areas were being depopulated and lesser cities declined.

Policy regarding the sale of land has actually spawned the worst abuses. Land which is used for farming is taxed at much lower rates than residential or commercial property. So owners frequently turn it into a "farm," growing any convenient crop and perhaps not even harvesting it. In the heart of Tokyo and other urban centers are enough "farms" to provide countless homes and keep land prices down. But the owners do not want to sell because they expect the price to rise or don't want to pay crushing inheritance taxes. In many cases, to pay off inheritance taxes, they have to divide land into small parcels and sell one or two. This only makes it harder to find decent-sized plots to put up decent-sized projects.

On top of all this is the speculation. The biggest push comes not from ordinary landowners but speculators who buy and sell at a terrific pace, often to one another, artificially bloating prices. They were encouraged in this by a ridiculous law (only recently repealed) that did not tax gains if they were used to purchase land within a year. And they were financed by the leading banks and trading companies. This kept prices on a steady roll. Admittedly, nothing goes up for ever and land prices have occasionally slipped a bit. But never much. The real estate operators, landowners, speculators and others tacitly agreed to hold the line. With so much money tied up in land, the government did not want prices to come under too much pressure either.

Only when skyrocketing land prices and housing costs became politically embarrassing did the government respond to popular demands. It did cool the market after the Tanaka years and Takeshita adopted some measures that impeded the rise of prices in Tokyo . . . but did nothing to keep the wave from spreading outward to other regions. Japan has also had, believe it or not, a housing policy with five-year housing plans. The 1981 plan sought to improve the quality and size of homes. The 1986 plan set the ambitious target of half of all Japanese families living in homes of American and European standards by the 21st century. This was to do away with the "rabbit hutch" image.

No need to elaborate on what happened to those plans. The situation today is worse than it was five or ten years ago. Japan has been moving steadily in the wrong direction and the Japanese population has had to endure it. There have, of course, been dark rumors that the people would simply not stand for this decline of living standards and loss of the one dream they most closely hold. They would rise and revolt.

That is silly. The LDP knows the population far better than to be scared by such claptrap. If the Japanese have meekly accepted so long, why should they change now?

Thus, when it comes to land and housing, the rating must be inferior. In fact, it should be even lower since Japan has performed worse than any advanced country and many developing ones in this sector. And there is little hope of improvement. While there is only modest pressure from the electorate for change, there is enormous pressure from vested interests to preserve the status quo. They include realtors, contractors, the whole construction industry, the farm lobby, the speculators and the banks. These are among the LDP's biggest supporters and most generous financial backers. And they will see to it that things go their way.

Glorious Plans And Mirages

I don't believe any Japanapologist has actually come out in favor of Japan's land and housing policy. In fact, I know of a world-renowned specialist in urban planning who was approached by the Japanese authorities to write a book describing Japan's purported successes in that field. Thank goodness he was rude enough to turn the offer down, explaining that he did not know of a single thing that had been done in Japan he could recommend to others. So we were spared a book entitled "Japan as No. 1 for Urbanism" or "Learning Urbanism from Japan."

But the claque has been extremely vigorous in praising and publicizing every effort to improve the situation through assorted eye-catching schemes. There has been no shortage of them and every time I write on the subject I have more to add. These are grandiose projects, proposed most often by the government, but increasingly now by the private sector, to overcome the concentration in Tokyo, reinvigorate the peripheral regions, and embellish the country while, in some cases, contributing solidly to economic progress.

The most famous plan, which included all four aspects, was promoted by Kakue Tanaka in the early 1970s. The prime minister called for a "remodelling of the archipelago" which would endow it with more ports, highways, bridges and other infrastructure, facilitate the development of backward regions, upgrade living areas and create a finer environment, etc., etc. He was backed strongly by the bureaucrats and businessmen and, for a while, it looked as if a spectacular renovation might take place. One of the first to jump on the bandwagon was Herman Kahn, who did not hesitate to proclaim:

"One thing seems certain, in addition to their economic and technological performance, the Japanese intend to make their environment into a work of art and a marvel of engineering. . . . the Japanese have a twenty-year program during which they intend to 'fix Japan.' I would guess that before the program is over they will have succeeded in doing so. They will be able to say that not only have they become the first truly post-industrial culture but they have achieved their advanced status in style—that the islands of Japan have become a truly worthy environment for the Japanese people. In fact, since a more attractive and liveable environment cannot be found anywhere in the world, if the Japanese are persuasive enough I may move there myself."[7]

Unfortunately—or perhaps fortunately—Tanaka was driven from office soon after and we never saw what the Japanese could do. But, that is not surprising. There never was a Tanaka plan, just Tanaka wishful thinking. By this I mean, there was no plan in the sense of specific projects regarding what should be built, where, when and, above all, with what money. There were just delightful ideas calculated to appeal to the public. And the only concrete result was a speculative binge that sent land prices up so high that it would have been impossible to implement the projects anyway (had they existed). I would therefore tend to think that "fortunately" is the appropriate word.

Somewhat more useful, and realistic, were the various Comprehensive National Development Plans that were issued periodically ever since 1962. They also sought to expand the infrastructure and contribute to decentralization. In the first instance, they did improve the situation by pouring trillions of yen into roads, harbors, water supply, sewerage systems and so on. Yet, somehow or other, they never quite hoisted Japan to the level of other advanced countries. While they managed to get industry out of the cities (greatly assisted by land costs that made it impractical to stay), they could not reverse or even stem the flow to Tokyo.

Thus, the most important effort has been to reduce the capital's drawing power. With 30 million people or a quarter of the population living within 50 kilometers of the emperor's palace, the need is evident. In fact, it was already obvious enough as of the 1960s to incite an endless series of proposals to move the capital somewhere else. They came from every possible source: LDP and Socialists, Ministries of Home Affairs, Construction, MITI and EPA, famous architects, academics and businessmen. It was suggested that the new capital should be located in Hamamatsu, nearer Nagoya or Osaka, around Ise Bay or, most often, at the foot of Mount Fuji.[8] The only thing they all had in common, which is why I won't bore you with the details, is that they were never put into practice.

The only measures actually implemented were considerably more modest. One was to transfer most of the government's research institutes out of Tokyo. Another was to strongly encourage universities to open second campuses out in the sticks. More recently, Prime Minister Takeshita decided that one institution or office attached to each ministry or agency should be relocated. But these were just a drop in the bucket which was constantly being filled yet further by the

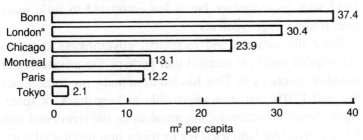

Park Space in Major Cities of the World

City	m² per capita
Bonn	37.4
London[a]	30.4
Chicago	23.9
Montreal	13.1
Paris	12.2
Tokyo	2.1

If parks and greenery have anything to do
with quality of life, forget it.

Source: Comparative International Statistics,
Bank of Japan, 1986.
Credit: *Facts and Figures of Japan 1989*, p. 87.

decision of more students, workers and companies to migrate
to Tokyo.

So, if Tokyo were to remain the capital, at least it was
necessary to make it more livable. For this reason, there has
been a profusion of other plans and projects. You may be
intrigued to learn that, in 1950, a plan was adopted to create
a vast "greenbelt" around the city. Alas, developers never
read the plan and nobody kept them from pushing the city
further and further out. In so doing, they destroyed most of
the greenery that remained. So, in 1975, an "improved" plan
called for holding on to what few patches of land could be
found. This, too, was largely ignored and now each Tokyoite
has barely enough park land to turn around in.

These failures did not keep Governor Shunichi Suzuki from
introducing a twenty-year plan for remaking Tokyo, not as
magnificent as the Tanaka plan but surely enough to please
admirers like Kahn. It was replete with ambitious targets like
doubling the size of greenery zones and providing rivers and
canals both to carry away rainwater and be stocked with fish.

There were also the usual slogans: "Tokyo—a town whose residents can live in a lively way" and "Tokyo—a town that inhabitants can call their home." The plan was launched in 1982 with great fanfare but it has amounted to little more than routine improvements.

Since the national and municipal governments failed to accomplish much, it seemed that perhaps the private sector could do a better job. That has led to so many proposals since the mid-1980s that it is impossible to keep track of them. Most consist of redeveloping areas along the rivers and harbors, converting land used for factories into residential communities and, most impressive, building artificial islands in Tokyo Bay. Among those with some hope of achievement in the coming years are the River City 21, Tokyo Teleport, Harumi Island and Ariake Harbor City.[9]

But they pale in comparison to several projects that would make the Egyptian Pharaohs blanch and Ferdinand De Lesseps turn green with envy. One is the man-made island that architect Kenzo Tange wants to build in Tokyo Bay. It would be 2,500 hectares large and could house as many as 350,000 people. The cost: a mere ¥12 trillion.[10] This was trumped by the "ocean city" plan sponsored by a group of business leaders and academics. It would require 100 million tons of steel and cost ¥50 trillion. The new city could accommodate a million people.[11] Even it was piddling compared to the audacious proposal of architect Kishin Kurokawa, a friend of Nakasone, who wished to build a 30,000 hectare island (i.e. half the size of the Tokyo ward area). It could be completed by the year 2025 at a cost of some ¥238 trillion.[12] To give a feel for the scale of these ventures, it might be mentioned that the new Osaka International Airport, the largest such project thus far, only ran into ¥1 trillion.

It is conceivable that the private sector, or at least its lunatic fringe, has bit off more than it can chew. And it is uncertain how many of the more extreme projects will ever be achieved.

But this is mere quibbling. The principal objection is that these projects are not a "solution," they only compound the problem. Every last one of them is designed to increase the concentration of population within the Tokyo catchment zone, whether in outlying prefectures, in less densely populated districts or on reclaimed land. This would only make the megalopolis an even larger part of the whole.

What is needed is the opposite. Some way of getting more people to live outside of Tokyo by developing or reviving other areas, many of which are becoming depopulated. This includes not only mountain and coastal villages but even Osaka, the second city, which is losing out to Tokyo. That is why Osaka also concocted an extraordinary project to re-shape and beautify. I saw it. A lovely color-coded plan indicating the location for a culture city, a technical city, an academic city and so on. The only drawbacks, minor ones I am certain, were that there was already something else built where those cities were to be located, there were no concrete arrangements to claim the land and, last but not least, there was no money to finance the construction. Once again, deeds would have trouble keeping up with words.

The most extravagant conceptualizations (without much materialization) have continued coming from the government. Almost every prime minister felt it his duty to offer a pet project, although none were of the dimensions of Tanaka's remodelling job. Ohira talked fondly of creating "garden cities" to promote "vigorous and diverse local societies by advancing richly verdant redevelopment while heeding protection from natural disasters in the cities and by advancing the creation of culturally attractive villages in the rural areas." I don't believe a single one was ever built. Ditto for the "regional plazas" proposed by Suzuki, with their "town center," sports and recreational facilities, health and medical installations, parks and green areas.[13] And then came Takeshita's program of "creating home towns" (*furusato sosei*).

Considering that he was only willing to budget ¥ 100 million for each, not much could be expected.[14]

Prime Minister Nakasone was too busy reforming, or at least expounding, to build castles in the air. But Toshiki Kaifu came up with an ambitious project, and one that had never been tried before, namely turning Japan into a "nation of culture." He intended to make up for the gross neglect of his predecessors whose culture budget was a mere fifth of the average level of advanced nations. He therefore established a special foundation to make Japan an international center of artistic and cultural activities while preserving its unique cultural heritage. The ultimate goal was to change Japan from "a nation of merchants to a nation of culture." Alas, Kaifu could not raise enough money to achieve that aim and, since there were no boondoggles and pork-barrel goodies, it was not very popular with LDP backers. But surely the intention was admirable.

Even more exciting concepts emanated from the bureaucracy. One was to create an "academic city" in Tsukuba, a few hours' drive from Tokyo, which was immortalized by Gene Gregory. "Where just a decade ago half-a-dozen country towns were clustered amid pine forests and farmland, there are now 51 governmental and private research institutes plus two universities . . ." which formed "one of the world's largest and best-equipped agglomerations of research institutions."[15] What he failed to stress, and was inadequately realized abroad, is that Japan had not actually created very much new since most of these institutions already existed and were simply relocated from Tokyo.

A similar trick was played by MITI even more blatantly in begetting the Technopolis. This was to be a "future city where importance is attached to relations between man and nature, which is open to the world, and where three different civilizations mingle with each other." These are the international city, the academic city and the industrial city. They were to become regional poles to "transfer the innovative power of the frontier industries." So much for the rhetoric. What did MITI actually do? It looked for local centers that already possessed schools, research institutes, parks and leisure areas, port and airports, etc. Then it waved a magic wand and dubbed them "technopolis." It did not cost the government much and it is still uncertain what the budding technopoli gained aside from PR.

The purpose of this exercise is not to debunk every effort at "fixing" Japan but to shatter any excessive illusions. There have been far too much wishful thinking, grandiose plans, public relations trickery and Potemkin villages whose purpose is to make the Japanese people forget their dissatisfaction and impress the outside world. This only gets in the way and makes it harder to tackle the essential problems. Worse, it wastes precious time.

As for the future, I do not expect any improvement and rather tend to fear a degradation of present conditions. It would take too much of a break with the past to bring about the radical changes that are necessary. And, the longer one waits, the harder it is to go against the currents carrying more people to Tokyo, concentrating more power and wealth there, and making it very difficult for any other region to get by. Moreover, when even ordinary public works projects are attempted, just putting up roads, schools or administrative buildings, they are burdened by incredibly high land costs that eat up the bulk of the budget. Japan is digging itself into a hole it will probably never get out of.

Looking ahead is therefore even more distasteful than looking back. The country will never have beautiful cities, uncluttered landscapes, cozy neighborhoods or ordinary amenities that are common in other places whose initial resources were often smaller but more wisely used. This is one of its most egregious failures and even rating it inferior is being generous.

NOTES

1. The phrase was first used by Sir Roy Denman, the EEC's director for external relations, in 1979.
2. These and other figures from Ministry of Construction.
3. *Japan Times*, December 21, 1982.
4. *Far Eastern Economic Review*, June 11, 1987.
5. *Yomiuri*, February 29, 1988.
6. These are my own observations which can be readily verified by anyone who wishes to do so.
7. Kahn, *The Emerging Japanese Superstate*, p. 212.
8. Kazuo Yawata, "A New Capital for Japan?," *Economic Eye*, March 1988, pp. 14–17.
9. *Far Eastern Economic Review*, July 30, 1987, p. 57.
10. *Japan Economic Journal*, July 19, 1986, p. 8.
11. *Ibid.*
12. *Far Eastern Economic Review*, July 30, 1987, pp. 58–61.
13. For more on the earlier promises and projects, see Woronoff, *Inside, Japan Inc.*, pp. 252–273.
14. *Yomiuri*, December 29, 1988.
15. *Far Eastern Economic Review*, March 25, 1985, p. 44.

13

Welfare
(What Is There To Be Entitled To?)

Desperately Seeking Welfare

Gee whiz. This time Ez Vogel has really come up with a Japanese miracle. It is a welfare system that does everything anyone could possibly want. It is cheap, rejecting the welfare state concept, and avoiding a heavy state burden. It provides ample coverage, but with only the very old and infirm becoming dependent on the state. It imbues people with a sense of purpose, self-respect and group effort while avoiding despair and degradation. And it does not create a feeling of entitlement. What is more, the public seems to be happy with the system.[1]

Such a system would, indeed, be a "miracle" in the purest sense, namely something that defies reason and expectations. So, before proclaiming it too widely, one should take a closer look at the situation.

It is true that the Japanese government, which had lagged far behind on social security and welfare, made a great leap forward during the 1960s and 1970s. During that period, it put together a system that compares favorably with most advanced countries. It established assorted pension plans for civil servants, company employees, self-employed and others. Most of these are contributory. But there are also schemes for those too poor, old or infirm to take care of themselves. There is an extensive network of health insurance that includes virtually everybody. Plus unemployment insurance.

Naturally, since there are various schemes, the contributions and benefits will differ. As a general rule, those who are best off are the civil servants, employees of large companies and members of farm cooperatives. Employees of small companies, temporary workers in general, owners of small shops and the like do considerably less well. This continues and accentuates the divisions that existed during their working lives and might rile some. But ordinary Japanese, who are accustomed to such distinctions and know from experience that they are not "entitled" to anything else accept it as inevitable.

The real problem, however, is how a government can keep down costs while running a comprehensive welfare system. One way is by making the benefits smallish, such as the meager sums paid out to jobless for quite short periods. Another is by limiting the beneficiaries of unpaid welfare, which is clearly done. The trickiest technique is unique to Japan. While most employees are expected to retire at the age of 55, pensions are only paid out as of 60, leaving citizens with a gap when they are not covered.

But the chief explanation of the thus far low-cost operation is much simpler. It evolved during a period when the economy was expanding rapidly and there were very few beneficiaries because most of the population was young and working. Such a felicitous situation could not possibly continue. There may be more unemployed at times. And it is certain that there will be more elderly. In fact, with a rapidly increasing life expectancy (75 for men, 81 for women), the population will soon be undergoing the fastest aging any country has ever experienced. From 11% in 1988, the share of people over 65 is projected to reach 24% by 2020.

This implies that, to keep the system intact and give the

public everything that has been promised, the government would have to expand medical and social security/welfare payments vastly over the coming years. From about 10% of national income in 1980, it should rise to 20% in the year 2000 and 32% by 2025.[2]

But the government balked at this. And the citizenry did not want to pay the contributions and taxes necessary. Thus, the highly touted ''age of welfare'' was quietly repealed and supposed ''reforms'' were introduced to pare down the benefits. Payments to fatherless families were decreased, income limitations were imposed for formerly free services, the aged would no longer get free medical care and everyone had to pay 10% of medical costs, expected to rise later to 20%. Then several pension plans were merged and the benefits reduced. Now efforts are being made to raise the age for receiving the employee's pension from 60 to 65.

That explains why Japan still lags most advanced nations with regard to social expenditures, often by a considerable margin. Only part of that can be traced to demographics. Much more was due to the fact that benefits were skimpy. In fact, when compared to other OECD members, Japan made a very poor showing. It spent only 16% of gross domestic product on the social welfare system while many European countries spent 30% and more and even the United States had reached 18%. The only place that was actually lower was Spain, rather odd company for a welfare ''miracle.''[3]

And this lowly position may actually worsen in the future if the government is unable to increase social security contributions and raise taxes appreciably, which seems likely. For then it will have to cut back sharply. Presently, social security benefits are roughly equal to those in advanced countries, largely because there are so few beneficiaries. This would quickly change with them falling to much lower levels, around 25% of the former wage, which would be completely inadequate.[4] For health services, beneficiaries would have to pay much more than 10% or 20%, perhaps 30% or 40%. As they say, there is no free lunch and there is also no such thing as a "cheap" welfare system.

Even then, no matter how hard it tries, the government will not be able to stem the mounting costs of welfare without thoroughly dismantling the system. It would thus be better to admit that a crisis looms ahead, work out a generally acceptable solution, and take whatever measures are necessary, including boosting the budget and imposing additional taxes. Instead, the response has repeatedly been to issue white papers and plans about the (comfortable, affluent, vital, harmonious, etc.) society of the 21st century without explaining how to get there.

Instead, the government increasingly hinted that state welfare was not the right path and individuals would have to do more for themselves. Older people were urged to work longer, which was good for them anyway. And families should pitch in, with the children looking after their parents and grandparents. This new age is to be one of "self-help" and "self-reliance." That concept was introduced by the 1983 and 1984 White Papers of the Ministry of Health and Welfare and expanded upon thereafter.

Was the population happy? If so, the applause was muted and old Ez would have stood out like a sore thumb for his comments. Most complained that it was impossible to get by on the scant pensions they received, that paying even 10% of medical fees was hard for some, that it was not so easy to get a decent job if you were over fifty, and so on. Nothing seems to have rankled more than the idea of retiring at 55 but not getting a pension until 60 and perhaps 65. As one employee griped in his letter to the editor, "are we expected to live on air for ten years until we turn 65?"[5] In a government survey on the coming of an aged society, the response was crystal-clear: 66% were worried, especially about pensions, health services and job opportunities.[6]

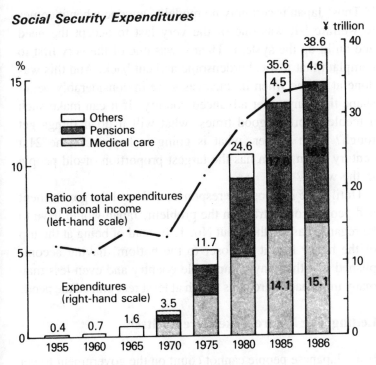

Social Security Expenditures

¥ trillion

The welfare dilemma: either raise taxes
or cut benefits... and fast.

Source: White Paper on Welfare,
Ministry of Health and Welfare, 1988.
Credit: *Facts and Figures of Japan 1989*, p. 73.

   On one point at least Vogel was right. There was no entitlement. Absolutely no entitlement. The government,
namely top politicians and elite bureaucrats, decided what
the welfare system would be like, who it would cover, what
it would provide, and how well it would be funded compared
to other activities. There was almost no input from the public
at large and efforts by the trade unions and opposition parties
were simply ignored, when they even bothered doing something. Whether this instilled a nobility in the Japanese that
was missing elsewhere is open to question.

266

Thus, Japan is certainly no model to anyone when it comes to welfare.[7] It was one of the very last to accept the need and build up the system. Then it was one of the very first to complain that it was burdensome and cut back. And this was done at a time when its finances were in considerably better shape than any other advanced country. If it can make such a feeble effort in good times, what will it do if things get rough? Even scarier, what is going to happen in the 21st century when Japan has the largest proportion of old people in the world?

Until there is a positive response, and until the government and people concentrate on the problem, Japan would have to be regarded as anything but No. 1. Instead of being at the top of the honor list, it is closer to the bottom, having accomplished less than any comparable country and even less than many more backward ones which at least recognized the need.

Letting The Future Take Care Of Itself

If the Japanese people cannot count on the government to get them through old age in a dignified manner, what can they do? That is the question aging Japanese have been putting to themselves for years and most are assiduously working on one solution or another. But it is uncertain how successful they will be since the possibilities are so limited.

In considering the alternatives, it is essential to constantly recall the dimensions of the problem. It is not just a matter of "rounding out" a fairly nice pension or social security check or making comfortable old age cozier. It may be necessary to cover the bulk of expenses from supplementary sources. Nor is this just for a few years. The money is needed most urgently from the time of official retirement at 50 or 55 to the age of 60, and eventually 65, when the state stipends come through. And then on to a ripe old age of 80 on the average, but 90 and 100 for some. And we are not talking of small numbers but ten, twenty, thirty million Japanese as we enter the 21st century.

What first comes to mind is the company pension schemes. They provide either a lump-sum benefit, an annuity or a mixture of the two on retirement. But they are not particularly generous. After 35 years of service, big companies may grant the equivalent of three or four years' wages, perhaps a bit more in some; small ones just offer a pittance.[8] Pensions naturally only apply to regular workers and those who have been with the company for an extended period, with white-collar employees receiving much more than blue-collar. There is usually nothing or close to it for temporary workers, part-timers or those who left after a few years (meaning most women).

Another solution, the most hopeful, is to find a post-retirement job so that a salary can cover current expenses. This will explain why so many Japanese work into their sixties and seventies, far more proportionately than in any other advanced nation. While under 12% of the elderly are employed in America and Europe, the figure is 22% in Japan. That is not, as the Japanese government and corporations insist, dutifully echoed by the Japanapologists, because Japanese simply like to work or don't feel a useful part of society otherwise. It is that they have to work if they want to survive. And this is the response they give in poll after poll.

Fortunately, and this is played up by the media, some Japanese are kept on by their company in a subsidiary position or given a job in enterprises specially established to carry the aged. Others are sent to suppliers and subcontractors. But it is not sufficiently emphasized that most of these jobs are rather second-rate, often menial ones, like services, repairs or night watchman. The wages they bring in are quite mediocre, tenure very uncertain, and the loss of status can be extremely painful for employees who have slaved away in the parent company. That is why many turn down the "generous" offer.

More serious is that, by passing along their older workers, the large companies are only solving the problem for their own personnel. The suppliers, subcontractors and existing service firms are either put out of business or have to make way for those who are parachuted down by laying off their own workers and failing to promote those who remain. They also have an increasingly aged staff, which does not help productivity. So, in effect, this is one last time for the big companies to take advantage of the small.

Thus, workers in small companies, temporary employees, part-timers and those who were not part of the "lifetime" employment system will find it exceedingly difficult to make ends meet and perhaps even find any job. This predicament will only worsen, for them and all the aged, as Japan's industries become less labor-intensive due to upgrading or transfer of manufacturing offshore. Mechanization and robotization also leave ever less room for those with limited skills. And terribly few old people will be able to assume the new jobs that open up and need more mental agility and specialized skills. Anyway. How long can you employ old people? Until 70? 80? 90? There has to be a point where this solution no longer functions.

Then, some observers naively think, they can live off their savings. Everybody knows that the Japanese are prodigious savers. That has been drummed in by repeated articles pointing to a savings rate of 18%, far higher than most Western levels. It was not mentioned, alas, that the savings rate has been declining steadily, from 23% a decade ago. And it is bound to fall yet further as younger generations appear which do not have the same cautious and frugal disposition. More and more purchases are now being made through credit cards, more and more people are taking out loans they will have to repay later on. Thus, while savings remain high, indebtedness has swollen even more rapidly.

So, by the time of retirement, the average Japanese household only has about ¥13 million stashed away. That may sound like a lot. But it just adds up to about two or three times the former annual salary. How long can a couple live off that? Six years if it accepts half-rations. Twelve years if it is even more parsimonious. It may get through the long wait for social security and a bit further. To think that this will suffice for the average life expectancy of 75-80 is too far-fetched to believe.

But, the couple can sell their home. That is probably worth a fortune. Yes, indeed, it may be worth a considerable amount of money. That is why Japanese are willing to sacrifice so much to buy one. Alas, if they sell their home, they will have to live somewhere else. And the price of a, by then, fairly dilapidated house and land will only bring in enough to buy a tiny condo in town and still have something modest left over. It is unlikely that this will cover needs very long.

Moreover, let us not forget that ever fewer Japanese own homes. Prices have skyrocketed out of reach for whole generations which now live in condos with no land. The price an old condo will fetch is not quite so large. And there will be many more who simply rent. What will they pay the rent with when they have no job?

Four solutions down, not because they are not feasible and helpful, they are simply inadequate. Let's try the next. It is the most fashionable. It fits in so nicely with Japanese traditions. It sounds so good. Even the government could suggest it as a superior solution to state aid. Let the family provide. Let old people live with their children. How wonderful! How admirable!

But, will it work? Most Japanese families, as has been pointed out, are none too affluent. They inhabit rather small houses or even smaller apartments. It is crowded to begin with. It would be even more so if mom and pop moved in. This would not only be a financial burden, it would be a social drain. The housewife, in addition to looking after the home and kids, would have to take care of two aged persons, her in-laws, with whom she might not be on the best of terms. The friction and antipathy of Japanese women to their mother-in-law is proverbial.

Even assuming this three-generation household functioned smoothly enough, there must come a time when the aging parents become ill or senile. It will then be necessary to have professional care. This cannot be provided by even the most willing and devoted of children. They will have to hire part or full-time nurses and paramedicals. Only the very richest could affort that.

Let us also not forget the time frame. With Japanese living on to 80 and 90, it is not merely a question of a three-generation household but a four-generation household. Children looking after parents that old will be in their 50s and 60s already, and need help from their own children. Can they all live together in a "rabbit hutch"? Can the grandchildren cover the costs of two older generations? Can the wife look after three or four old, perhaps ill and senile dependents?

In addition, there will be more and more old people who outlive their children and could thus not stay with them under any circumstances. Others will not move in because they are too proud or, with ever greater frequency, have children who do not want or cannot afford to keep them. There are already nearly four million households consisting solely of a man and/or woman 65 or older. This category is the fastest growing in the country. So, for many, the family is not even an option.

The difficulties are so great and the impossibility so manifest that one can only wonder what sort of government could ever expect individual families to cope. Perhaps conceding this, the authorities have now come up with another savior: the private sector. Just let private entrepreneurs set up old age homes and "silver villages." The aged can go there.

Sorry to shatter this illusion as well. I know it may be getting tedious for readers. But, given land and construction

271

costs, these homes and villages must either be dreadfully expensive or built way out in the sticks. This happens to be the case, which explains why so few Japanese can afford them or would care to move that far away from their family, friends and neighborhood. Moreover, very few facilities have actually been completed and much of this is just another exercise in cooperative public-private wishful thinking.

That may explain why a desperate Ministry of International Trade and Industry grasped at the straw of setting up colonies for aged Japanese abroad. The land and construction costs would be much lower, personnel cheaper and more abundant, and the climate perhaps more congenial. This only overlooked some minor drawbacks. Most Japanese have never lived abroad and would have trouble adjusting. It would still be necessary to provide Japanese-style food, Japanese-speaking personnel, and Japanese management, which is expensive and hard to find. It would also be necessary to find receptive host countries. Yet, while many accepted Japanese cars and VTRs, none were eager to have Japanese old folks exported to their shores.

What is this? Six down. Not many more to go.

Charity? Most countries, advanced and backward, would think of charitable organizations, church, community or voluntary associations, stepping in to help solve the problem. But, for all its economic accomplishments, Japan has pitifully little philanthropy. Shinto and Japanese-style Buddhism have not inculcated charity as an obligation or noble gesture although some of the "new religions" promote more active solidarity and the Christian community also practices it. Otherwise, care for others is pretty much limited to the family. This would leave an awful lot of old people out in the cold.

What happens to the losers? Some pretty horrible things. There are increasing numbers of hobos, vagrants, bag ladies and the like wandering about the larger cities and spending the night in parks and subway stations. Others live alone in

272

their old *home* and take care of themselves as long as they can. Then, one day, they don't come out and nobody looks in to see what is wrong. Some weeks later, there is an ugly stench and the police find that they have passed away. For those who cannot face such trials or do not want to be a "nuisance" to their family or friends, suicide is the most graceful way out.

This is no exaggeration. It is what is already happening and every year these distasteful phenomena will become more widespread. The inability to provide for a decent old age is the biggest blot on Japan's record, one so ominous it covers many of the more positive achievements. It is shameful that the government should perform so poorly, and that the population should do no better. It is even more disgraceful that foreign "friends" can present this gross dereliction of duty as having a good side. More honest observers, foreign and Japanese, will increasingly stigmatize it as Japan's worst failure.

Notes

1. Vogel, *Japan As Number One*, pp. 184 & 201–3.
2. *Japan Times*, June 3, 1982.
3. *Financial Times*, July 6, 1988.
4. Nikkeiren foresaw that the decrease could be even more drastic if the system were not revamped. See *Report of the Committee for the Study of Labor Questions*, March 1983.
5. *Yomiuri*, December 14, 1988.
6. *Japan Times*, April 8, 1983.
7. For more on the welfare system, see Woronoff, *Politics, The Japanese Way*, pp. 287–304.
8. *General Survey of Retirement Allowance Schemes*, Ministry of Labor.

14

(Japan As No. 23,
Or 57, Or Whatever)

Learning From Japan . . . Sometimes

My goodness! Isn't it amazing! When you view Japan very selectively, considering only those sectors that are outstanding and focusing on the aspects that are best, and then embellish the whole lot, Japan looks like No. 1. But, when you take the overall situation, all sectors good and bad, including all aspects good and bad, the result is strikingly different. It turns out that the wonderland we have heard so much of, and which we visited briefly in the introduction, was not only too good to be true, it wasn't true at all.

This means that labeling Japan No. 1 is a bit silly. It is probably even worse. The most significant thing about my rating is not that I have added lots of nasty features which were ignored by those who praise Japan but rather that things I rank poorly are often among those which get top grades with the Japan boosters. The conflict is not that they have shown the good and I have added the bad but that much of what they claim to be good is regarded in my book as bad.

Let us take another look at Vogel's carefully selected short list of areas where Japan is No. 1. The political system, summed up as "higher interests and fair shares," is only superior to outright domination but hardly as good as a real working democracy. Welfare, he calls it "security without entitlement," certainly lacks the entitlement but it is dubious whether the security will be there when needed. The state, "meritocratic guidance and private initiative," would only function the way it's supposed to with better politicians, bureaucrats and businessmen than Japan presently boasts.[1]

No wonder we have not put them at the top of our report card. They leave much to be desired. Other sectors, which were not terribly admirable and thus overlooked by the Japanapologists, where our rating is not very high are internationalization, quality of life and amenities. These are important items. They were not added just to quibble or make Japan look bad. If it cannot accomplish more in areas where others have been fairly successful, it most certainly does not deserve the No. 1 spot.

Of course, there are categories where Japan has done quite well, admittedly with the corrections we inserted. They are, in Vogel's quaint terminology, the large company ("identification and consensus"), basic education ("quality and equality") and crime control ("enforcement and public support"). On these subjects, one can imagine admirers getting enthusiastic about what has been achieved even if one regrets their tendency to gloss over petty failings and drawbacks.

This is mentioned not so much because Japan, like everywhere else, offers both good and bad. And is thus as often No. 23 or No. 57 as No. 1. What is most disturbing is that the authors and commentators who peddle Japan are not just making a neutral contribution to our understanding. They are scoring didactic points. They are earnestly recommending that we "learn from Japan." In fact, they often go further and seriously agitate for changes in their own country to bring it more into line with Japan.

It is one thing to say, "look what Japan is doing; isn't that interesting." It is quite another to stridently insist, "what Japan is doing is much better; we must learn from

Good old Ron witnessing the
"real" Japan close up.

it.'' In such cases, the evidence that Japan really is superior must be more convincing than thus far. It is also necessary to remember that, even if Japan is doing well (which some may not concede), it is still very difficult and risky to copy it.

After all, there are tremendous cultural differences. Western societies are more individualistic, Westerners are taught to pursue personal ambitions, conformity is condemned and spontaneity praised. Westerners are more equalitarian and are only willing to subordinate their interests to broader ones under certain circumstances. There may

276

also be legal distinctions which inhibit the adoption of Japanese methods. Many countries have legislation that forbids discrimination by race, sex and age. There is a stricter division of political powers and a greater separation between the public and private sectors. There are tougher antitrust laws. Corruption is not only a punishable crime, politicians actually get punished for it and also criticized by the media and public.

Beyond this, the goals may differ. Other peoples do not seek what the Japanese do. Take something as basic as corporate strategy. Most foreign companies strive for profits rather than market share. When they educate their youth, foreigners like to provide broad training to foster a rounded personality. Very few think it is admirable to live for the company rather than the family, nation or oneself. And hardly any can conceive that work should be the sole purpose in life and that leisure has to be sacrificed.

While most of these objections are formulated within a Western context, it would be mistaken to assume that the Japanese system would go down well in the rest of Asia. True, the East Asian countries have a similar Confucian ethic. But most are more individualistic, especially the Chinese. They still put family above company. And they are not quite willing to sacrifice all for economic growth, especially when they notice that this had not brought the Japanese a secure or comfortable lifestyle.

However, these complications are not enumerated to keep foreigners from learning from Japan. I do not in the least believe that our salvation comes from being ''more like us.''[2] We are already too much like ourselves. There is no point in Americans becoming more American, French more French or Koreans more Korean. That would only exaggerate the existing characteristics and push them further in the same direction. Much more can be gained by seeing how others do things, including the Japanese. And then adopting whatever can be used while heeding the difficulties just mentioned.

For example, "lifetime employment" may be hard to transplant, whether for an individualistic West or developing countries that lack the social structures. But there is absolutely no reason why companies cannot aim for steadier employment conditions, keeping workers who show loyalty, and offering more promotion in-house as a suitable reward. There is certainly more room for consensus, especially in companies run by hard-nosed managers who think it is their prerogative to decide everything. There is no need to fall into the opposite extreme of committees, or even more wasteful *nemawashi*, but certainly more consultation and feed-back would help. Market share, while not as desirable as profits, should definitely be taken into account because it shapes future profit in many ways.

It is obvious that there are advantages to techniques like quality control circles, productivity campaigns, suggestion boxes, just-in-time delivery and so on. Any company that does not use them is foolish. In limited doses, and when fairly compensated, they also appeal to the workers and suppliers. Nor does it hurt to have employees who are flexible enough to do several jobs on the shop floor or in the office and who are not impeded by strict work rules or jurisdictional conflicts between unions. Once again, with due explanation and reward for extra effort.

Industrial policy has not always been constructive in Japan, especially because it was overdone in a society which is already excessively conformist and where companies already tend to follow (or copy) one another. In a society which is less structured, with everyone going his own way (and proud of it), it would be useful to have some body that could develop an overall vision and make concrete suggestions. It would be to the good to adopt some common priorities and run a few joint projects. If nothing else, this would spark a debate on national economic policy.

Education, the most widely propagated theme, is the hardest to adapt, given greatly differing national perspectives. Yet, no one could object to putting more stress on the basics, augmenting the share of math and science in an increasingly technological age, and providing more practical skills. It would have even more impact in places like the United States, which have completely ignored the need for strict standards, to hold more and stiffer exams (as long as they test knowledge and not rote memory). The biggest contribution would simply be to make children spend more hours at school and do more homework. This would increase not only the educational input but raise the profile of school over against competing activities like sports, television, sex and drugs.

These are just a few examples. There are many more. Beyond these specific instances, however, we can all learn from Japan more broadly by moving our society a bit in its direction so that we come closer to the middle. Crossing over to the other side, actually behaving like the Japanese, would be pointless. Thus, Westerners could moderate their individualism and think more of society, they could be somewhat less spontaneous and show more self-control, they might sacrifice their own interests to broader ones and accept a bit less leisure if something useful could be gained. Developing countries, Asian or not, could certainly show more discipline without necessarily displaying the single-mindedness of the Japanese in forging productive machinery at all costs.

In short, I do not object to learning from Japan. I do not object to learning from anyone. But let us at least borrow what is good while avoiding what is bad. And let us remember that, no matter how good, some aspects will be very hard to assimilate and should perhaps be discarded. Alas, none of this will be possible until the state of knowledge (or ignorance) on Japan is completely reversed and we can see the *honne* through the *tatemae*.

Friends—Or Enemies—Of Japan?

It would seem that the Japanese should be delighted with the present wave of pop literature. After all, it portrays Japan in a very favorable light, enhances its finer points and ignores the less attractive ones, and even goes so far as to proclaim Japan as No. 1, a position it longed for but was too timid to claim. Coming from foreigners, the flattery should be that much more appreciated.

Still, the Japanese were not entirely happy about this phenomenon. After all, they knew that much of what was produced in those laudatory books or TV documentaries was not *honne* but *tatemae*. It was not the truth but some pretense, some illusion, some splendiferous version of the Japan they all wished existed but sadly conceded was not real. And those who concocted the myths were often ignorant or paid for their efforts. So there was little joy in being told that Japan had the world's best economy, management, bureaucracy, education, crime enforcement, etc., etc. when they knew it was not so.

Of course, the reception varied. It goes without saying that the elite, the top politicians, bureaucrats and businessmen were more than pleased to have foreigners peddle their *tatemae* and make it appear as if they really had some validity. Also, while trying to maintain a humble mien, they were happy to obtain international recognition for their signal contributions to this acknowledged success. It was not often they were praised by other Japanese who were not flunkies, so such flowery compliments from foreign friends were highly appreciated. But even they did not quite swallow the line. So much was stated in the lead to *The Wheel Extended*,

Toyota's quarterly review, which usually echoes the establishment position:

"The candid response of many Japanese to Vogel's conclusion is that the problems he mentions are serious challenges still confronting Japan today. To say that the nation has dealt with them successfully (i.e., solved them) distorts the facts."[3]

Ordinary people were even less pleased. After all, they were also subjected to the *tatemae* which the elite constantly tried to foist on them, with considerably less success because most Japanese can distinguish better and guess what the *honne* is. Thus, while they often read these Japanapologetic books for curiosity sake, they did not necessarily like them. They were merely amazed—and amused—that *gaijin* could write such rubbish and still be recognized as authorities in their home country.

Every now and then, Japanese readers would come upon comments that just made them gasp or which they choked on because they had personally suffered from the reality. For example, older men gagged at the notion of lifetime employment as they scrambled for post-retirement jobs, employees of smaller companies were vexed by the idea that the company "family" looked after one and all, women giggled at the notion of a harmonious family as they waited for their hubby to finally come home, and citizens were flabbergasted at the talk of an efficient bureaucracy and democratic government.

The most aggrieved were those Japanese who agitated for improvement and reforms. They knew it did not help to have the "friends" of Japan praise the very institutions they were trying to renovate: government, education, criminal justice, social and sexual equality, internationalization, the family, etc. And they did not like the way these foreigners mixed in the debates and repeatedly backed the status quo, showing they were "friends" of the elite but not the people. In such circumstances, the comments regarding Vogel and company were frequently unprintable.

By the way, this is not just my view of things. As we worked our way through the report card, referring to items which were highly touted by the Japanapologists, we readily found Japanese in positions of respect and authority who disagreed. If you will remember, we have not quoted unknowns or rebels but university professors, recognized specialists, top politicians, bureaucrats and businessmen, many of them definitely establishment types. We also cited dozens of public opinion polls and surveys as well as comments from the media. There was no lack of criticism of supposed strong points from the Japanese.

Yet, the Japanapologists remain oblivious to these opposing views. Despite their proclaimed mastery of the subjects and familiarity with the language and literature, they are the ones who do not draw on Japanese sources, who do not quote the polls and who obviously do not mix enough with ordinary people to gather anecdotal evidence. Worse, they systematically discard everything that goes against their theses. And no attempt to explain the facts, to dispel the myths, seems to work.

I have attended numerous strange encounters between foreigners and Japanese in which the opinions of the opinionated *gaijin* were vastly more positive and optimistic. I have seen these outsiders steadfastly reject the arguments of the insiders and then claim that their benighted counterparts were simply too modest about successes while exaggerating failures. In short, they insisted that the foreign "friends" knew more about the country than did the Japanese.

Once again, should you not trust my views, you might care to hear what a serious and respected Japanese had to say about the "World and Japan" forum he attended. Jiro Ushio, quoted below, was chairman of Ushio Electric, vice-chairman of Keizai Doyukai, and a stolid member of the establishment not given to loose criticism. But even he was aghast. "Almost to a man, non-Japanese delegates exhibited immense faith in Japanese performance. The Japanese participants, in stark contrast, were laden with anxiety about the state of affairs in Japan."[4]

Why this annoyance and concern? Well, for one, the wave of adulation has not only had positive effects. What Japan wants most, and this has been repeatedly stated, is "understanding." Admittedly, in Japanese the word connotes actual acceptance of the situation. But what they get here is overkill. The Japanapologists go so far that they create new misunderstandings which only strain relations with the outside world.

This is best explained with examples. The Japanese were extremely proud of their industrial policy, promptly dubbed targeting. But it was soon regarded as an insidious trick to compete unfairly and wipe out foreign rivals . . . which was not the desired result. Then it became impossible to dispel the idea that Japan was rich, immensely rich. That unleased an avalanche of demands that Japan buy more imported goods, provide additional aid, forgive debts, spend more on arms or environmental protection, participate in a space station, and contribute to all sorts of worthy causes. Alas, there was not enough money for all that.

This also hurts on the person-to-person level. When foreigners hear of the extraordinary educational system, and then attend college only to find out that it is mediocre, they get more than annoyed. When foreigners are recruited by Japanese companies, they actually expect to be treated much better than elsewhere and, if they are not, they get bitter. When foreigners are duly impressed with tales of manipulation by elite bureaucrats, they get more frustrated than otherwise when nothing is accomplished. When foreigners are convinced that Japan's economic power can make it a political leader as well, they are disappointed—and displeased—that nothing much comes of it.

In short, time and again, the effort to embellish Japan has backfired and many Japanese leaders were forced to admit the truth, which did not sound anywhere near as good as the official line and was even more embarrassing when it was realized that there was such a discrepancy. Now many concede that if Japan cannot live up to its modern myth, it should not try to spread one.

They also get annoyed by the frightful cost of supporting the myth-makers in style. True, the Japanapologists love Japan for its intrinsic virtues. But this is not free. You still have to subsidize their travel and stay, the cost of holding countless seminars and conferences, the need to endow foreign chairs of Japanese studies, etc. There are also the rounds of cocktail parties and excursions organized for foreign journalists, businessmen and visiting dignitaries. And also the masses of publications, often glossy and thick, distributed in huge quantities to anyone who can be influenced. None of that is cheap, certainly not at today's prices. And the bill is perhaps getting too high.

The most serious problems reach somewhat further. One is that all this flattery is having an insidious effect on some Japanese. Of course, they do not believe the Japanapologists implicitly. They know what is wrong with Japan and, just because some crazy *gaijin* are foolish enough not to, it does not lead them to believe that the problems have been solved. What does happen, however, is that they get the feeling that things in Japan are much better than abroad. They have no way of checking that out. Few enough are well-travelled or mix extensively with the locals even when they are abroad. So there is a growing impression that, even if we Japanese are not perfect, certainly we are much better than the rest.

This cannot help creating a degree of arrogance among the Japanese. More and more have taken to lecturing other peoples and countries on how they should solve their problems and how they should show the determination and discipline which the Japanese displayed in overcoming crisis after crisis. This arrogance, despite a supposed tradition of humility, has become increasingly visible to outsiders. And it does not sit well with them. Especially not when some have a long enough memory to recall other periods when Japan gave out gratuitous advice and then used its power to impose its will.

While there is little chance that Japan will be able to have its way abroad, there are dangers domestically. Throughout this book, it has been shown that there are serious problems that must be solved and reforms that must finally be accomplished. But this tempting concept that Japan is No. 1 only gets in the way. It supports those who, for their own reasons, wish to perpetuate the status quo and keep things as they are. It undercuts those who feel that it is necessary to change and create a society for the 21st century. In short, it is retrograde and stands in the way of progress.

It also contributes to cutting Japan off from the rest of the world. Once upon a time, the Japanese felt acutely that they had to learn from outside. They then engaged in a "learn from America" fad. Now, it seems, America should learn from them. So should everybody else. And there is little point in Japan taking lessons from the United States, or Britain, or France, or Korea. Alas, if it does not seek fresh ideas and novel solutions abroad, where else is it to find them? Surely not in a Japan that is clannish, inward looking, discourages innovation and imagination and promptly hammers in every nail that stands out!

So this wave of adulation and flattery (or perhaps sycophancy and opportunism) has not been positive in many respects. In fact, the minuses probably outweigh the pluses by now. And the Japanese are bound to suffer more than the foreigners unless something can be done to rectify the situation.

Containing the Apologists

From everything we have seen so far, certain conclusions are fairly clear. First of all, it is evident that the glorified view of Japan produced by the Japanapologists is much closer to *tatemae* than *honne*, to illusion than reality, to falsehood than truth. In fact, it is one of the most extraordinary hoaxes of the 20th century, foisted on a gullible public at a time when Japan is no longer a closed country but one that can be freely visited. Yet, our knowledge of Japan today is not only no better than a century ago but in some ways worse. Of course, we have the facts and figures, the statistics and documents, but our interpretation is completely off. There is no Japan which is No. 1 and the very idea that this can be proclaimed— and widely believed—shows the effectiveness of the Japan claque.

It is also pretty clear that this new misunderstanding of Japan, less explicable and excusable than ignorance in the time of Perry or MacArthur, is not to the benefit of outsiders. They make one mistake after the other by assuming that Japan has become a model for education, management, economic development, politics and so on. If they actually do business in Japan, or have to represent their country there or, as is increasingly the case, marry into a Japanese family, this ignorance can be very costly and painful. But it is not particularly good for the Japanese either. They do not gain by assuming that the situation is better than it actually is or that Japan has somehow attained a superior height from which it can look down on all other nations.

What is not clear is how to put an end to Japanapology. After all, it is no longer just one view of Japan, one of many schools of thought that are contending for public acceptance. The apologists are among the foremost authorities on Japan while the rest, especially the supposed Japan-bashers, are assumed to be little more than carping critics or gadflies.

Japan as No. 1 has become the conventional wisdom. Its precepts are assumed correct and anything else must first be proven. It is no longer necessary to demonstrate that Japan is superior. And it is increasingly difficult to show that it has serious failings.

More worrisome even than Japanapology becoming the conventional wisdom (or collective ignorance) is that the apologists have taken over the machinery. They run the departments and institutes of Japan studies. They screen manuscripts for publishers and write reviews to define which books are good and bad. They are consulted by the media. Their advice is even curried by business and government. This makes it much easier to blackball or ostracize anybody who does not agree with them or might show them up for the fakes they are.

Still, something must be done. The first thing, obviously, is to patiently document just what is wrong (and also what is right) with Japan. It can be done in articles and books, lectures and private conversations. The opponents are often voices in the wilderness, lonely and raucous ones, but at least those voices should not be stilled. Gradually, with a political scandal here and social conflicts there, more observers will realize that the situation is not so great. Moreover, the number of foreigners working and living in Japan is increasing rapidly. Most arrive with the Japan as No. 1 scenario in mind. But they quickly learn how mistaken they were and, having once been fooled, they also try to disseminate the truth.

It would be nice if the Japanese contributed more. Let them obey the rules of courtesy among themselves, mouthing the *tatemae* when it is appropriate. But, with foreigners, they should try harder to express the *honne*. Genuine foreign friends will find out anyway so nothing is gained by denying reality. Still, until the people come around to that, it is always possible to know what they actually think by reading Japanese dailies and weeklies and just observing what Japanese do in practice as opposed to theory.

Anyway, the primary source of Japanapology is not the Japanese but foreign apologists. Some of them are admittedly rather dumb and simply do not know the truth. They repeat the empty compliments they have learned and served them so well thus far. You can, of course, try to point out the flaws in their arguments. But that is unlikely to help much if they haven't figured things out yet. At least, if they are so misguided, you can stop consulting them and perhaps, if they are professors, as so many are, suggest that they be replaced by someone who does know the truth.

There should gradually be some improvement in the media coverage of Japan. More and more publications and channels have their own correspondents on the spot. More and more of them are staying longer or coming back for a second and third stint. The better they know Japan, the more likely they are to uncover the truth. Also, having been faced so often with the facile lies that are used on the newcomer, they are more likely to make an effort to find out for themselves and dig deeper. In addition, more of them now insist on producing critical material even if the editors back home prefer fluff.

Businessmen and diplomats are also under greater pressure to know exactly what is happening. That is their job. The former must generate profits, the latter defend the national interest, and that cannot be done on the basis of naive assumptions but hard facts. Here, too, more are staying for longer periods and more are aware that there are two levels of perception and only the *honne* will help them accomplish their work.

The trickiest problems arise with the academics. They are the biggest purveyors of untruths. And it is hard to see just how to alter this. After all, one of the most durable *tatemae* of the Western world is that scholars seek the truth, test all alternatives, merge thesis and antithesis into synthesis. But that is obviously not happening. To the contrary, they tend to support one another as they push Japanapology from one extreme to the next. And they undercut and stigmatize anyone who may disagree. How can you reform the academics?

If a journalist writes an erroneous article, you can send a letter to the editor. If a diplomat makes a nasty mistake, he can be recalled. If a businessman does not know what is going on, he will probably lose money and his job as well. But, oddly enough, academics can make mistakes, gross and manifest ones, time and again, and get away with it. For they operate on the basis of peer review. Once the overall community has been converted to a given position, they regularly coopt members with the same views. And thus there is no one to criticize them. Indeed, the critics are neatly kept out of the academic establishment by those who are already in it.

There is not much the students can do. I have personally spoken to hundreds of students who complain that their professors simply do not know what they are talking about. But the students do not dare correct their *sensei* for fear of flunking out. And those who succeed are frequently bootlickers since that is the surest way of getting a doctorate and later on an academic post. Perhaps the university administrators should do something.

The real hitch is not that some apologists are ignorant but that they are on the make. Japanapology is not only a source of fame but wealth. There are numerous "professional *gaijin*" in Japan who earn a living simply by saying and doing the right things. The Japanese do not admire or respect them. But they can be useful. There are even more foreigners who are paid to help Japan in its efforts to win friends and influence people abroad. They make money by writing, lecturing, consulting, obtaining information, arranging introductions, etc. Some have amassed tidy sums, including illustrious professors, complacent ambassadors and clever lobbyists. Just how far this can go was shown when former president Reagan obtained $2 million for giving two interviews.

So, if money is a major consideration, at least the Japan-apologists should be kept away from the sources thereof or it should be made harder to cash in. This would mean, in academia, that professors of Japan studies should not also be collecting funds. That should be the task of someone who does not teach. And, if they do get some of the money, it should be ensured that this does not influence what they teach. There might thus be an end to seminars and conferences whose purpose is to promote Japanese causes. As for the erstwhile ambassadors, civil servants, politicians, etc., they might be legally precluded from working for a foreign power until a decent time had elapsed. When it comes to supposedly neutral bodies (Japan Society, Asia Society, think tanks and institutes) whose support is more subtle and diffuse, they might be required to register as foreign agents if they receive ample funds from Japan.

By now, a bit of public outrage and outcry would seem long overdue. That academics became advocates rather than specialists was already improper. That some should actually become propagandists for Japanese causes is even more inex-cusable. They are supposed to teach the truth and anything else is a betrayal of their trust. The same applies to journalists who distort facts to get a hot story. Or business consultants and management gurus who give clients a false idea of how the system works and thereby deliver them to the tender mercies of Japanese competitors. It is even more reprehen-sible when politicians or officials collaborate with the Japa-nese in the hope of a suitable reward. That can be regarded as treachery, if not treason.

It should already be perfectly evident that Japanapology is more than just a scholarly fluke or intellectual aberration among those who are supposed to be informing their fellow citizens about this great and important country. By twisting

facts and creating myths, they are doing a disservice to their
own country and also to Japan. Certainly, they deserve a
reprimand and, in some cases, even stiffer penalties, although
that is unlikely to occur. But at least they should cease being
respected and trusted as experts and authorities.

NOTES

1. See Vogel, *Japan As Number One*.
2. See James Fallows, *More Like Us*.
3. *The Wheel Extended*, January-March 1981, p. 1.
4. *Japan Times*, October 11, 1984.

Bibliography

Although it is a bit unusual, I am including two bibliographies which shall simply be called Alternative A and Alternative B. These neutral words seem more appropriate than labelling them *tatemae* and *honne*, or Japanapology and Japan-bashing, or pro and con, or any other loaded terminology. The first group clearly takes a more positive, favorable, approving stance; the second a more negative, critical, sometimes harsh position. There are good and bad books in each category so inclusion in one or the other is not necessarily a judgement as to their intrinsic value. But the second group does tend to be more objective and truthful on the whole.

Do not be misled by the fact that there are about as many entries listed under each category. There are vastly more books which could come under Alternative A, so many that it was pointless to include them all. Anyway, they are relatively well known already and you can tell their position almost from the title and book jacket. Far fewer books would fit in Alternative B, and these are often less well known, so the list is more comprehensive.

Both categories of books are needed to get both sides of the story. Even if you disagree with one version, that is no excuse to deny its existence or hide the existence of the books that present it. I therefore hope that this practice will be followed by other authors, whether in a single or alternative bibliographies. It is indispensable to show readers the whole range of opinion no matter where one may stand personally. This comment is intended particularly for the Japanapologists who have gone out of their way to create the impression that they are not only the mainstream but that countercurrents scarcely exist.

Alternative A

Abegglen, James C., *Management And Labor, The Japanese Solution*, Tokyo, Kodansha International, 1973.
———, *The Japanese Factory*, Glenco, Free Press, 1958.
Abegglen, James C., and Stalk, George, *Kaisha, The Japanese Corporation*, New York, Basic Books, 1985.
Athos, A.G., and Pascale, R., *The Art of Japanese Management*, New York, Simon and Schuster, 1981.
Bayley, David, *Forces of Order: Police Behavior in Japan and the United States*, Berkeley, University of California Press, 1976.
Ballon, Robert J., *The Japanese Employee*, Tokyo, Tuttle, 1969.
Benedict, Ruth, *The Chrysanthemum and the Sword*, Tokyo, Tuttle, 1954.
Clifford, William, *Crime Control in Japan*, Boston, D.C. Heath, 1976.
Christopher, Robert C., *Second To None, American Companies In Japan*, New York, Crown Publishers, 1987.
———, *The Japanese Mind: The Goliath Explained*, New York, Linden Press, 1983.
Cummings, William, *Education and Equality in Japan*, Princeton, Princeton University Press, 1980.
Curtis, Gerald L., *The Japanese Way of Politics*, New York, Columbia University Press, 1988.
Dore, Ronald, *Flexible Rigidities*, London, Athlone Press, 1986.
———, *Taking Japan Seriously*, Stanford, Stanford University Press, 1987.
Dore, Ronald, and Sako, Mari, *How The Japanese Learn To Work*, London, Routledge, 1989.
Duke, Benjamin, *The Japanese School*, New York, Praeger, 1986.
Feigenbaum, Edward A., and McCorduck, Pamela, *The Fifth Generation: Artificial Intelligence and Japan's Computer Challenge to the World*, Reading, Addison-Wesley, 1983.
Forbis, William H., *Japan Today*, Tokyo, Tuttle, 1975.
Gibney, Frank, *Japan: The Fragile Superpower*, Tokyo, Tuttle, 1975.
Johnson, Chalmers, *MITI And The Japanese Miracle*, Stanford, Stanford University Press, 1982.
Kahn, Herman, *The Emerging Japanese Superstate*, Harmondsworth, Penguin Books, 1970.

Lynn, Richard, *Educational Achievement in Japan, Lessons for the West*, Armonk, M.E. Sharpe, 1988.

Ouchi, William, *Theory Z*, Reading, Addison-Wesley, 1981.

Reischauer, Edwin O., *The Japanese*, Cambridge, Harvard University Press, 1981.

———, *The Japanese Today*, Cambridge, Harvard University Press, 1988.

———, *My Life Between Japan And America*, New York, Harper and Row, 1986.

Tanaka, Kakuei, *Building A New Japan*, Tokyo, Simul Press, 1972.

Vogel, Ezra F., *Comeback*, New York, Simon and Schuster, 1985.

———, *Japan As Number One*, Cambridge, Harvard University Press, 1979.

White, Merry, *The Japanese Educational Challenge: A Commitment to Children*, New York, Free Press, 1987.

Zengage, Thomas R., and Ratcliffe, C. Tait, *The Japanese Century, Challenge and Response*, London, Longman, 1989.

Alternative B

Apter, David E., and Sawa, Nagayo, *Against the State, Politics and Social Protest in Japan*, Cambridge, Harvard University Press, 1984.

Bulletin of Concerned Asian Scholars, *The Other Japan*, Armonk, M.E. Sharpe, 1988.

Chalmers, Norma J., *Industrial Relations in Japan: The Peripheral Sector*, London, Routledge, 1989.

Clark, Rodney, *The Japanese Company*, New Haven, Yale University Press, 1979.

Dale, Peter N., *The Myth of Japanese Uniqueness*, London, Routledge, and New York, St. Martin's Press, 1986.

Emmott, Bill, *The Sun Also Sets, Why Japan Will Not Be Number One*, London, Simon & Schuster, 1989.

Fallows, James, *More Like Us: Making America Great Again*, Boston, Houghton Mifflin, 1989.

Fukutake, Tadashi, *Japanese Society Today*, Tokyo, University of Tokyo Press, 1981.

Hanami, Tadashi, *Labor Relations in Japan Today*, Tokyo, Kodansha International, 1979.

Kamata, Satoshi, *Japan In The Passing Lane*, New York, Random House, 1980.

Kaplan, David E., and Dubro, Alec, *Yakuza: The Explosive Account of Japan's Underworld*, Reading, Addison-Wesley, 1986.

McCormack, Gavan, and Sugimoto, Yoshio (eds.), *Democracy in Contemporary Japan*, Armonk, M.E. Sharpe, 1986.

294

Mouer, Ross, and Sugimoto, Yoshio, *Images of Japanese Society*, London, KPI, 1986.

Nagai, Michio, *Higher Education in Japan: Its Take-Off and Crash*, Tokyo, University of Tokyo Press, 1971.

Nakane, Chie, *Japanese Society*, Berkeley, University of California Press, 1970.

Prestowitz, Clyde V., *Trading Places: How We Allowed Japan To Take the Lead*, New York, Basic Books, 1988.

Rohlen, Thomas P., *For Harmony and Strength*, Berkeley, University of California Press, 1974.

———, *Japan's High Schools*, Berkeley, University of California Press, 1983.

Seidensticker, Edward, *This Country, Japan*, Tokyo, Kodansha International, 1979.

Sethi, S. Prakash, Namiki, Nobuaki, Swanson, Carl L., *The False Promise of the Japanese Miracle*, New York, Pitman Publishing, 1984.

Seward, Jack, *More About The Japanese*, Tokyo, Lotus Press, 1984.

———, *The Japanese*, Tokyo, Lotus Press, 1984.

Steiner, Kurt, Krauss, Ellis S., and Flanagan, Scott C. (eds.), *Political Opposition and Local Politics in Japan*, Princeton, Princeton University Press, 1980.

Tasker, Peter, *Inside Japan: Wealth, Work and Power in the New Japanese Empire*, London, Sidgwick & Jackson, 1987.

Taylor, Jared, *Shadows of the Rising Sun*, New York, William Morrow, 1983.

van Wolferen, Karel, *The Enigma of Japanese Power*, New York, Alfred A. Knopf, 1989.

Vogel, Ezra F., (ed.), *Modern Japanese Organization and Decision-Making*, Berkeley, University of California Press, 1975.

Wolf, Marvin J., *The Japanese Conspiracy*, New York, Empire Books, 1983.

Woronoff, Jon, *Japan: The Coming Economic Crisis*, Tokyo, Yohan, 1979.

———, *Japan: The Coming Social Crisis*, Tokyo, Yohan, 1980.

———, *Japan's Commercial Empire*, Tokyo, Lotus Press, New York, M. E. Sharpe, and London, Macmillan, 1986.

———, *Japan's Wasted Workers*, Tokyo, Lotus Press, and New York, Rowman & Allenheld, 1981.

———, *Inside Japan Inc.*, Tokyo, Lotus Press, 1982.

———, *The Japan Syndrome*, Tokyo, Lotus Press, and New Brunswick, Transaction Publishers, 1985.

———, *Politics, The Japanese Way*, Tokyo, Lotus Press, London, Macmillan, New York, and St. Martin's Press, 1987.

———, *World Trade War*, Tokyo, Lotus Press, and New York, Praeger/Greenwood, 1985.

Index

Books by Jon Woronoff

WEST AFRICAN WAGER

ORGANIZING AFRICAN UNITY

HONG KONG: CAPITALIST PARADISE

KOREA'S ECONOMY, MAN-MADE MIRACLE

JAPAN: THE COMING SOCIAL CRISIS

JAPAN: THE COMING ECONOMIC CRISIS

JAPAN'S WASTED WORKERS

INSIDE JAPAN, INC.

WORLD TRADE WAR

JAPAN'S COMMERCIAL EMPIRE

THE JAPAN SYNDROME

ASIA'S "MIRACLE" ECONOMIES

POLITICS, THE JAPANESE WAY